# NoSQL
# for Mere
# Mortals®

 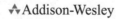

# NoSQL

## for Mere

## Mortals®

Dan Sullivan

## ✦ Addison-Wesley

Hoboken, NJ ▪ Boston ▪ Indianapolis ▪ San Francisco

New York ▪ Toronto ▪ Montreal ▪ London ▪ Munich ▪ Paris ▪ Madrid

Capetown ▪ Sydney ▪ Tokyo ▪ Singapore ▪ Mexico City

U.S. Corporate and Government Sales
(800) 382-3419
corpsales@pearsontechgroup.com

For questions about sales outside the U.S., please contact:

International Sales
international@pearsoned.com

Visit us on the Web: informit.com/aw

Library of Congress Control Number: 2015935038

ISBN-13:       978-0-13-402321-2
ISBN-10:       0-13-402321-8

Text printed in the United States on recycled paper at Edwards Brothers Malloy, Ann Arbor, Michigan.

First printing, April 2015

Editor-in-Chief: Greg Wiegand

Acquisitions Editor: Joan Murray

Development Editor: Mark Renfrow

Managing Editor: Sandra Schroeder

Senior Project Editor: Tonya Simpson

Copy Editor: Karen Annett

Indexer: WordWise Publishing Services

Proofreader: Chuck Hutchinson

Technical Reviewer: Theodor Richardson

Editorial Assistant: Cindy Teeters

Cover Designer: Alan Clements

Compositor: Mary Sudul

*For Katherine*

# About the Author

**Dan Sullivan** is a data architect and data scientist with more than 20 years of experience in business intelligence, machine learning, data mining, text mining, Big Data, data modeling, and application design. Dan's project work has ranged from analyzing complex genomics and proteomics data to designing and implementing numerous database applications. His most recent work has focused on NoSQL database modeling, data analysis, cloud computing, text mining, and data integration in life sciences. Dan has extensive experience in relational database design and works regularly with NoSQL databases. Dan has presented and written extensively on NoSQL, cloud computing, analytics, data warehousing, and business intelligence. He has worked in many industries, including life sciences, financial services, oil and gas, manufacturing, health care, insurance, retail, power systems, telecommunications, pharmaceuticals, and publishing.

# Contents

# Preface

It is difficult to avoid discussions about data. Individuals are concerned about keeping their personal data private. Companies struggle to keep data out of the hands of cybercriminals. Governments and businesses have an insatiable appetite for data. IT analysts trip over themselves coming up with new terms to describe data: Big Data, streaming data, high-velocity data, and unstructured data. There is no shortage of terms for ways to store data: databases, data stores, data warehouses, and data lakes. Someone has gone so far as to coin the phrase data swamp.

While others engage in sometimes heated discussions about data, there are those who need to collect, process, analyze, and manage data. This book is for them.

NoSQL databases emerged from unmet needs. Data management tools that worked well for decades could not keep up with demands of Internet applications. Hundreds and thousands of business professionals using corporate databases were no longer the most challenging use case. Companies such as Google, Amazon, Facebook, and Yahoo! had to meet the needs of users that measured in the millions.

The theoretically well-grounded relational data model that had served us so well needed help. Specialized applications, like Web crawling and online shopping cart management, motivated the enhancement and creation of nonrelational databases, including key-value, document, column family, and graph databases. Relational databases are still needed and face no risk of being replaced by NoSQL databases.

Instead, NoSQL databases offer additional options with different performance and functional characteristics.

This book is intended as a guide to introduce NoSQL databases, to discuss when they work well and when they do not, and, perhaps most important, to describe how to use them effectively to meet your data management needs.

You can find PowerPoints, chapter quizzes, and an accompanying instructor's guide in Pearson's Instructor Resource Center (IRC) via the website pearsonhighered.com.

# Acknowledgments

This book is the product of a collaboration, not a single author as the cover may suggest. I would like to thank my editor, Joan Murray, for conceiving of this book and inviting me into the ranks of the well-respected authors and publishing professionals who have created the For Mere Mortals series.

Tonya Simpson patiently and professionally took a rough draft of *NoSQL for Mere Mortals* and turned it into a polished, finished product. Thanks to Sondra Scott, Cindy Teeters, and Mark Renfrow of Pearson for their help in seeing this book to completion. Thank you to Karen Annett for copyediting this book; I know I gave you plenty to do.

Thanks to Theodor Richardson for his thoughtful and detail-oriented technical edit.

My family was a steadfast support through the entire book writing process.

My father-in-law, Bill Aiken, is my number-one fan and my constant source of encouragement.

I am thankful for the encouragement offered by my children Nicole, Charles, and Kevin and their partners Katie and Sara.

I would like to especially thank my sons, Nicholas and James. Nicholas read chapters and completed review questions as if this were a textbook in a course. He identified weak spots and was a resource for improving the explanations throughout the text. James, a professional technology writer himself, helped write the section on graph databases. He did not hesitate to make time in his schedule for yet another unexpected request for help from his father, and as a result, the quality of those chapters improved.

Neither this book nor the other professional and personal accomplishments I have had over the past three decades could have occurred without the ever-present love and support of my partner, Katherine. Others cannot know, and probably do not even suspect, that much of what I appear to have done myself is really what we have accomplished together. This book is just one of the many products of our journey.

Dan Sullivan
Portland, Oregon
2015

# Introduction

Databases are like television. There was a time in the history of both when you had few options to choose from and all the choices were disappointingly similar. Times have changed. The database management system is no longer synonymous with relational databases, and television is no longer limited to a handful of networks broadcasting indistinguishable programs.

Names like PostgreSQL, MySQL, Oracle, Microsoft SQL Server, and IBM DB2 are well known in the IT community, even among professionals outside the data management arena. Relational databases have been the choice of data management professionals for decades. They meet the needs of businesses tracking packages and account balances as well as scientists studying bacteria and human diseases. They keep data logically organized and easily retrieved. One of their most important characteristics is their ability to give multiple users a consistent view of data no matter how many changes are under way within the database.

Many of us in the database community thought we understood how to live with databases. Then life changed. Actually, the Internet changed. The Internet emerged from a military-sponsored network called ARPANET to become a platform for academic collaboration and eventually for commercial and personal use. The volume and types of data expanded. In addition to keeping our checking account balances, we want our computers to find the latest news, help with homework, and summarize reviews of new films. Now, many of us depend on the Internet to keep in touch with family, network with colleagues, and pursue professional education and development.

It is no surprise that such radical changes in data management requirements have led to radically new ways to manage data. The latest generation of data management tools is collectively known as NoSQL databases. The name reflects what these systems are not instead of what they are. We can attribute this to the well-earned dominance of relational databases, which use a language called SQL.

NoSQL databases fall into four broad categories: key-value, document, column family, and graph databases. (Search-oriented systems, such as Solr and Elasticsearch are sometimes included in the extended family of NoSQL databases. They are outside the scope of this book.)

Key-value databases employ a simple model that enables you to store and look up a datum (also known as the value) using an identifier (also known as the key). BerkleyDB, released in the mid-1990s, was an early key-value database used in applications for which relational databases were not a good fit.

Document databases expand on the ideas of key-value databases to organize groups of key values into a logical structure known as a document. Document databases are high-performance, flexible data management systems that are increasingly used in a broad range of data management tasks.

Column family databases share superficial similarities to relational databases. The name of the first implementation of a column family database, Google BigTable, hints at the connection to relational databases and their core data structure, the table. Column family databases are used for some of the largest and most demanding, data-intensive applications.

Graph databases are well suited to modeling networks—that is, things connected to other things. The range of use cases spans computers communicating with other computers to people interacting with each other.

This is a dynamic time in database system research and development. We have well-established and widely used relational databases that are good fits for many data management problems. We have long-established alternatives, such as key-value databases, as well as more recent designs, including document, column family, and graph databases.

One of the disadvantages of this state of affairs is that decision making is more challenging. This book is designed to lessen that challenge. After reading this book, you should have an understanding of NoSQL options and when to use them.

Keep in mind that NoSQL databases are changing rapidly. By the time you read this, your favorite NoSQL database might have features not mentioned here. Watch for increasing support for transactions. How database management systems handle transactions is an important distinguishing feature of these systems. (If you are unfamiliar with transactions, don't worry. You will soon know about them if you keep reading.)

## Who Should Read This Book?

This book is designed for anyone interested in learning how to use NoSQL databases. Novice database developers, seasoned relational data modelers, and experienced NoSQL developers will find something of value in this book.

Novice developers will learn basic principles and design criteria of data management in the opening chapters of the book. You'll also get a bit of data management history because, as we all know, history has a habit of repeating itself.

There are comparisons to relational databases throughout the book. If you are well versed in relational database design, these comparisons might help you quickly grasp and assess the value of NoSQL database features.

For those who have worked with some NoSQL databases, this book may help you get up to speed with other types of NoSQL databases. Key-value and document databases are widely used, but if you haven't encountered column family or graph databases, then this book can help.

If you are comfortable working with a variety of NoSQL databases but want to know more about the internals of these distributed systems, this book is a starting place. You'll become familiar with implementation features such as quorums, Bloom filters, and anti-entropy. The references will point you to resources to help you delve deeper if you'd like.

This book does not try to duplicate documentation available with NoSQL databases. There is no better place to learn how to insert data into a database than from the documentation. On the other hand, documentation rarely has the level of explanation, discussion of pros and cons, and advice about best practices provided in a book such as *NoSQL for Mere Mortals*. Read this book as a complement to, not a replacement for, database documentation.

## The Purpose of This Book

The purpose of this book is to help someone with an interest in data to use NoSQL databases to help solve problems. The book is built on the assumption that the reader is not a seasoned database professional. If you are comfortable working with Excel, then you are ready for the topics covered in this book.

With this book, you'll not only learn about NoSQL databases, but also how to apply design principles and best practices to solve your data management requirements. This is a book that will take you into the internals of NoSQL database management systems to explain how distributed databases work and what to do (and not do) to build scalable, reliable applications.

The hallmark of this book is pragmatism. Everything in this book is designed to help you use NoSQL databases to solve problems. There is a bit of computer science theory scattered through the pages but only to provide more explanation about certain key topics. If you are well versed in theory, feel free to skip over it.

## How to Read This Book

For those who are new to database systems, start with Chapters 1 and 2. These will provide sufficient background to read the other chapters.

If you are familiar with relational databases and their predecessors, you can skip Chapter 1. If you are already experienced with NoSQL, you could skip Chapter 2; however, it does discuss all four major types of NoSQL databases, so you might want to at least skim the sections on types you are less familiar with.

Everyone should read Part II. It is referenced throughout the other parts of the book. Parts III, IV, and V could be read in any order, but there are some references to content in earlier chapters. To achieve the best understanding of each type of NoSQL database, read all three chapters in Parts II, III, IV, and V.

Chapter 15 assumes familiarity with the content in the other chapters, but you might be able to skip parts on NoSQL databases you are sufficiently familiar with. If your goal is to understand how to choose between NoSQL options, be sure to read Chapter 15.

## How This Book Is Organized

Here's an overview of what you'll find in each part and each chapter.

### Part I: Introduction

NoSQL databases did not appear out of nowhere. This part provides a background on relational databases and earlier data management systems.

**Chapter 1**, "Different Databases for Different Requirements," introduces relational databases and their precursor data management systems along with a discussion about today's need for the alternative approaches provided by NoSQL databases.

**Chapter 2**, "Variety of NoSQL Databases," explores key functionality in databases, challenges to implementing distributed databases, and the trade-offs you'll find in different types of databases. The chapter includes an introduction to a series of case studies describing realistic applications of various NoSQL databases.

## Part II: Key-Value Databases

In this part, you learn how to use key-value databases and how to avoid potential problems with them.

**Chapter 3**, "Introduction to Key-Value Databases," provides an overview of the simplest of the NoSQL database types.

**Chapter 4**, "Key-Value Database Terminology," introduces the vocabulary you need to understand the structure and function of key-value databases.

**Chapter 5**, "Designing for Key-Value Databases," covers principles of designing key-value databases, the limitations of key-value databases, and design patterns used in key-value databases. The chapter concludes with a case study describing a realistic use case of key-value databases.

## Part III: Document Databases

This part delves into the widely used document database and provides guidance on how to effectively implement document database applications.

**Chapter 6**, "Introduction to Document Databases," describes the basic characteristics of document databases, introduces the concept of schemaless databases, and discusses basic operations on document databases.

**Chapter 7**, "Document Database Terminology," acquaints you with the vocabulary of document databases.

**Chapter 8**, "Designing for Document Databases," delves into the benefits of normalization and denormalization, planning for mutable documents, tips on indexing, as well as common design patterns. The chapter concludes with a case study using document databases for a business application.

## Part IV: Column Family Databases

This part covers Big Data applications and the need for column family databases.

**Chapter 9**, "Introduction to Column Family Databases," describes the Google BigTable design, the difference between key-value, document, and column family databases as well as architectures used in column family databases.

**Chapter 10**, "Column Family Database Terminology," introduces the vocabulary of column family databases. If you've always wondered "what is anti-entropy?" this chapter is for you.

**Chapter 11**, "Designing for Column Family Databases," offers guidelines for designing tables, indexing, partitioning, and working with Big Data.

## Part V: Graph Databases

This part covers graph databases and use cases where they are particularly appropriate.

**Chapter 12**, "Introduction to Graph Databases," discusses graph and network modeling as well as the benefits of graph databases.

**Chapter 13**, "Graph Database Terminology," introduces the vocabulary of graph theory, the branch of math underlying graph databases.

**Chapter 14**, "Designing for Graph Databases," covers tips for graph database design, traps to watch for, and methods for querying a graph database. This chapter concludes with a case study example of graph database applied to a business problem.

## Part VI: Choosing a Database for Your Application

This part deals with applying what you have learned in the rest of the book.

**Chapter 15**, "Guidelines for Selecting a Database," builds on the previous chapters to outline factors that you should consider when selecting a database for your application.

## Part VII: Appendices

**Appendix A**, "Answers to Chapter Review Questions," contains the review questions at the end of each chapter along with answers.

**Appendix B**, "List of NoSQL Databases," provides a nonexhaustive list of NoSQL databases, many of which are open source or otherwise free to use.

The Glossary contains definitions of NoSQL terminology used throughout the book.

# Part I
# *Introduction*

# Different Databases for Different Requirements

*"There is nothing new in the world except the history you do not know."*
—HARRY S. TRUMAN

## Topics Covered In This Chapter

Relational Database Design

Early Database Management Systems

The Relational Database Revolution

Motivations for Not Just/No SQL (NoSQL) Databases

Case Study

The history of information technology is a story of increasingly faster computation and greater volumes of data storage. An important sub-plot of this story is the evolution of data management technologies. Anyone who started to work with data management systems in the past two decades might understandably assume that data management is synonymous with relational database management systems. It is not. Prior to the advent of the relational database management systems, such as Microsoft Access, Microsoft SQL Server, Oracle relational database, and IBM's DB2, computer scientists and information technology professionals created a variety of data management systems based on different organizing principles. The data management community has recently taken on new types of data management problems that have prompted the development of new kinds of data management systems. These are collectively known as NoSQL databases.

NoSQL gets its name from SQL (pronounced "sequel"), which is a language used with most relational database management systems. The "No" in NoSQL can mean literally there is no SQL used in a database, or it can mean "not just SQL." For our purposes, we will consider the non-SQL aspects of NoSQL databases.

> ❖ **Note** If you are interested in learning more about SQL, see John L. Viescas and Michael J. Hernandez's *SQL Queries for Mere Mortals* (Addison-Wesley, 2007).

This chapter introduces the basic concepts of data management and database systems. It begins with a discussion of early database management systems. The limitations of these early data management systems motivated the development of a new kind of database: the relational database. Relational databases were a major advance over earlier types of data management systems. For example, relational databases help avoid inconsistencies in data, known as data anomalies, that could be introduced in some data management systems under seemingly normal operating conditions. Relational databases have so successfully solved a wide range of data management problems that they have been widely used across industries and application areas.

## Relational Database Design

Relational databases are well designed to support hundreds and even thousands of users simultaneously. Even large enterprises can support complex applications serving thousands of users. As businesses and researchers developed new types of applications designed for the Web, they realized that relational databases were not always meeting their needs.

Web applications may need to support tens of thousands of users or more. Some of the most important features of relational databases, such as ensuring anyone reading data will have a consistent view of the data, require time, storage, and computational resources. These types of features are vital to some applications.

For example, if you were to transfer $100 from your savings account to your checking account, it requires two steps: Deduct $100 from your savings account and add $100 to your checking account. If you were to read your account balances after the $100 was deducted from your savings account but before it was added to your checking account, you would appear to be missing $100. Relational databases can group a set of operations, like deducting from savings and adding to checking accounts, as a single operation. If you were to read your balances, you would see the balances either before or after the transfer—never in the middle of the set of operations.

## E-commerce Application

Now consider an e-commerce application. Customers use a web application to select products from a vendor's catalog. As you select products, they are added to a "shopping cart." Of course, there is no literal shopping cart; it is a metaphor for a data structure that manages the customer's selection. For this kind of data management operation, a fairly simple data structure will suffice. You would need a unique identifier for each customer and a list of items selected. (You might also want other details, such as the date and time an item was added to the cart so you can remove items after some period of inactivity, but we'll ignore those additional details for now.)

A data model using key-value pairs would work well here. The unique customer ID would be the key, which is how you look up or find data. The values would be the list of items in the cart. Because there is no need to support operations like transfers between bank accounts, you do not need to support the additional data management features found in relational databases.

Different applications require different types of databases. This fact has driven the development of data management systems for decades. As you shall see, history repeats itself. Some of the features found in early database management systems appear again in some NoSQL databases. This fact is more than just an interesting coincidence. Relational databases largely displaced early types of data management systems because the relational model addresses limitations of early systems.

As you evaluate NoSQL databases, you should consider how the newer NoSQL databases address the limitations of relational databases as well as any limitations they have in common with earlier data management systems.

## Early Database Management Systems

Early data management systems include file and database systems that were designed prior to the advent of relational databases in the 1970s. These include

- Flat file data management systems
- Hierarchical data management systems
- Network data management systems

Flat file–based systems were the earliest form of computerized data management. The hierarchical and network models improved on the flat file approach to data management.

## Flat File Data Management Systems

A *file* is an organized set of data stored on a long-term storage medium such as a disk or, at the time, magnetic tape. At the time flat files were commonly used data management, but magnetic tape was also in widespread use. For this reason, early data management files had to accommodate the physical constraints of physical systems.

### Organization of Flat File Data Management Systems

Although there are multiple ways of storing data on magnetic tape, this section just considers block storage for simplicity. Magnetic tape is a long, thin magnetized plastic material that was a popular means of recording audio from the 1950s to the 1970s. It was adapted to store digital data as well. A magnetic tape is divided into a series of blocks with gaps between them (see Figure 1.1). Data is written to blocks by recording heads in a tape drive. Data is read by moving the tape over heads as well.

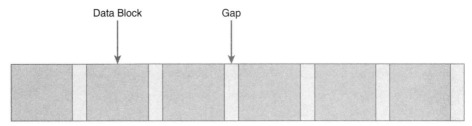

**Figure 1.1** *Magnetic tapes store data in sequential blocks.*

It is a relatively simple operation to start reading a tape at a particular block and then read the following blocks in sequence. This is known as sequential access to data. This method optimizes the amount of data read relative to the amount of movement of the tape. You can think of a block as a chunk of data that the tape drive reads. Blocks may contain data about multiple entities, such as people, products, and locations. If a business needs to track customers' names, addresses, and phone numbers, it could use a file-based storage method. The programmers working on the project may decide to leave a fixed amount of storage space for each customer:

- Customer ID—10 characters

- Customer name—40 characters

- Customer address—100 characters

- Customer phone number—10 characters

To store each customer's information, 160 characters are required. If a block on the tape is 800 characters long, you could store five customer records in each block (see Figure 1.2).

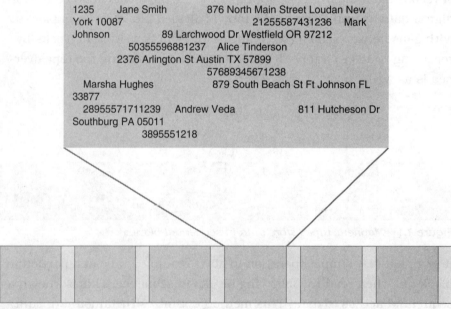

1235     Jane Smith          876 North Main Street Loudan New York 10087                    21255587431236     Mark Johnson          89 Larchwood Dr Westfield OR 97212          50355596881237     Alice Tinderson          2376 Arlington St Austin TX 57899                    57689345671238          Marsha Hughes          879 South Beach St Ft Johnson FL 33877          28955571711239     Andrew Veda               811 Hutcheson Dr Southburg PA 05011               3895551218

**Figure 1.2**   *A block is a chunk of data read by tape or disk drive in a single read operation.*

## Random Access of Data

Sometimes it is necessary to access data on different parts of the tape. For example, looking up the addresses of several customers may require moving the tape to several different positions, some of which can be quite far from each other. This is known as random access (see Figure 1.3).

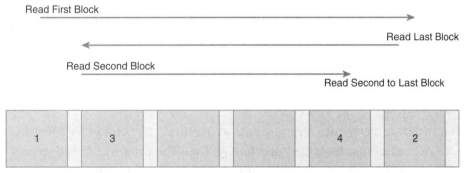

**Figure 1.3**  *Random access to blocks on tape can take more time than sequential access because there can be more tape movement relative to the amount of data read.*

Random access is more efficient on disk drives. Read-write heads of disk drives may need to move to be in the correct position to read a data block, but there is less movement than with tapes. Disk read-write heads only need to move at most the radius of the disk. Tape drives may need to move the full length of a tape to retrieve a data block.

## Limitations of Flat File Data Management Systems

The programs that use flat files largely determine the organization of data. A team of developers, for example, may decide that they want to organize the file by customer record ordered by customer ID. This makes for efficient addition of new customers. As each new customer is created, the customer can be added to the end of the tape. If you need to produce a list of customers ordered by customer ID, you could start at the beginning of the tape and sequentially read each record. If you need to produce a customer list ordered alphabetically by customer name, it is a more difficult process. You could, for example, read all the data from tape to memory (assuming it would all fit) and then sort the records in memory.

One of the problems with file-based data management systems is that they can lead to duplicated data. Another team of developers may need customer data but want to organize records by customer name instead of customer ID. Another developer who needs access to customer data may not know other customer files exist or does not want to use someone else's file because the structure of the file might change. If that were to happen, programmers have to update their programs to reflect the new structure.

If a programmer wrote a program that assumed the customer record was organized as described previously, then the program would expect to find the customer address to start at 51 characters after the start of the record; the first 10 characters would be taken up by the customer ID, and the following 40 by customer name. Now, imagine the programmers who designed the original file layout decided they needed 50 characters for a customer name. They changed the organization of the file to be

- Customer ID—10 characters

- Customer name—50 characters

- Customer address—100 characters

- Customer phone number—10 characters

They then created a new file with the new organization, copied the data from the original file to a new version, and replaced the old version with the new version. Programs designed to work with the original file format would start reading the customer address at character 51, which is now part of the customer name.

Another problem with flat file management is that it is difficult to share files that contain information that should be kept confidential from some users. An employee file that contains the names, addresses, phone numbers, employee IDs, and position title of all employees would be useful to a number of different parts of an organization. However, if the file also contained salary information, then that data should be accessed only by those who have a job responsibility that requires it, such as someone working on payroll or in human resources. In this scenario, the easiest solution may be to have two copies of the employee file: one with salary data and one without.

The proposed solution introduces another problem: The data in the two files may become inconsistent. If an employee moves and informs the human resources department of her new address, that department might update the file its employees use; that is, the one with salary information. Unless the employee or someone in human resources informs the person responsible for updating the other version of the employee file, the data in the two files will be inconsistent. One file will have the employee's new address while the other file will contain the employee's old address.

To summarize, the limitations of flat file data management systems include the following:

- It is inefficient to access data in any way other than by the way data is organized in the file; for example, by customer ID.

- Changes to file structure require changes to programs.

- Different kinds of data have different security requirements.

- Data may be stored in multiple files, making it difficult to maintain consistent sets of data.

Attempts to address the limitations of flat file data management systems led to the development of hierarchical data model and network data model systems.

## Hierarchical Data Model Systems

One of the limitations of flat file–based data management systems is that they can be inefficient to search. Hierarchical data models address this problem by organizing data in a hierarchy of parent-child relationships.

### Organization of Hierarchical Data Management Systems

A hierarchy starts with a root node that links to the top layer of data nodes or records. These top-layer records can have child records that contain additional data about the parent record. The logical organization is shown in Figure 1.4.

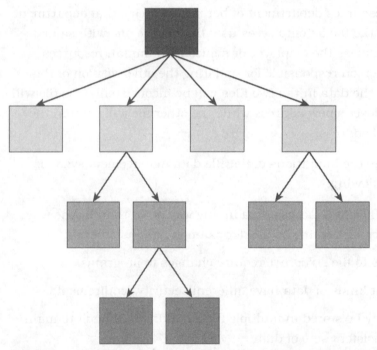

**Figure 1.4**   *The hierarchical model is organized into a set of parent-child relations.*

Consider the kind of data the loan department of a bank may track. It has customers and each customer has one or more loans. For each customer, the loan department would want to track the customer's name, address, and phone number. For each loan, the loan department should track the amount of the loan, the interest rate, the date the loan was made, and the date the loan is due. Customers can have more than one loan at a time, and a loan might have multiple customers associated with it. Figure 1.5 shows the logical organization of such a database.

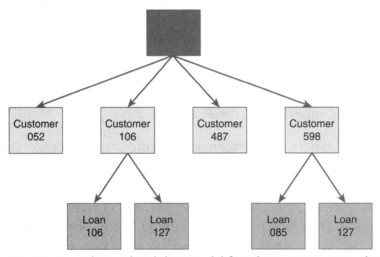

**Figure 1.5**   *A hierarchical data model for a loan management database.*

An advantage of the hierarchical model over flat files is that searching is more efficient. Rather than having to scan over all the data on a tape to search for a block of data, a program using a hierarchical model could scan just customer records in search of a particular customer's loan record. Once the customer record is found, the program could search through the customer's loans looking for the particular loan of interest.

**Limitations of Hierarchical Data Management Systems**

Hierarchical data management systems work well when the entities you are managing can be organized into parent-child relationships, specifically, one parent to one or more children. One customer with one loan is easily managed. One customer with three loans is easily managed. Two customers with one loan, such as two business partners taking out a short-term business loan, are not so easily represented.

In the case of two customers on the same loan, the hierarchical data management system would have to duplicate information about the loan under both customers. This creates three problems. First, it makes inefficient use of storage space to duplicate data.

In addition, like duplicated data in the case of flat file management systems, it can lead to inconsistent data if care is not taken to ensure that any changes are applied to all copies of the data.

Also, there is a potential for errors when aggregating data. For example, to find the total value of all outstanding loans, a programmer could not just read all loan records and add all loan amounts together. Because some loans have multiple copies, one for each customer, simply adding all copies of all loan records will sum to a total loan amount greater than the actual amount. The programmer must take steps to count each loan only once.

To address the limitations of hierarchical models, data management system designers turned to network data model systems.

## Network Data Management Systems

A network data model is like a hierarchical data model in that it uses links between records; however, unlike hierarchical data models, you are not restricted to having one parent record. Also, unlike flat file data management systems and hierarchical data management systems, network data models have two essential components: a schema and the database itself.

**Organization of Network Data Management Systems**

A network is made up of data records linked together. The data records are known as nodes and the links are known as edges. The collection of nodes and edges is known as a graph. Network data models have two important constraints on how you use edges. Edges have a direction to them. This allows you to represent parent-child relations. Parent-child relations are also known as one-to-many relations (see Figure 1.6). Furthermore, network data models allow for multiple parents, such as two customers on a loan. It can also represent two customers with two loans without duplicating data. This is known as a many-to-many relation.

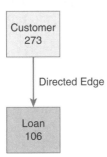

**Figure 1.6**  *A parent-child relationship is represented by a directed edge.*

Another constraint is that you cannot have cycles in the graph. That is, if you start at a node, follow a link to another node, then follow a link from that node, and so on, you will never return to the starting node. Graphs that have directed edges and no cycles are known as directed acyclic graphs (see Figure 1.7).

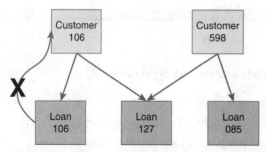

**Figure 1.7**    *This graph has cycles and, therefore, is not a directed acyclic graph and not a model of a network data management system.*

Additional constraints on which nodes can link to other nodes arise from the entities you are trying to model. For example, in a banking database, customers can have addresses, but loans and bank accounts do not. In a human resources database, employees can have positions in the organization, but departments cannot. The kinds of nodes that can link to other nodes are defined in a structure called a schema (see Figure 1.8).

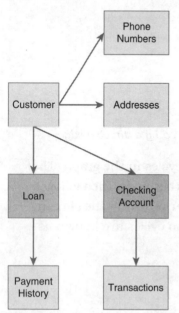

**Figure 1.8**    *A simple network schema shows which entities can link to other entities.*

The other part of a network data management system is the database itself. This is where the actual data is stored according to the structure of the schema. One of the advances of network databases over previous approaches is that it became standardized in 1969 by the Conference on Data Systems Languages (CODASYL) Consortium. This standard became the basis for most implementations of network databases.

**Limitations of Network Data Management Systems**

The chief limitation of network databases is that they can be difficult to design and maintain. Depending on how nodes are linked, a program may need to traverse a large number of links to get to the node with the needed data. For example, if you must start at a customer record to get to a loan record and then to a loan payment history record, you must traverse two links from customer to loan payment history. As data models become more complex, the number of links and the length of paths can become substantially longer.

Also, if after a network database is deployed, a database designer determines another entity or node type is needed, then programs that access the network database will have to be updated. Adding nodes to the schema and the database changes the paths that programs must traverse to get to particular nodes.

## Summary of Early Database Management Systems

Early database management systems include flat file, hierarchical, and network databases.

Flat file databases tend to keep data about a single entity together in a single record. This is a simple structure but can lead to duplicated data and inefficient retrieval. It is difficult to implement security controls to protect confidential data in flat file management systems.

Hierarchical data management systems allow for parent-child relationships. This can help avoid duplicating data about parents because only one copy of a parent record is needed. Because data is organized into different records, data retrieval can be more efficient. For example, searching for a customer in a loan database might require scanning all customer records, but at least the program does not have to scan over loan data as well.

❖ **Note** Although hierarchical data management systems avoid some duplication found in flat file management systems, there is still a potential for duplicate data. This can occur, for example, in the case of a loan database that must model multiple customers on a single loan.

Network data management improves on hierarchical databases by allowing multiple parents. Network data management systems also incorporate schemas that define valid relations between node types. The ability to represent parent-child and many-to-many relations is an advantage over flat file and hierarchical data management systems.

The disadvantages of early database management systems include duplicate data, difficulty implementing security, inefficient searching, and difficulty maintaining program code to access databases. The reason programs have to change when the structure of the database changes is that there is no independence between the logical organization of a database and the way the data is physically stored on tape or disk. As you will see in the next section, the structural independence of the logical and physical organization of the database is a major advance in data management provided by relational database management systems.

# The Relational Database Revolution

Although network and hierarchical data management systems improved on flat file data management systems, it was not until 1970 when E. F. Codd published a paper on the design of a new type of database that data management technology radically changed. There are many important aspects of relational database design that are improvements over previous data management models. Relational databases were based on a formal mathematical model that used relational algebra to describe data and their relations. Relational databases separated the logical organization of data structures from the physical storage of those structures. Codd and others developed rules for designing relational databases that eliminated the potential for some types of data anomalies, such as inconsistent data.

❖ **Note** There are many aspects of relational databases that deserve in-depth review. This section, however, provides only a minimal, high-level review of key points. For more on relational databases, see Michael J. Hernandez's *Database Design for Mere Mortals: A Hands-On Guide to Relational Database Design* (Addison Wesley, 2003).

## Relational Database Management Systems

A relational database management system is an application made up of multiple programs that manage data and allow users of the application to add, update, read, and delete data. Unlike flat file data stores where each time a new file for storage was created, a programmer had to develop a program to manipulate the data, relational database management systems are designed to use a common language to manipulate data. That language is called SQL and is standardized across relational database management systems. Although SQL is a language used with relational databases, it is sometimes used as shorthand for "relational" as in "SQL database" or "NoSQL."

Most of the users of relational database management systems (RDBMSs) do not work directly with the database software. Instead, they work with applications created by software developers and those applications interact with the RDBMS. To explain relational databases, it helps to separately describe the features of the RDBMS and a typical database application.

## Organization of Relational Database Management Systems

A relational database management system is a set of programs for managing data and programs that manipulate that data. The minimal requirements for implementing an RDBMS include four components:

- Storage management programs
- Memory management programs
- Data dictionary
- Query language

Together, these four components provide the core data management and data retrieval services of an RDBMS.

### Storage Management Programs

Database systems store data persistently on disks and flash drives for long-term storage. Database storage may be directly attached to a server or other device running a database. For example, a laptop running the MySQL database can persistently store data on the local disk drive. In large enterprises, IT departments may offer shared storage. In such cases, large disk arrays are managed as a single resource and database servers can save data to and read data from these storage arrays (see Figure 1.9).

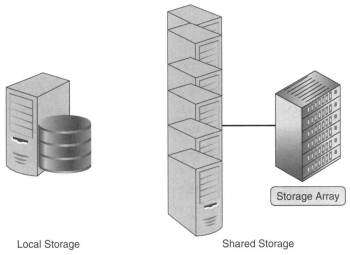

Local Storage          Shared Storage

**Figure 1.9** *Local storage versus shared network storage.*

Regardless of what type of storage system is used, the RDBMS has to track where each piece of data is stored. One of the drawbacks of tape-based storage was the need to sequentially search a tape to retrieve data. Disk and flash devices are not so restricted. This has allowed RDBMS designers to improve retrieval methods.

Like flat file–based data stores, RDBMSs, at the most basic level, read and write blocks of data. Disk technologies made it easier to create and use indexes to data. Indexes are data sets that contain location information about blocks of data saved by the database. Indexes are based on some attribute contained in the data, such as a customer ID or customer name. Indexes point to the location on disk or flash memory that contains the record holding information about the entity referenced in the index. For example, an index with the data "Smith, Jane 18277372" would indicate that the block of data with information about Jane Smith is located at disk position 18277372.

The storage management programs in an RDBMS do much more than keep track of the location of data. They can also optimize the placement of data on disks, compress data to save storage, and make copies of data blocks so data is not lost in case a data block on a disk goes bad.

### Memory Management Programs

RDBMSs are also responsible for managing data in memory. Often, the size of data stored in a database is larger than available memory. The RDBMS memory management components are responsible for bringing and keeping data in memory as long as it is needed and deleting it when it is no longer needed or to make space for additional data. Because reading data from memory is order of magnitudes faster than reading it from disk, the overall performance of the RDBMS is highly influenced by its ability to use memory efficiently and effectively.

### Data Dictionary

The data dictionary is the part of the RDBMS that keeps track of information about the structure of data stored in the database (see Figure 1.10). This includes information about multiple levels of database structures, including

- Schemas
- Tables
- Columns
- Indexes
- Constraints
- Views

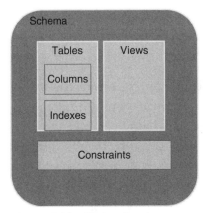

**Figure 1.10**  *Data structures managed by a data dictionary.*

A *schema* is a collection of tables, views, indexes, and other structures that are all related to a set of data. Typically, you would have separate schemas for separate major types of applications, such as a schema for inventory of products, for accounts receivable, or for employees and their benefits.

Tables are structures that have data about entities. Entities describe a physical or logical thing related to the business or operation supported by an RDBMS. Entities for a human resources schema might include employees, managers, and departments. An inventory schema might include warehouses, products, and suppliers.

Tables are made up of columns. Columns contain a single unit of information. An employee table might contain the following: employee first name, last name, street address, city, state, zip code, date of birth, and salary. Columns have a type associated with them to indicate the kind of data that can be stored. First name, for example, may be character data, date of birth would be a date type, and salary would be some type of number or currency type.

Indexes, as described earlier, are data structures used by the RDBMS to improve the speed at which the RDBMS can retrieve data. An employee table would probably have an index on the employee's last name to enable rapid lookup of employee data by last name.

Constraints are rules that further restrict the values of data that can go in a column. Data types associated with columns prevent the wrong type of data from being saved to a column. A program might mistakenly try to write a number to the employee first name column, but the database would prevent it. A negative number would be a valid number or currency value and allowed in the salary column. You could add a constraint to the salary column to specify that a salary must be greater than 0. Constraints are generally based on business rules about the entities and operations the data is representing.

Views are collections of related columns from one or more tables as well as values calculated for data in columns. Views can be used to restrict the data that a user sees. For example, if an employee table has salary information, you can create a view that includes all non-salary columns from the employee table. Users who need access to employees' names and addresses can use that view instead of the employee table. Views can also combine data from multiple tables, such as a table with employee names and a table with details about promotions all employees have received.

### Query Language

A query language in an RDBMS performs two types of operations: defining data structures and manipulating data. SQL is the query language of relational databases and includes statements for performing both types of operations.

### SQL Data Definition Language

SQL includes statements that allow programmers to create and delete schemas, tables, views, indexes, constraints, and other data structures. It also provides statements for adding and removing columns from tables, and granting access to read or write tables. The following is a sample statement for creating a schema:

```
CREATE SCHEMA humresc
```

The following is a sample statement for creating a table:

```
CREATE TABLE employees (
    emp_id  int,
    emp_first_name varchar(25),
    emp_last_name varchar(25),
    emp_address varchar(50),
    emp_city varchar(50),
    emp_state varchar(2),
    emp_zip varchar(5),
    emp_position_title varchar(30)
    )
```

The specifics of these statements are not important at this point, but they do show the declarative style of SQL. Instead of telling the computer how to create a data structure, such as creating a free block of data at a particular address, you tell the RDBMS what kind of data structure you want. In the first case, the statement creates a schema with the name humresc (short for human resources). In the second statement, a table called employee is created with eight columns. Varchar is a variable-length character type. The number with each varchar term is the maximum length of the column. Int, short for integer, indicates that the emp _ id is an integer.

*SQL Data Manipulation Language*
Once you have a schema with tables, you can start to add data and manipulate it. The SQL data manipulation language includes statements for

- Inserting data
- Updating data
- Deleting data
- Selecting (that is, reading) data

The following is a sample `INSERT` statement for the employee table:

```
INSERT INTO employee (emp_id, first_name, last_name)
  VALUES (1234, 'Jane', 'Smith')
```

This statement adds a row to the employee table with an `emp _ id` of 1234, a first name of `'Jane'`, and a last name of `'Smith'`. The other columns of the table would be `NULL`, a special data value used to indicate the column has no value specified.

Updating and deleting statements allow users to change values in existing rows or remove existing rows.

To read data from a database, use the `SELECT` statement. For example:

```
SELECT emp_id, first_name, last_name
FROM    employee
```

would produce output such as

```
emp_id          first_name                 last_name
-----------------------------------------------------------------
1234            Jane                       Smith
```

The data manipulation data statements are capable of expressing complex operations and targeting specific rows of data using fairly complex logic in the `SELECT`, `UPDATE`, and `DELETE` statements.

Relational database management systems provide storage management, memory management, a data dictionary, and a query language. Although programmers and software developers may be comfortable working directly with SQL, database applications allow any computer user to work with relational databases.

### Organization of Applications Using Relational Database Management Systems

Working with broad concepts, you can think of business applications that use relational databases as having three major components:

- A user interface

- Business logic

- Database code

The user interface is designed to support the workflow of users. For example, a person using a human resources application might need to look up an employee's salary, change an employee's position, or add a new employee. The user works with menus and other user interface abstractions to invoke data entry forms, update the data as needed, and save changes to the database. There is no exposure to SQL or to the RDBMS.

The business logic is the part of the program that performs calculations and checks business rules. A business rule, for example, might check the age of an employee to verify the employee is over 21 before assigning the position "bartender" to that employee. Business rules can be implemented in programming languages, such as Python, Visual Basic, or Java, or in SQL.

Database code is the set of SELECT, INSERT, UPDATE, and DELETE (and so on) statements that perform operations on the database. The statements correspond to the operations that users can perform through the user interface.

Database applications make the functionality of relational databases, and other types of databases, accessible to nonprogrammers.

### Limitations of Relational Databases

Relational databases have been the dominant type of database used for database applications for decades. Relational databases addressed many of the limitations of flat file–based data stores, hierarchical databases, and network databases. With the advent of the Web, however, the limitations of relational databases became increasingly problematic.

Companies such as Google, LinkedIn, Yahoo!, and Amazon found that supporting large numbers of users on the Web was different from supporting much smaller numbers of business users, even those in large enterprises with thousands of users on a single database application.

Web application developers working with large volumes of data and extremely large numbers of users found they needed to support

- Large volumes of read and write operations

- Low latency response times

- High availability

These requirements were difficult to realize using relational databases. These were not the first database users who needed to improve performance. The problem is that techniques used in the past did not work at the scale of operations, users, and data that businesses now demanded. In the past, if a relational database was running slowly, it could be upgraded with more CPUs, additional memory, or faster storage devices. This is a costly option and works only to a point. There are limits to how many CPUs and memory can be supported in a single server. Database designers could redesign the database schema to use techniques that would improve performance but at the cost of increasing the risk of data anomalies. (These techniques are known as *denormalization*.)

Another option is to use multiple servers with a relational database. This is possible, but operating a single relational database management system over multiple servers is a complex operation. This makes long-term management difficult. There are also performance issues when supporting a series of operations that run on different servers but all have to complete successfully or all fail. These sets of operations that succeed or fail together are known as transactions. As the number of servers in a database cluster increases, the cost of implementing transactions increases.

In spite of these difficulties, some companies, such as Facebook, use the MySQL relational database for some of its operations. They, however, have a dedicated MySQL staff that are pushing and expanding the limits of MySQL. Most organizations do not have such resources. For those organizations, if relational databases are not meeting needs, then it may be time to consider a NoSQL database.

# Motivations for Not Just/No SQL (NoSQL) Databases

Pressing real-world problems motivated the data management professionals and software designers who created NoSQL databases. Web applications serving tens of thousands or more users were difficult to implement with relational databases. Four characteristics of data management systems that are particularly important for large-scale data management tasks are

- Scalability

- Cost

- Flexibility

- Availability

Depending on the needs of a particular application, some of these characteristics may be more important than others.

### Scalability

Scalability is the ability to efficiently meet the needs for varying workloads. For example, if there is a spike in traffic to a website, additional servers can be brought online to handle the additional load. When the spike subsides and traffic returns to normal, some of those additional servers can be shut down. Adding servers as needed is called scaling out.

When you work with relational databases, it is often challenging to scale out. Additional database software may be needed to manage multiple servers working as a single database system. Oracle, for example, offers Oracle Real Applications Clusters (RAC) for cluster-based databases. Additional database components can add complexity and cost to operations.

Alternatively, database administrators could choose to scale up, which is upgrading an existing database server to add additional processors, memory, network bandwidth, or other resources that would improve performance on a database management system or replacing an existing server with one with more CPUs, memory, and so on (see Figure 1.11).

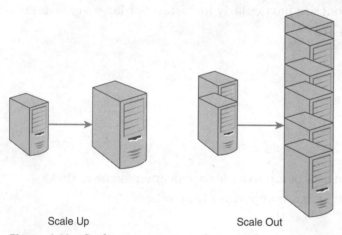

Scale Up                          Scale Out

**Figure 1.11**  *Scaling up versus scaling out.*

Scaling out is more flexible than scaling up. Servers can be added or removed as needed when scaling up. NoSQL databases are designed to utilize servers available in a cluster with minimal intervention by database administrators. As new servers are added or removed, the NoSQL database management system adjusts to use the new set of available servers. Scaling up by replacing a server requires migrating the database management to a new server. Scaling up by adding resources would not require a migration, but would likely require some downtime to add hardware to the database server.

## Cost

The cost of database licenses is an obvious consideration for any business or organization. Commercial software vendors employ a variety of licensing models that include charging by the size of the server running the RDBMS, by the number of concurrent users on the database, or by the number of named users allowed to use the software. Each of these models presents challenges for users of the database system.

Web applications may have spikes in demand that increase the number of users utilizing a database at any time. Should users of the RDBMS pay for the number of peak users or the number of average users? How should they budget for RDBMS licenses when it is difficult to know how many users will be using the system six months or a year from now? Users of open source software avoid these issues. The software is free to use on as many servers of whatever size needed because open source developers do not typically charge fees to run their software. Fortunately for NoSQL database users, the major NoSQL databases are available as open source.

Third-party companies provide commercial support services for open source NoSQL databases so businesses can have software support as they do with commercial relational databases.

## Flexibility

Relational database management systems are flexible in the range of problems that can be addressed using relational data models. Industries as different as banking, manufacturing, retail, energy, and health care all make use of relational databases. There is, however, another aspect of relational databases that is less flexible.

Database designers expect to know at the start of a project all the tables and columns that will be needed to support an application. It is also commonly assumed that most of the columns in a table will be needed by most of the rows. For example, all employees will have names and employee IDs. There are times that the problems modeled are less homogeneous than that.

Consider an e-commerce application that uses a database to track attributes of products. Computer products would have attributes such as CPU type, amount of memory, and disk size. Microwave ovens would have attributes such as size and power. A database designer could create separate tables for each type of product or define a table with as many different product attributes as she could imagine at the time she designs the database.

Unlike relational databases, some NoSQL databases do not require a fixed table structure. For example, in a document database, a program could dynamically add new attributes as needed without having to have a database designer alter the database design.

▶ *Refer to Chapter 2, "Distributed Systems and the Variety of NoSQL Databases," for more information on working with a document database.*

## Availability

Many of us have come to expect websites and web applications to be available whenever we want to use them. If your favorite social media or e-commerce site were frequently down when you tried to use it, you would likely start looking for a new favorite.

NoSQL databases are designed to take advantage of multiple, low-cost servers. When one server fails or is taken out of service for maintenance, the other servers in the cluster can take on the entire workload (see Figure 1.12). Performance may be somewhat less, but the application will still be available. If a database is running on a single server and it fails, the application will become unavailable unless there is a backup server. Backup servers keep replicated copies of data from the primary server in case the primary server fails. If that happens, the backup can take on the workload that the primary server had been processing. This can be an inefficient configuration because a server is kept in reserve in the event of a failure but otherwise is not helping to process the workload.

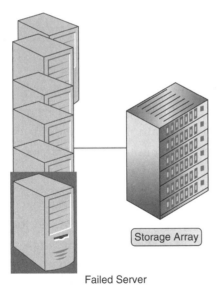

Storage Array

Failed Server

**Figure 1.12**  *High-availability NoSQL clusters run multiple servers. If one fails, the others can continue to support applications.*

Database designers turned to NoSQL systems when existing RDBMSs failed to meet their needs. Scalability, cost, flexibility, and availability are increasingly important concerns for application developers, and their choice of database management systems reflects this.

## Summary

Data management systems have evolved to meet changing application requirements subject to the constraints of the existing compute and storage technologies at their times. Early data management systems were based on records stored in flat files. These provided a basic capability of persistent storage of data, but suffered from a number of drawbacks, including slow search and retrieval operations, redundant data, and poor security. Hierarchical databases were an improvement over flat files. These systems allowed for parent-child relations between records. This helped reduce, but not eliminate, the potential for redundant data. Network databases further improved on hierarchical databases by allowing for multiple parent–multiple child relations. These are commonly known as many-to-many relations.

The development of relational databases represented a radical improvement over flat file, hierarchical, and network databases. Relational databases are based on a sound mathematical foundation. Rules for designing relational databases eliminate the potential for a range of data anomalies, such as inconsistent data. Relational databases virtually replaced all other types of data management systems in business applications.

In spite of the widespread successful use of relational databases, the exponential growth of e-commerce and social media led to the need for data management systems that were scalable, low cost, flexible, and highly available. Achieving some of these objectives with relational databases is possible in some cases, but often with difficulty and potentially high costs.

NoSQL databases were created to address the limitations of relational database management systems. NoSQL databases are unlikely to displace relational databases the way RDBMSs displaced flat file, hierarchical, and network databases. The two will likely complement each other and adapt features from each other as they both continue to be applied to increasingly complex and demanding applications.

## Case Study

Throughout this book, you will develop a case study around a set of applications needed by a transportation management company. The company, TransGlobal Transport and Shipping, is a fictional company with realistic requirements. As you examine each of the major types of NoSQL databases, you will consider how each can be applied to a specific application for TransGlobal Transport and Shipping.

The four major applications are

- Building a shipment order
- Managing customer manifests, or a detailed description of items in a shipment
- Maintaining a customer database
- Optimizing transportation routes

As you will see, different sets of requirements can demand different types of database systems. In this case, the four types of NoSQL databases will be used to meet the information management needs of TransGlobal Transport and Shipping.

▶ *Refer to Chapter 2, "Distributed Systems and the Variety of NoSQL Databases," to learn more about the four types of NoSQL databases.*

# Review Questions

1.  If the layout of records in a file data management system changes, what else must change?

2.  What kind of relation is supported in a hierarchical data management system?

    a. Parent-child

    b. Many-to-many

    c. Many-to-many-to-many

    d. No relations are allowed.

3.  What kind of relation is supported in network data management systems?

    a. Parent-child

    b. Many-to-many

    c. Both parent-child and many-to-many

    d. No relations are allowed.

4.  Give an example of a SQL data manipulation language statement.

5.  Give an example of a SQL data definition language statement.

6.  What is scaling up?

7.  What is scaling out?

8.  Are NoSQL databases likely to displace relational databases as relational databases displaced earlier types of data management systems?

9.  Name four required components of a relational database management system (RDBMS).

10. Name three common major components of a database application.

11. Name four motivating factors for database designers and other IT professionals to develop and use NoSQL databases.

# References

Codd, E. F. A Relational Model of Data for Large Shared Data Banks. *Communications of the ACM* 13, no. 6 (June 1970).

Intuit. "A Timeline of Database History." http://quickbase.intuit.com/articles/timeline-of-database-history.

# Bibliography

Hernandez, Michael J. *Data Design for Mere Mortals: A Hands-On Guide to Relational Database Design.* Reading, MA: Addison-Wesley, 2007.

Viescas, John L., and Michael J. Hernandez. *SQL Queries for Mere Mortals.* Reading, MA: Addison-Wesley, 2007.

# 2

# Variety of NoSQL Databases

*"Nothing is pleasant that is not spiced with variety."*
—Francis Bacon

## Topics Covered In This Chapter

Data Management with Distributed Databases

ACID and BASE

A Variety of Distributed Databases

NoSQL databases solve a wide variety of data management problems by offering several types of solutions. NoSQL databases are commonly designed to use multiple servers, but this is not a strict requirement. When systems run on multiple servers, instead of on just one computer, they are known as distributed systems (see Figure 2.1).

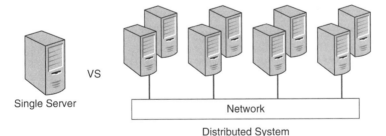

Figure 2.1  *Single server versus distributed system.*

This chapter starts with a review of common features and challenges faced by distributed databases. Because NoSQL databases are often used in distributed environments, this chapter spends some time examining the challenges of using multiple servers to manage data in a single logical database. Much of what is discussed in the following section on distributed systems does not apply if you run your NoSQL database on a single server.

Chapter 1, "Different Databases for Different Requirements," introduced the motivations for NoSQL, including the need for scalability, flexibility, cost control, and availability. A common way to meet these needs is by designing data management systems to work across multiple servers, that is, as a distributed system.

In addition to the other benefits of NoSQL databases, distributed systems offer some level of operational simplicity. You can add and remove servers as needed rather than adding or removing memory, CPUs, and so on from a single server. Also, some NoSQL databases include features that automatically detect when a server is added or removed from a cluster.

Many NoSQL databases take advantage of distributed systems, but they may employ different data management strategies. There are four major types of key NoSQL databases:

- Key-value databases, for example, work with a simple model based on keys, which are identifiers for looking up data, and values, the data that is associated with keys.

- Document databases also use identifiers to look up values, but the values are typically more complex than those typically stored in key-value databases. Documents are collections of data items stored together in a flexible structure.

- Column family databases have some of the characteristics of relational databases, such as organizing data into collections of columns. Column family databases trade some of the functionality of relational databases, such as the ability to link or join tables, for improved performance.

- Graph databases are well suited to model objects and relationships between objects.

Because distributed systems are the foundation of many NoSQL databases, it is important to explore some of the issues associated with managing data in a distributed system. After I outline the challenges and limitations associated with distributed databases, you will learn about key-value, document, column family store, and graph databases and compare them with relational databases.

# Data Management with Distributed Databases

Before getting into the details of distributed databases, let's look at a simplified view of databases in general. Databases are designed to do two things: store data and retrieve data. To meet these objectives, the database management systems must do three things:

- Store data persistently
- Maintain data consistency
- Ensure data availability

In this section, you will learn how distributed systems meet these objectives. You will also learn about limitations of distributed systems, with particular attention to balancing consistency, availability, and protection for network failures that leaves some servers in a cluster unreachable.

## Store Data Persistently

Data must be stored persistently; that is, it must be stored in a way that data is not lost when the database server is shut down. If data were only stored in memory—that is, RAM—then it would be lost when power to the memory is lost. Only data that is stored on disk, flash, tape, or other long-term storage is considered persistently stored, as shown in Figure 2.2.

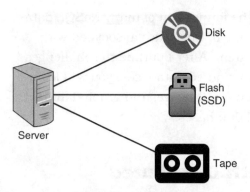

Persistently Stored Data

**Figure 2.2**   *Persistently stored data is stored on disk, flash, or other long-term storage medium.*

Data must be available for retrieving. You can retrieve persistently stored data in a number of different ways. Data stored on a flash device is read directly from its storage location. The movable parts of the disk and tape drives are put in position so that the read heads of the device are over the block of data to be read.

You could design your database to simply start at the beginning of a data file and search for the record you need when a read operation is performed. This would lead to painfully long response times and a waste of valuable compute resources. Rather than scan the full table for the data, you can use database indexes, which are like indexes at the end of a book, to quickly find the location of a particular piece of data. Indexes are a central element of databases.

## Maintain Data Consistency

It is important to ensure that the correct data is written to a persistent storage device. If the write or read operation does not accurately record or retrieve data, the database will not be of much use. This is rarely a problem unless there is a hardware failure. A more common issue with reading and writing occurs when two or more people are using the database and want to use the same data at the same time.

Consider a small business with two partners, Alice and Bob. Alice is using a database application to update the company's financial records. She has just received a number of payments from customers and posted them to the accounting system. The process requires two steps: updating the customer's balance due and updating the total funds available to the business. At the same time Alice is doing that, Bob is placing an order for more supplies. Bob wants to make sure there are sufficient funds before he commits to an order, so he checks the balance of total funds available. What balance will Bob see?

Ideally, Bob would see the balance of funds available that includes the most recent payments. If he issues his query while Alice is updating the customer balance and total funds available, then Bob would see the balance without the new payments. The reason for this is that the database is designed to be consistent. Bob could see the balance before or after Alice updates both the customer balance record and the funds available record, but never when only one of the two has been updated (see Figure 2.3).

It would be inconsistent for the database to return results that indicated a customer had paid the balance due on her account without also including that payment in the funds available record. Relational database systems are designed to support these kinds of multistep procedures that have to be treated as a single operation or transaction.

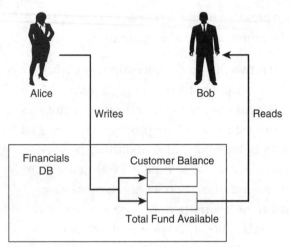

**Figure 2.3**    *Data should reflect a consistent state.*

## Ensure Data Availability

Data should be available whenever it is needed. This is difficult to guarantee. Hardware may fail. An operating system on the database server may need patching. You might need to install a new version of the database management system. A database that runs on a single server can be unavailable for a large number of reasons.

One way to avoid the problem of an unavailable database server is to have two database servers: One is used for updating data and responding to queries while the other is kept as a backup in case the first server fails. The server that is used for updating and responding to queries is called the primary server, and the other is the backup server. The backup server starts with a copy of the database that is on the primary server. When the database is in use, any changes to the primary database are reflected in the backup database as well.

For example, if Alice and Bob's company used a backup database server, then when Alice updated a customer's account, those same changes would be made to the backup server. This would require the database to write data twice: once to the disk used by the primary server and then one more time to the disk used by the backup server in an operation known as a two-phase commit (see Figure 2.4).

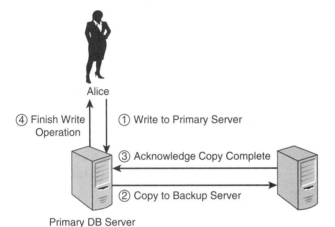

Alice

④ Finish Write Operation

① Write to Primary Server

③ Acknowledge Copy Complete

② Copy to Backup Server

Primary DB Server

**Figure 2.4**   *Two-phase commits are complete only when operations on both databases are complete.*

Recall that a database transaction is an operation made up of multiple steps and that all steps must complete for the transaction to complete. If any one of the multiple steps fails, then the entire transaction fails. Updating two databases makes every update a multistep process.

When the company used a single server, there was just one step in updating the number of a particular product in the warehouse. For example, the number of black desk chairs could be updated from 100 to 125 in a single operation. Now that the company is using a backup database, the number of chairs would have to be updated on the primary server and the backup server.

The process for updating both databases is similar to other multi-step transactions: Both databases must succeed for the operation to succeed. If the primary database is updated to reflect 125 black desk chairs in the warehouse but the update fails on the backup database, then the primary database resets the chair count back to 100. The primary and the backup databases must be consistent. This is an example of a two-phase commit. In the first phase of the operation, the database writes, or commits, the data to the disk of the primary server. In the second phase of the operation, the database writes data to the disk of the backup server.

With data consistent on two database servers, you can be sure that if the primary database fails, you can switch to using the backup database and know that you have the same data on both. When the primary database is back online, the first thing it does is to update itself so that all changes made to the backup database while the primary database was down are made to the primary database. The primary database is usable when it is consistent with the backup database.

The advantage of using two database servers is that it enables the database to remain available even if one of the servers fails. This is helpful but is not without costs. Database applications, and the people who use them, must wait while a write operation completes.

Because, in the case of a two-phase commit, a write operation is not complete until both databases are updated successfully, the speed of the updates depends on the amount of data written, the speed of the disks, the speed of the network between the two servers, and other design factors (see Figure 2.5).

> ❖ **Note**  You can have consistent data, and you can have a high-availability database, but transactions will require longer times to execute than if you did not have those requirements.

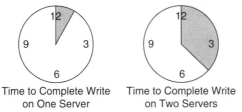

Time to Complete Write on One Server    Time to Complete Write on Two Servers

**Figure 2.5**  *Consistency and availability require more time to complete transactions in high-availability environments.*

## Consistency of Database Transactions

The term *consistency* with respect to database transactions refers to maintaining a single, logically coherent view of data. When you transfer $100 from your savings account to your checking account, the bank's software may subtract $100 from your savings account in one step and add $100 to your checking account in another. At no time would it be correct to say you have $100 less in your savings account without also reflecting an additional $100 in your checking account.

Consistency has also been used to describe the state of copies of data in distributed systems. For example, if two database servers each have copies of data about products stored in a warehouse, it is said they are consistent if they have the same data. This is different from the kind of consistency that is needed when updating data in a transaction.

❖ **Note** To avoid confusion going forward, let's define a database server as a computer that runs database management software. That database management software will be called a database management system.

Database management systems can run on one or more computers. When the database management system is running on multiple computers, it is called a distributed database. The term *database* in this context is synonymous with *database management system*.

## Availability and Consistency in Distributed Databases

You might be starting to see some of the challenges to maintaining a database management system that uses multiple servers. When two database servers must keep consistent copies of data, they incur longer times to complete a transaction. This is acceptable in applications that require both consistency and high availability at all times. Financial systems at a bank, for example, fall into this category. There are applications, however, in which the fast database operations are more important than maintaining consistency at all times. For example, an e-commerce site might want to maintain copies of your shopping cart on two different database servers. If one of the servers fails, your cart is still available on the other server.

Imagine you are programming the user interface for an e-commerce site. How long should the customer wait after clicking on an "Add to My Cart" button? Ideally, the interface would respond immediately so the customer could keep shopping. If the interface feels slow and sluggish, the customer might switch to another site with faster performance. In this case, speed is more important than having consistent data at all times.

One way to deal with this problem is to write the updates to one database and then let the program know the data has been saved. The interface can indicate to the customer that the product has been added to the cart. While the customer receives the message that the cart has been updated, the database management system is making a copy of the newly updated data and writing it to another server. There is a brief period of time when the customer's cart on the two servers is not consistent, but the customer is able to continue shopping anyway. In this case, we are willing to tolerate inconsistency for a brief period of time knowing that eventually the two carts will have the same products in it. This is especially true with online shopping carts because there is only a small chance someone else would read that customer's cart data anyway (see Figure 2.6).

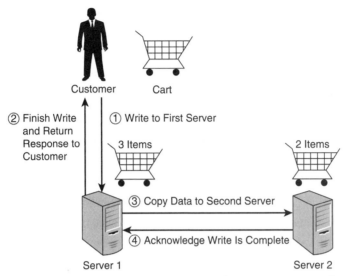

**Figure 2.6**  *Data structures, such as shopping carts, can be inconsistent for short periods of time without adversely affecting system effectiveness. In this example, Server 2 is inconsistent with Server 1 until step 3 is complete.*

## Balancing Response Times, Consistency, and Durability

NoSQL databases often implement eventual consistency; that is, there might be a period of time where copies of data have different values, but eventually all copies will have the same value. This raises the possibility of a user querying the database and getting different results from different servers in a cluster. For example, assume Alice has updated a customer's address in a database that implements eventual consistency. Immediately after Alice updates the address, Bob reads that customer's address. Will he see the new or old address? The answer is not as simple as it is when working with a relational database and strict consistency.

NoSQL databases often use the concept of quorums when working with reads and writes. A *quorum* is the number of servers that must respond to a read or write operation for the operation to be considered complete.

When a read is performed, the NoSQL database reads data from, potentially, multiple servers. Most of the time, all of the servers will have consistent data. However, while the database copies data from one of the servers to the other servers storing replicas, the replica servers may have inconsistent data.

One way to determine the correct response to any read operation is to query all servers storing that data. The database counts the number of distinct response values and returns the one that meets or exceeds a configurable threshold. For example, assume data in a NoSQL database is replicated to five servers and you have set the read threshold to 3 (see Figure 2.7). As soon as three servers respond with the same response, the result is returned to the user.

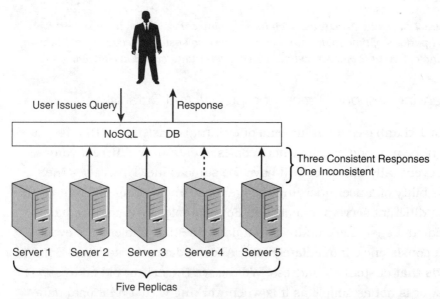

**Figure 2.7**   *NoSQL databases can mitigate the risk of inconsistent data by having servers vote on the correct response to a query.*

You can vary the threshold to improve response time or consistency. If the read threshold is set to 1, you get a fast response. The lower the threshold, the faster the response but the higher the risk of returning inconsistent data.

In the preceding example, if you set the read threshold to 5, you would guarantee consistent reads. In that case, the query would return only after all replicas have been updated and could lead to longer response times.

Just as you can adjust a read threshold to balance response time and consistency, you can also alter a write threshold to balance response time and durability. *Durability* is the property of maintaining a correct copy of data for long periods of time. A write operation is considered complete when a minimum number of replicas have been written to persistent storage.

❖ **Caution** If the write threshold is set to 1, then the write is complete once a single server writes the data to persistent storage. This leads to fast response times but poor durability. If that one server or its storage system fails, the data is lost.

Assume you are working the five-server cluster described previously. If data is replicated across three servers and you set the write threshold to 3, then all three copies would be written to persistent storage before the write completes. If you set the threshold to 2, your data would be written to two servers before completing the write operation and the third copy would be written at a later time.

Setting the write threshold to at least 2 provides for durability while setting the number of replicas higher than the threshold helps improve durability without increasing the response time of write operations.

## Consistency, Availability, and Partitioning: The CAP Theorem

This book is one of many books written "for mere mortals," that is, people who are not necessarily specialists in the subject area. In these books, technical terminology is kept to a minimum and discussions are designed to provide practical, useful knowledge. There are times, however, when a brief discussion of a fundamental principle is worth the need to delve into a more subject-oriented discussion. This is one of those times.

The CAP theorem, also known as Brewer's theorem after the computer scientist who introduced it, states that distributed databases cannot have consistency (C), availability (A), and partition protection (P) all at the same time. *Consistency*, in this case, means consistent copies of data on different servers. *Availability* refers to providing a response to any query. *Partition protection* means if a network that connects two or more database servers fails, the servers will still be available with consistent data.

You saw in a previous example of the e-commerce shopping cart that it is possible to have a backup copy of the cart data that is out of sync with the primary copy. The data would still be available if the primary server failed, but the data on the backup server would be inconsistent with data on the primary server if the primary server failed prior to updating the backup server (see Figure 2.8).

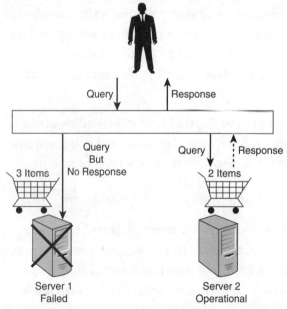

**Figure 2.8** *Data can be available but not consistent.*

You also saw in an earlier example of the two-phase commit that you can have consistency but at the risk of the most recent data not being available for a brief period of time. While the two-phase commit is executing, other queries to the data are blocked. The updated data is unavailable until the two-phase commit finishes. This favors consistency over availability (see Figure 2.9).

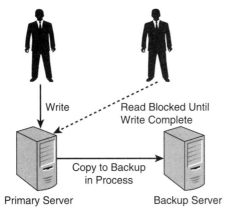

Write

Read Blocked Until
Write Complete

Copy to Backup
in Process

Primary Server                    Backup Server

**Figure 2.9**   *Data can be consistent but not available.*

Partition protection deals with situations in which servers cannot communicate with each other. This would be the case in the event of a network failure. This splitting of the network into groups of devices that can communicate with each other from those that cannot is known as partitioning. (*Partitioning*, like *consistency*, has multiple meanings in data management. It is important to remember that when talking about the CAP theorem, *partitioning* has to do with the inability to send messages between database servers.) If database servers running the same distributed database are partitioned by a network failure, then you could continue to allow both to respond to queries and preserve availability but at the risk of them becoming inconsistent. Alternatively, you could disable one so that only one of the servers responds to queries. This would avoid returning inconsistent data to users querying different servers but at the cost of availability to some users.

From a practical standpoint, network partitions are rare, at least in local area networks. You can imagine a wide area network with slow network connections and low throughput (for example, older satellite connections to remote areas) that could experience network outages. This means that from a pragmatic perspective, database application designers have to deal with the trade-offs between consistency and availability more than issues with partitioning.

Designers of NoSQL database management systems have to determine how to balance varying needs for consistency, availability, and partitioning protection. This is not a one-time decision for the database management system. NoSQL database designers can provide configuration mechanisms that allow users of the database to specify their preferred settings rather than making a single choice for all users of the database management system.

Application designers could make use of NoSQL database configuration options to make the availability-consistency trade-off decision at fine-grained levels, such as based on different types of data in the database. The only limitation is the configuration options provided in the NoSQL database management system used by the application.

## ACID and BASE

In the world of chemistry, acids are chemicals with a pH of less than 7 and bases are chemicals that have a pH of greater than 7. However, the use of the terms ACID and BASE when discussing databases has nothing to do with chemistry. ACID is an acronym derived from four properties implemented in relational database management systems. BASE is an acronym for properties common to NoSQL databases.

### ACID: Atomicity, Consistency, Isolation, and Durability

A is for *atomicity*. Atomicity, as the name implies, describes a unit that cannot be further divided. The word *atom* comes from the Greek *atomos*, which means indivisible. In the earlier discussion about transactions, such as transferring funds from your savings account to your checking account, you learned that all the steps had to complete or none of them completed. In essence, the set of steps is indivisible. You have to complete all of them as a single indivisible unit, or you complete none of them.

C is for *consistency*. In relational databases, this is known as strict consistency. In other words, a transaction does not leave a database in a state that violates the integrity of data. Transferring $100 from your savings account to your checking account must end with either (a) $100 more in your checking account and $100 less in your savings account or (b) both accounts have the same amount as they had at the start of the transaction. Consistency ensures no other possible state could result after a transfer operation.

I is for *isolation*. Isolated transactions are not visible to other users until transactions are complete. For example, in the case of a bank transfer from a savings account to a checking account, someone could not read your account balances while the funds are being deducted from your savings account but before they are added to your checking account. Databases can allow different levels of isolation. This can allow, for example, lost updates in which a query returns data that does not reflect the most recent update because the update operation has not completely finished.

D is for *durability*. This means that once a transaction or operation is completed, it will remain even in the event of a power loss. In effect, this means that data is stored on disk, flash, or other persistent media.

Relational database management systems are designed to support ACID transactions. NoSQL databases typically support BASE transactions, although some NoSQL databases also provide some level of support for ACID transactions.

## BASE: Basically Available, Soft State, Eventually Consistent

BA is for *basically available*. This means that there can be a partial failure in some parts of the distributed system and the rest of the system continues to function. For example, if a NoSQL database is running on 10 servers without replicating data and one of the servers fails, then 10% of the users' queries would fail, but 90% would succeed. NoSQL databases often keep multiple copies of data on different servers. This allows the database to respond to queries even if one of the servers has failed.

S is for *soft state*. Usually in computer science, the term *soft state* means data will expire if it is not refreshed. Here, in NoSQL operations, it refers to the fact that data may eventually be overwritten with more recent data. This property overlaps with the third property of BASE transactions, eventually consistent.

E is for *eventually consistent*. This means that there may be times when the database is in an inconsistent state. For example, some NoSQL databases keep multiple copies of data on multiple servers. There is, however, a possibility that the multiple copies may not be consistent for a short period of time. This can occur when a user or program updates one copy of the data and other copies continue to have the old version of the data. Eventually, the replication mechanism in the NoSQL database will update all copies, but in the meantime, the copies are inconsistent.

The time it takes to update all copies depends on several factors, such as the load on the system and the speed of the network. Consider a database that maintains three copies of data. A user updates her address in one server. The NoSQL database management system automatically updates the other two copies. One of the other copies is on a server in the same local area network, so the update happens quickly. The other server is in a data center thousands of miles away, so there is a time delay in updating the third copy. A user querying the third server while the update is in progress might get the user's old address while someone querying the first server gets the new address.

## Types of Eventual Consistency

Eventual consistency is such an important aspect of NoSQL databases, it is worth further discussion.

There are several types of eventual consistency:

- Casual consistency
- Read-your-writes consistency
- Session consistency
- Monotonic read consistency
- Monotonic write consistency

### Casual Consistency

Casual consistency ensures that the database reflects the order in which operations were updated. For example, if Alice changes a customer's outstanding balance to $1,000 and one minute later Bob changes it to $2,000, all copies of the customer's outstanding balance will be updated to $1,000 before they are updated to $2,000.

### Read-Your-Writes Consistency

Read-your-writes consistency means that once you have updated a record, all of your reads of that record will return the updated value. You would never retrieve a value inconsistent with the value you had written. Let's say Alice updates a customer's outstanding balance to $1,500. The update is written to one server and the replication process begins updating other copies. During the replication process, Alice queries the customer's balance. She is guaranteed to see $1,500 when the database supports read-your-writes consistency.

### Session Consistency

Session consistency ensures read-your-writes consistency during a session. You can think of a session as a conversation between a client and a server or a user and the database. As long as the conversation continues, the database "remembers" all writes you have done during the conversation. If the session ends and you start another session with the same server, there is no guarantee it will "remember" the writes you made in the previous session. A session may end if you log off an application using the database or if you do not issue commands to the database for so long that the database assumes you no longer need the session and abandons it.

### Monotonic Read Consistency

Monotonic read consistency ensures that if you issue a query and see a result, you will never see an earlier version of the value. Let's assume Alice is yet again updating a customer's outstanding balance. The outstanding balance is currently $1,500. She updates it to $2,500. Bob queries the database for the customer's balance and sees that it is $2,500. If Bob issues the query again, he will see the balance is $2,500 even if all the servers with copies of that customer's outstanding balance have not updated to the latest value.

### Monotonic Write Consistency

Monotonic write consistency ensures that if you were to issue several update commands, they would be executed in the order you issued them. Let's consider a variation on the outstanding balance example. Alice is feeling generous today and decides to reduce all customers' outstanding balances by 10%. Charlie, one of her customers, has a $1,000 outstanding balance. After the reduction, Charlie would have a $900 balance. Now imagine if Alice continues to process orders. Charlie has just ordered $1,100 worth of material. His outstanding balance is now the sum of the previous outstanding balance ($900) and the amount of the new order ($1,100) or $2,000.

Now consider what would happen if the NoSQL database performed Alice's operations in a different order. Charlie started with a $1,000 outstanding balance. Next, instead of having the discount applied, his record was first updated with the new order ($1,100). His outstanding balance becomes $2,100. Now, the 10% discount operation is executed and his outstanding balance is set to $2,100–$210 or $1890.

Monotonic write consistency is obviously an important feature. If you cannot guarantee the order of operations in the database, you would have to build features into your program to guarantee operations execute in the order you expect.

## Four Types of NoSQL Databases

Distributed databases come in several forms. Distributed relational databases exist but are not within the scope of this book. Instead, the focus here is on NoSQL databases. The most widely used types of NoSQL databases are

- Key-value pair databases
- Document databases
- Column family store databases
- Graph databases

NoSQL databases do not have to be implemented as distributed systems. Many can run on a single server. Some of the most interesting and appealing features of NoSQL databases, however, require a distributed implementation. When availability and scalability are top concerns, it makes sense to implement a NoSQL database across multiple servers. As soon as you enter the realm of distributed systems, you are faced with decisions and trade-offs not found in single-server implementations. As you design your NoSQL databases and related applications, consider how you want to balance your need for scalability, availability, consistency, partition protection, and durability. These topics are central to NoSQL databases and are addressed repeatedly throughout this book.

## Key-Value Pair Databases

Key-value pair databases are the simplest form of NoSQL databases. These databases are modeled on two components: keys and values.

### Keys

Keys are identifiers associated with values. They are analogous to tags you get when you check luggage at the airport. The tag you receive has an identifier associated with your luggage. With your tag, you can find your luggage more efficiently than without it. Imagine you have a connecting flight and your luggage did not make it to your connecting flight. If your luggage doesn't have a tag, an airline employee searching for your bag would have to look through all undelivered bags to determine which is yours.

Now imagine that the airline organizes undelivered bags by tag number. If the airline employee knows your ticket number, she or he could go right to that spot in the luggage area to retrieve your bag.

Airlines generate luggage tags when you check a bag. If you were assigned the task of designing a ticket-generating program, you might decide to have tickets with two parts: a flight number and a sequential number.

> ❖ **Note** This is an oversimplified scheme because it does not account for flights with the same number that occurs on different days, but we will continue with it anyway.

The first customer checking bags on flight 1928 might be assigned ticket 1928.1 for her first bag and 1928.2 for her second bag. The second customer also has two bags and he is assigned 1928.3 and 1928.4 (see Figure 2.10).

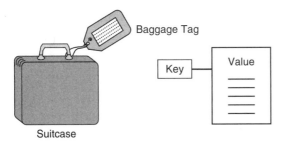

**Figure 2.10**  *Airline tags for checked bags are analogous to keys used to store data in a key-value database.*

You can use a similar approach when generating keys in a key-value database. Let's assume you are building a key-generating program for an e-commerce website. You realize you need to track five pieces of information about each visitor to your site: the customer's account number, name, address, number of items in the shopping cart, and customer type indicator. The customer type indicator identifies customers enrolled in the company's loyalty program.

All of these values are associated with a customer, so you can generate a sequential number for each customer. For each item you are storing, you create a new key by appending the name of the item you are storing to the customer number. For example, data about the first customer in the system would use keys 1.accountNumber, 1.name, 1.address, 1.numItems, and 1.custType (see Figure 2.11).

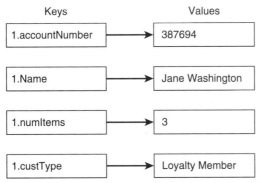

**Figure 2.11**  *Key-value databases are modeled on a simple, two-part data structure consisting of an identifier and a data value.*

This approach would work when you have a relatively simple database. If you need to track other entities, such as product information, warehouses, and shipping providers, you might want to use a similar sequential numbering system. Take warehouses, for example. You might want to track the closest warehouse to a customer that has the products listed in the shopping cart. This can help determine an estimated delivery date. For each warehouse, you need to track its warehouse number and its address. If you use a sequential number generator for warehouses that is different from the one used with customers, you could generate the following keys for the first warehouse: 1.number and 1.address.

The 1.address key is used for both a customer and a warehouse. This will cause problems because data about customers and warehouses will be saved with the same key. If you add a warehouse to your key-value database using 1.address and then save a customer's address using 1.address, the next time you look up the warehouse's address, you will find a customer's address instead.

One way to address this problem is to use a key-naming convention that includes the entity type. For example, you could use the prefix *cust* for customer and *wrhs* for warehouse. You can append the sequentially generated numbers to these prefixes to create unique keys. The keys for the customer data would look like the following:

- cust1.accountNumber

- cust1.name

- cust1.address

- cust1.numItems

- cust1.custType

- cust2.accountNumber

- cust2.name

- cust2.address

- cust2.numItems

- cust2.custType

and so on. Similarly, the keys for the warehouse data would be

- wrhs1.number

- wrhs1.address

- wrhs2.number

- wrhs2.address

The important principle to remember about keys is that they must be unique. Of course, someone building a key-value database at Company A might use the same keys as someone at Company B. This is not a problem because the two databases are separate. There is no chance of one company reading or writing to the other database. In database terminology, the keys in these two companies are in different name-spaces. A *namespace* is a collection of identifiers. Keys must be unique within a namespace.

A namespace could correspond to an entire database. In this case, all keys in the database must be unique. Some key-value databases provide for different namespaces within a database. This is done by setting up data structures for separate collections of identifiers within a database. This book refers to these data structures as *buckets* (see Figure 2.12).

❖ **Note** If you are familiar with SQL databases, you might notice a similarity to schemas in relational databases.

Database

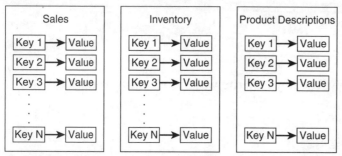

**Figure 2.12**   *Key-value databases may support separate namespaces within a single database.*

## Values

*Values* are data stored along with keys. Like luggage, values in a key-value database can store many different things. Values can be as simple as a string, such as a name, or a number, such as the number of items in a customer's shopping cart. You can store more complex values, such as images or binary objects, too.

Key-value databases give developers a great deal of flexibility when storing values. For example, strings can vary in length. Cust123.address could be "543 N. Main St." or "543 North Main St. Portland, OR 97222." Values can also vary in type. An employee database might include photos of employees using keys such as Emp328.photo. That key could have a picture stored as a binary large object (BLOB) type or a string value such as "Not available." Key-value databases typically do not enforce checks on data types of values.

Because key-value databases allow virtually any data type in values, it is important for software developers to implement checks in their programs. For example, a program that expects either a BLOB or a string with a value of "Not available" might not function as expected if the string "No photo" is used instead. A programmer might decide to support any BLOB or string as valid values, but it is up to the programmer to determine the range of valid values and enforce those choices as needed.

## Differences Between Key-Value and Relational Databases

Key-value databases are modeled on minimal principles for storing and retrieving data. Unlike in relational databases, there are no tables, so there are no features associated with tables, such as columns and constraints on columns. There is no need for joins in key-value databases, so there are no foreign keys. Key-value databases do not support a rich query language such as SQL.

Some key-value databases support buckets, or collections, for creating separate namespaces within a database. This can be used to implement something analogous to a relational schema, especially when combined with a key-naming convention like the one described previously.

If you have developed relational data models, you might have noticed parallels between the key-naming convention and tables, primary keys, and columns. The key-naming convention described previously basically uses the convention of concatenating a table name or symbol, a primary key, and a column name. For example, the key 'cust123.address' would be equivalent to a relational table named cust or customer, with a column called address, and a row identified by the primary key ID of 123 (see Figure 2.13).

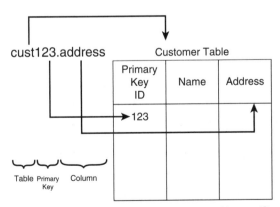

**Figure 2.13**  *The key-naming convention outlined above maps to patterns seen in relational database tables.*

## Document Databases

Document databases, also called document-oriented databases, use a key-value approach to storing data but with important differences from key-value databases. A document database stores values as documents. In this case, documents are semistructured entities, typically in a standard format such as JavaScript Object Notation (JSON) or Extensible Markup Language (XML). It should be noted that when the term *document* is used in this context, it does not refer to word processing or other office productivity files. It refers to data structures that are stored as strings or binary representations of strings.

### Documents

Instead of storing each attribute of an entity with a separate key, document databases store multiple attributes in a single document.

Here is a simple example of a document in JSON format:

```
{
    firstName: "Alice",
    lastName: "Johnson",
    position: "CFO",
    officeNumber: "2-120",
    officePhone: "555-222-3456",
}
```

One of the most important characteristics of document databases is you do not have to define a fixed schema before you add data to the database. Simply adding a document to the database creates the underlying data structures needed to support the document.

The lack of a fixed schema gives developers more flexibility with document databases than they have with relational databases. For example, employees can have different attributes than the ones listed above. Another valid employee document is

```
{
    firstName: "Bob",
    lastName: "Wilson",
    position: "Manager",
    officeNumber: "2-130",
    officePhone: "555-222-3478",
    hireDate: "1-Feb-2010",
    terminationDate: "12-Aug-2014"
}
```

The attributes `hireDate` and `terminationDate` are in Bob's document but not Alice's. This is not a problem from the database perspective. Developers can add attributes as needed, but their programs are responsible for managing them. If you expect all employee documents to have first and last names, you should implement a check in your code that adds employee documents to ensure that the rule is enforced.

### Querying Documents

You might be wondering, why couldn't you store JSON or XML documents in key-value databases? Because key-value databases have few restrictions on the type of data stored as a value, you could store a JSON document as a value. The only way to retrieve such a document is by its key, however.

Document databases provide application programming interfaces (APIs) or query languages that enable you to retrieve documents based on attribute values. For example, if you have a database with a collection of employee documents called "employees," you could use a statement such as the following to return the set of all employees with the position Manager:

```
db.employees.find( { position:"Manager" })
```

As with relational databases, document databases typically support operators such as AND, OR, greater than, less than, and equal to.

## Differences Between Document and Relational Databases

As noted, a key distinction between document and relational databases is that document databases do not require a fixed, predefined schema.

Another important difference is that documents can have embedded documents and lists of multiple values within a document. For example, the employee documents might include a list of previous positions an employee held within the company. For example:

```
{
    firstName: "Bob",
    lastName: "Wilson",
    positionTitle: "Manager",
    officeNumber: "2-130",
    officePhone: "555-222-3478",
    hireDate: "1-Feb-2010",
    terminationDate: "12-Aug-2014"
    PreviousPositions: [
        {      \position: "Analyst",
         StartDate:"1-Feb-2010",
        endDate:"10-Mar-2011"
        } {
            position: "Sr. Analyst",
            startDate: "10-Mar-2011"
            endDate:"29-May-2013"
        } ]
}
```

Embedding documents or lists of values in a document eliminates the need for joining documents the way you join tables in a relational database. If there are cases where you stored a list of document identifiers in a document and want to look up attributes in the documents associated with those identifiers, then you would have to implement that operation in your program.

Document databases are probably the most popular type of NoSQL database. They offer support for querying structures with multiple attributes, like relational databases, but offer more flexibility with regard to variation in the attributes used by each document.

The next section discusses the column family database, which is another type of NoSQL database that shares some important characteristics with relational databases.

## Column Family Databases

Column family databases are perhaps the most complex of the NoSQL database types, at least in terms of the basic building block structures. Column family databases share some terms with relational databases, such as rows and columns, but you must be careful to understand important differences between these structures.

These differences are discussed in Chapters 9 through 11. In the meantime, let's examine the basic building blocks of column family databases.

### Columns and Column Families

A column is a basic unit of storage in a column family database. A column is a name and a value. (Some column family databases keep a time stamp along with a name and value, but let's ignore that for now.) See Figure 2.14.

**Figure 2.14**  *A column consists of a name and a value. In this example, the column is named lastName and has a value of "Wilson."*

A set of columns makes up a row. Rows can have the same columns, or they can have different columns, as shown in Figure 2.15.

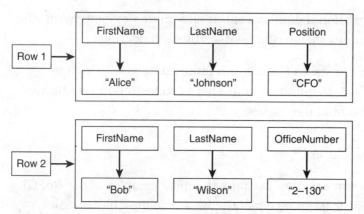

**Figure 2.15**  *A row consists of one or more columns. Different rows can have different columns.*

When there are large numbers of columns, it can help to group them into collections of related columns. For example, first and last name are often used together, and office numbers and office phone numbers are frequently needed together. These can be grouped in collections called *column families*.

As in document databases, column family databases do not require a predefined fixed schema. Developers can add columns as needed. Also, rows can have different sets of columns and super columns. Column family databases are designed for rows with many columns. It is not unusual for column family databases to support millions of columns.

### Differences Between Column Family and Relational Databases

Column family databases and relational databases are superficially similar. They both make use of rows and columns, for example. There are important differences in terms of data models and implementation details.

One thing missing from column family databases is support for joining tables. You might have noticed that the term *table* has not been used when describing column family databases. This is intentional. Tables in relational databases have a relatively fixed structure, and the relational database management system can take advantage of that structure when optimizing the layout of data on drives and when retrieving data for read operations. Unlike a relational database table, however, the set of columns in a column family table can vary from one row to another.

In relational databases, data about an object can be stored in multiple tables. For example, a customer might have name, address, and contact information in one table; a list of past orders in another table; and a payment history in another. If you needed to reference data from all three tables at once, you would need to perform a join operation between tables. Column family databases are typically denormalized, or structured so that all relevant information about an object is in a single, possibly very wide, row.

Query languages for column family databases may look similar to SQL. The query language can support SQL-like terms such as SELECT, INSERT, UPDATE, and DELETE as well as column family–specific operations, such as CREATE COLUMNFAMILY.

The next section discusses a fourth type of NoSQL databases known as graph databases, which are well suited for addressing problems that require representing many objects and links between those objects. Social media, a transportation network, and an electric grid are just a few examples of areas where graph databases may be used.

## Graph Databases

Graph databases are the most specialized of the four NoSQL databases discussed in this book. Instead of modeling data using columns and rows, a graph database uses structures called nodes and relationships (in more formal discussions, they are called vertices and edges). A *node* is an object that has an identifier and a set of attributes. A *relationship* is a link between two nodes that contain attributes about that relation.

## Nodes and Relationships

There are many ways to use graph databases. Nodes can represent people, and relationships can represent their friendships in social networks. A node could be a city, and a relationship between cities could be used to store information about the distance and travel time between cities. Figure 2.16 includes an example of flying times between several cities.

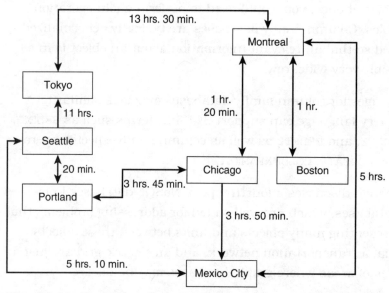

**Figure 2.16**   *Properties of relationships or nodes store attributes about relations between linked nodes. In this case, attributes include flying times between cities.*

Both the nodes and relationships can have complex structures. For example, each city can have a list of airports along with demographic and geographic data about the city, as shown in Figure 2.17.

```
┌─────────────────────────────┐
│          Chicago            │
├─────────────────────────────┤
│ Airports : [                │
│                             │
│    ⎧ Name :                 │
│    ⎨ "O' Hare"              │
│    ⎩ Symbol : ORD},         │
│                             │
│       {Name : Midway,       │
│        Symbol : MDW}        │
│        ]                    │
│                             │
│ Population : 2,715,000,     │
│ Area : 234 Sq. Miles        │
└─────────────────────────────┘
```

**Figure 2.17** *Nodes can also have attributes to describe the node. In this case, attributes include information about the airports in the city along with population and geographic area.*

Graph databases get their name from a branch of mathematics called graph theory. *Graph theory* is the study of objects represented by vertices and relations represented by edges. Graph theory is not related to the study of charts and other visualizations sometimes referred to as graphs.

### Differences Between Graph and Relational Databases

Graph databases are designed to model adjacency between objects. Every node in the database contains pointers to adjacent objects in the database. This allows for fast operations that require following paths through a graph.

For example, if you wanted to find all possible ways to fly from Montreal to Mexico City using the graph you saw in Figure 2.16, you could start at the Montreal node and follow each of the adjacent nodes to Boston, Chicago, and Tokyo, and then to Mexico City. At the Boston node, you would find no relationship with Mexico City and assume that there are no direct flights available from Boston to Mexico City. From Chicago, a direct flight to Mexico City would take 3 hours and 50 minutes. That time, plus the 1 hour and 20 minutes to fly to Chicago would leave a total flying time of 5 hours and 10 minutes.

Flying from Montreal to Tokyo to get to Mexico City is possible but hardly efficient. Because the relationship between Montreal and Tokyo shows a 13 hour 30 minute flight, over twice as long as the Montreal to Chicago to Mexico City route, you can safely stop following other routes from Tokyo to Mexico City. From Chicago, you could fly to Portland, but like Boston, this does not lead to a direct flight to Mexico City. Finally, a direct flight from Montreal to Mexico City would take 5 hours, the fastest route available.

Performing this same kind of analysis in a relational database would be more involved. We could easily represent the same data shown in Figure 2.16 using a table such as the one shown in Table 2.1.

**Table 2.1   Flight Times Between Cities Modeled as a Relational Table**

| City 1 | City 2 | Flying Time |
| --- | --- | --- |
| Montreal | Boston | 1 hr. |
| Montreal | Chicago | 1 hr. 20 min. |
| Montreal | Tokyo | 13 hr. 30 min. |
| Montreal | Mexico City | 5 hr. |
| Chicago | Mexico City | 3 hr. 50 min. |
| Chicago | Portland | 3 hr. 45 min. |
| Portland | Seattle | 20 min. |
| Seattle | Tokyo | 11 hr. |
| Seattle | Mexico City | 5 hr. 10 min. |

Querying is more difficult. You would have to write multiple SQL statements or use specialized recursive statements if they are provided (for example, Oracle's CONNECT BY clause in SELECT statements) to find paths using the table representation of the data.

Graph databases allow for more efficient querying when paths through graphs are involved. Many application areas are efficiently modeled as graphs and, in those cases, a graph database may streamline application development and minimize the amount of code you would have to write.

The most widely used types of NoSQL databases are key-value, document, column family, and graph databases. The following chapters describe each of these in depth and present examples of typical use cases for each.

## Summary

NoSQL databases are often deployed using clusters of servers. When applications run on multiple servers and coordinate their work across servers, they are known as distributed systems. When you use NoSQL databases in a distributed manner, you will have to decide how to address the challenges that come with that type of implementation. Distributed systems help improve scalability and availability but make it more difficult to ensure consistency of data across servers. There are also potential problems if there is a network failure and some servers cannot send messages to other servers in the distributed database system.

The nature of distributed systems has led NoSQL database designers to choose a different set of principles for building data management systems. Rather than support atomic, consistent, isolated, and durable transactions (ACID), NoSQL databases achieve basic availability, soft state, eventually consistent (BASE). (Some NoSQL databases are working to support ACID transactions, at least in some cases.)

The four types of NoSQL databases described in this chapter all must address the challenges of distributed systems. The types of NoSQL database systems differ primarily in the basic data structures used to model data. The different data structure choices lead to different implementation details. Developers who work with NoSQL databases should understand how the nature of distributed systems could affect their applications, and they should know how to choose among NoSQL databases for their requirements. The rest of this book is dedicated to informing you about those topics.

## Review Questions

1.  What is a distributed system?

2.  Describe a two-phase commit. Does it help ensure consistency or availability?

3.  What do the *C* and *A* in the CAP theorem stand for? Give an example of how designing for one of those properties can lead to difficulties in maintaining the other.

4.  The *E* in BASE stands for eventually consistent. What does that mean?

5.  Describe monotonic write consistency. Why is it so important?

6.  How many values can be stored with a single key in a key-value database?

7.  What is a namespace? Why is it important in key-value databases?

8.  How do document databases differ from key-value databases?

9.  Describe two differences between document databases and relational databases.

10. Name two data structures used in column family databases.

11. What are the two fundamental data structures in a graph database?

12. You are assigned the task of building a database to model employees and who they work with in your company. The database must be able to answer queries such as how many employees does Employee A work with? And, does Employee A work with anyone who works with Employee B? Which type of NoSQL database would naturally fit with these requirements?

# References

Brewer, Eric. "CAP Twelve Years Later: How the 'Rules' Have Changed." *Computer* vol. 45, no. 2 (Feb 2012): 23–29

Chodorow, Kristina. *MongoDB: The Definitive Guide*. Sebastopol, CA: O'Reilly Media, Inc., 2013.

Hewitt, Eben. *Cassandra: The Definitive Guide*. Sebastopol, CA: O'Reilly Media, Inc., 2010.

Robinson, Ian, Jim Webber, and Emil Eifrem. *Graph Databases*. Sebastopol, CA: O'Reilly Media, Inc., 2013.

Vogel, Werner. 2008. "Eventually Consistent—Revisited" (December). http://www.allthingsdistributed.com/2008/12/eventually_consistent.html

# Bibliography

Hernandez, Michael J. *Data Design for Mere Mortals: A Hands-On Guide to Relational Database Design*. Reading, MA: Addison-Wesley, 2007.

Viescas, John L., and Michael J. Hernandez. *SQL Queries for Mere Mortals*. Reading, MA: Addison-Wesley, 2007.

# Part II
# Key-Value Databases

■ ■ ■ ■ ■ ■ ■ ■ ■ ■ ■

# 3

# Introduction to Key-Value Databases

*"Everything should be made as simple as possible, but no simpler."*
—ALBERT EINSTEIN

## Topics Covered In This Chapter

From Arrays to Key-Value Databases

Essential Features of Key-Value Databases

Properties of Keys

Characteristics of Values

Key-value databases are the simplest of the NoSQL databases and are a good place to start a detailed examination of NoSQL database options. As the name implies, the design of this type of data store is based on storing data with identifiers known as keys. This chapter introduces key-value data structures by starting with an even simpler data structure: the array.

A key-value data store is a more complex variation on the array data structure. Computer scientists have extended the concept of an array by relaxing constraints on the simple data structure and adding persistent data storage features to create a range of other useful data structures, including associative arrays, caches, and persistent key-value databases.

In this chapter, you learn about key characteristics of key-value data stores as well as about keys and values themselves. You also see some important operational characteristics of key-value databases.

Before jumping into database-specific topics, the next section sets the stage for key-value databases with a slight diversion into introductory data structures.

# From Arrays to Key-Value Databases

Relational databases did not spring from the mind of computer scientists at the dawn of computing. Chapter 1, "Different Databases for Different Requirements," describes the development of databases as a series of increasingly more complex systems that are better able to manage increasingly more complex data management challenges. The high points of that progression are relational and NoSQL databases.

It helps to start an examination of key-value databases by starting with a simple data structure and showing how adding features to a simple data structure can lead to a simple but even more useful type of database.

## Arrays: Key Value Stores with Training Wheels

One of the first data structures taught to computer science students is the array. After scalar variables, like integers and characters, the array is one of the simplest. An array is an ordered list of values. Each value in the array is associated with an integer index. The values are all the same type. For example, an array could be an ordered list of integers, characters, or Boolean values. Figure 3.1 shows an array of 10 Boolean elements.

| | |
|---|---|
| 1 | True |
| 2 | True |
| 3 | False |
| 4 | True |
| 5 | False |
| 6 | False |
| 7 | False |
| 8 | True |
| 9 | False |
| 10 | True |

**Figure 3.1**  *An array is an ordered list of elements. All elements are of the same type. The value of each element of the array is read and set by reference to its index.*

The syntax for reading and setting array values varies by programming language. In this book, to read the first element of an array named exampleArray, you would use

```
exampleArray[0]
```

❖ **Note** It is common practice in programming languages to use zero instead of one as the first element of an array.

The convention for reading from an array is to use the name of the array followed by an [, an integer index, and then a ]. To set the value of an array element, use the same syntax for reading an element and follow it with an assignment symbol, in this case a '=', and the value to be assigned to that element. For example,

```
exampleArray[0] = 'Hello world.'
```

sets the first element of exampleArray to the string of characters 'Hello world.' Additional elements can be set with the following commands:

```
exampleArray[1] = 'Goodbye world.'
exampleArray[2] = 'This is a test.'
```

```
exampleArray[5] = 'Key-value database'
exampleArray[9] = 'Elements can be set in any order.'
```

exampleArray is an array in which all elements are strings of characters. You could not, for example, set an element of exampleArray to a real number. The following command would generate an error:

```
exampleArray[6] = 3.1415
```

You might see the two following limitations when working with arrays:

- The index can only be an integer.

- The values must all have the same type.

Sometimes it is useful to have a data structure that does not have these limitations.

## Associative Arrays: Taking Off the Training Wheels

An associative array is a data structure, like an array, but is not restricted to using integers as indexes or limiting values to the same type. You could, for example, have commands such as the following:

```
exampleAssociativeArray['Pi'] = 3.1415
exampleAssociativeArray['CapitalFrance'] = 'Paris'
exampleAssociativeArray['ToDoList'] = { 'Alice' : 'run
  reports; meeting with Bob', 'Bob' : 'order inventory;
  meeting with Alice' }
exampleAssociativeArray[17234] = 34468
```

Associative arrays generalize the idea of an ordered list indexed by an identifier to include arbitrary values for identifiers and values (see Figure 3.2). As the previous examples show, keys can be strings of characters or integers. Depending on the programming language or database, you may be able to use keys with even more complex data structures, such as a list of values.

| 'Pi' | 3.14 |
|---|---|
| 'CapitalFrance' | 'Paris' |
| 17234 | 34468 |
| 'Foo' | 'Bar' |
| 'Start_Value' | 1 |

**Figure 3.2**  *An associative array shares some characteristics of arrays but has fewer constraints on keys and values.*

In addition, note that values stored in the associative array can vary. In the previous examples, there is a real number, a character string, a list, and an integer. The identifiers are generally referred to as keys. As you might have already guessed, associative arrays are the basic structure underlying the concept of key-value databases.

> ❖ **Note** Associative arrays go by a number of different names, including dictionary, map, hash map, hash table, and symbol table.

## Caches: Adding Gears to the Bike

Key-value databases build on the concept of an associative array, but there are important differences. Many key-value data stores keep persistent copies of data on long-term storage, such as hard drives or flash devices. Some key-value data stores only keep data in memory. These are typically used so programs can access data faster than if they had to retrieve data from disk drives (see Figure 3.3). The first time a piece of data is retrieved from a disk, for example, as the result of a SQL query in a relational database, it is stored in the cache along with a set of unique keys. A SQL query such as the following retrieves name and shipping address information from a relational table called customers:

```
SELECT
    firstName,
    lastName,
    shippingAddress,
    shippingCity,
```

```
    shippingState,
    shippingZip
from
    customers
where
    customerID = 1982737
```

Only the information for the customer with the `customerID` of `1982737` is retrieved.

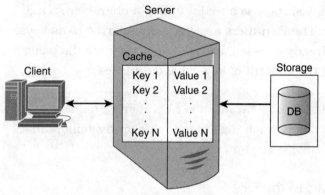

**Figure 3.3**   *Caches are associative arrays used by application programs to improve data access performance.*

The program could run faster if it retrieved data from memory rather than from the database. The first time the program fetches the data, it will need to read from the disk but after that the results can be saved in memory.

> ❖ **Tip** If the program is relatively simple and only needs to track one customer at a time, then the application programmer could use character-string variables to store the customer name and address information. When a program must track many customers and other entities at the same time, then using a cache makes more sense.

An in-memory cache is an associative array. The values retrieved from the relational database could be stored in the cache by creating a key for each value stored. One way to create a unique key for each piece of data for each customer is to concatenate a unique identifier with the name of the data item. For example, the following stores the data retrieved from the database in an in-memory cache:

```
customerCache['1982737:firstname'] = firstName
customerCache['1982737:lastname'] = lastName
customerCache['1982737:shippingAddress'] = shippingAddress
customerCache['1982737:shippingCity'] = shippingCity
customerCache['1982737:shippingState'] = shippingState
customerCache['1982737:shippingZip'] = shippingZip
```

Because the `customerID` is part of the key, the cache can store data about as many customers as needed without creating separate program variables for each set of customer data.

Programs that access customer data will typically check the cache first for data and if it is not found in the cache, the program will then query the database. Here is sample pseudocode for a `getCustomer` function:

```
define getCustomer(p_customerID):
    begin
        if exists(customerCache['1982737:firstName]),
            return(
                    customerCache[p_customerID
                      +':lastname'],
                    customerCache[p_customerID
                      +':shippingAddress'],
                    customerCache[p_customerID
                      +':shippingCity'],
                    customerCache['p_customerID
                      +':shippingState'],
                    customerCache[p_customerID
                      +'':shippingZip']
                    );
    else
            return(addQueryResultsToCache(p_customerID,
                'SELECT
                    firstName,
                    lastName,
```

```
                        shippingAddress,
                        shippingCity,
                        shippingState,
                        shippingZip
                FROM
                        customers
            WHERE
                        customerID = p_customerID')
     end;
);
```

The pseudocoded function takes one parameter, p_customerID, which is a unique identifier of the customer. The if statement checks if there exists a key in the cache that consists of the customer identifier passed in as a parameter and the character string 'firstName'. If it does exist, then it is safe to assume that all the attributes about the customer are in the cache and can be returned from the cache. If the customer's first name is not in the cache, the function executes another function called addQueryResultsToCache. This function takes a key, and SQL query returns the data associated with that key. The function also stores a copy of the returned data in the cache so it is available next time the getCustomer function is called.

> ❖ **Caution** Like arrays in programming languages, when the server is shut down or the cache terminates, the data in memory is lost. The next time the application starts, it will have to reload the cache with data by executing statements like the SQL statement in the getCustomer function.

Although caches are types of key-value data stores, they are outside the scope of this book. The following discussion about key-value databases applies to key-value stores that save data persistently.

## In-Memory and On-Disk Key-Value Database: From Bikes to Motorized Vehicles

Caches are helpful for improving the performance of applications that perform many database queries. Key-value data stores are even more useful when they store data persistently on disk, flash devices, or other long-term storage. They offer the fast performance benefits of caches plus the persistent storage of databases.

Key-value databases impose a minimal set of constraints on how you arrange your data. There is no need for tables if you do not want to think in terms of groups of related attributes.

❖ **Note** The one design requirement of a key-value database is that each value has a unique identifier in the form of the key. Keys must be unique within the namespace defined by the key-value database. The namespace can be called a bucket, a database, or some other term indicating a collection of key-value pairs (see Figure 3.4).

**Database**

| Bucket 1 | | Bucket 2 | | Bucket 3 | |
|---|---|---|---|---|---|
| 'Foo1' | 'Bar' | 'Foo1' | 'Baz' | 'Foo1' | 'Bar7' |
| 'Foo2' | 'Bar2' | 'Foo4' | 'Baz3' | 'Foo4' | 'Baz3' |
| 'Foo3' | 'Bar7' | 'Foo6' | 'Baz2' | 'Foo7' | 'Baz9' |

**Figure 3.4** *Keys of a key-value database must be unique within a namespace.*

Developers tend to use key-value databases when ease of storage and retrieval are more important than organizing data into more complex data structures, such as tables or networks.

❖ **Note** Developers could readily implement networks and table-like data structures using key-value databases as a foundation. A developer could use a key-naming convention that uses a table name, primary key value, and an attribute name to create a key to store the value of an attribute, as shown in the following example:

```
customer:1982737:firstName
customer:1982737:lastName
customer:1982737:shippingAddress
customer:1982737:shippingCity
customer:1982737:shippingState
customer:1982737:shippingZip
```

Next, the developer can create a set of functions that emulate the operations performed on a table, such as creating, reading, updating, or deleting a row. One example of pseudocode for a `create` function is

```
define addCustomerRow(p_tableName, p_primaryKey,
  p_firstName, p_lastName, p_shippingAddress,
  p_shippingCity, p_shippingState, p_shippingZip)
  begin
    set [p_tableName+p_primary+'firstName'] = p_firstName;
    set [p_tableName+p_primary+'lastName'] = p_lastName;
    set [p_tableName+p_primary+'shippingAddress'] =
      p_shippingAddress;
    set [p_tableName+p_primary+'shippingCity'] =
      p_shippingCity;
    set [p_tableName+p_primary+'shippingState'] =
      p_shippingState;
    set [p_tableName+p_primary+'shippingZip'] =
      p_shippingZip;
  end;
```

The reading, updating, and deleting functions are equally as easy to write. (You will write a `delete` function later in the chapter as an exercise.)

# Essential Features of Key-Value Databases

A variety of key-value databases is available to developers, and they all share three essential features:

- Simplicity
- Speed
- Scalability

These characteristics sound like an ideal combination that should be embraced by every database, but as you will see, there are limitations that come along with these valued features.

## Simplicity: Who Needs Complicated Data Models Anyway?

Key-value databases use a bare-minimum data structure. You might wonder, why would anyone want to use a bare-minimum database when you could use a feature-rich relational database? The answer is that sometimes you do not need all those extra features.

Think about word processors. Microsoft Word, for example, has an impressive list of features, including a wide array of formatting options, spelling and grammar checkers, and even the ability to integrate with other tools like reference and bibliography managers.

These are just the kinds of tools you want in your word processor if you are writing a book or lengthy term paper. But what if you are writing a six-item to-do list on your phone? A full-featured word processor is more than you need. A simple text editor would do the job just as well. The same kind of situation can occur when design applications use a database for storage.

Often, developers do not need support for joining tables or running queries about multiple entities in the database. If you were implementing a database to store information about a customer's online shopping cart, you could use a relational database, but it would be simpler to use a key-value database. You would not have to define a database schema in SQL. You would not have to define data types for each attribute you'd like to track.

If you discover that you would like to track additional attributes after you have written your program, you can simply add code to your program to take care of those attributes. There is no need to change database code to tell the database about the new attribute. Key-value databases have no problem working with adding new attributes as they come along.

In key-value databases, you work with a simple data model. The syntax for manipulating data is simple. Typically, you specify a namespace, which could be a database name, a bucket name, or some other type of collection name, and a key to indicate you want to perform an operation on a key-value pair. When you specify only the namespace name and the key, the key-value database will return the associated value. When you want to update the value associated with a key, you specify the namespace, key, and new value.

Key-value databases are flexible and forgiving. If you make a mistake and assign the wrong type of data, for example, a real number instead of an integer, the database usually does not complain. This feature is especially useful when the data type changes or you need to support two or more data types for the same attribute. If you need to have both numbers as strings for customer identifiers, you can do that with code such as the following:

```
shoppingCart[cart:1298:customerID]  =  1982737
shoppingCart[cart:3985:customerID]  =  'Johnson, Louise'
```

One of the advantages of simple data structures in computer science is that they are often associated with fast operations.

## Speed: There Is No Such Thing as Too Fast

Major database vendors create tools to help developers and database administrators identify slow-running queries. Books are written on tuning databases. Software engineers comb their code for opportunities to cut down on the time required to run their code. It seems like no one wants to wait for his or her data.

Key-value databases are known for their speed. With a simple associative array data structure and design features to optimize performance, key-value databases can deliver high-throughput, data-intensive operations.

One way to keep database operations running fast is to keep data in memory. Reading and writing data to RAM is much faster than writing to a disk. Of course, RAM is not persistent storage, so if you lose power on your database server, you will lose the contents of RAM. Key-value databases can have the advantages of fast write operations to RAM and the persistence of disk-based storage by using both.

When a program changes the value associated with a key, the key-value database can update the entry in RAM and then send a message to the program that the updated value has been saved. The program can then continue with other operations. While the program is doing something else, the key-value database can write the recently updated value to disk. The new value is saved to disk unless there is a power loss or some other failure between the time the application updates the value and the key-value database stores the value on disk (see Figure 3.5).

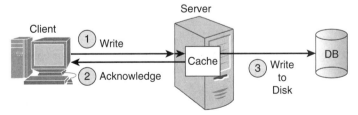

**Figure 3.5** *Write operations can return control to the calling application faster by first writing inserts and updates to RAM and then updating disk storage.*

Similarly, read operations can be faster if data is stored in memory. This is the motivation for using a cache, as described earlier. Because the size of the database can exceed the size of RAM, key-value stores have to find ways of managing the data in memory.

> ❖ **Tip** Compressing data is one way of increasing the effective storage capacity of memory, but even with compression there may not be sufficient memory to store a large key-value database completely in RAM.

When the key-value database uses all the memory allocated to it, the database will need to free some of the allocated memory before storing copies of additional data. There are multiple algorithms for this, but a commonly used method is known as least recently used (LRU). The idea behind the LRU algorithm is that if data has not been used in a while, it is less likely to be used than data that has been read or written more recently. This intuition makes sense for many application areas of key-value databases (see Figure 3.6).

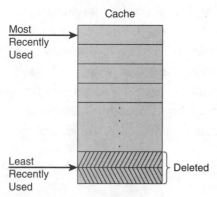

**Figure 3.6** *Least recently used algorithms delete data that has not been read or written as recently as other data.*

Consider a key-value database used to store items in customers' online carts. Assume that once a customer adds an item to the cart, it stays there until the customer checks out or the item is removed by a background cleanup process. A customer who finished shopping several hours ago may still have data in memory. More than likely, that customer has abandoned the cart and is not likely to continue shopping. Compare that scenario with a customer who last added an item to the cart five minutes ago. There is a good chance that customer is still shopping and will likely add other items to the cart or continue to the checkout process shortly.

## Scalability: Keeping Up with the Rush

It is important for key-value databases, and other types of NoSQL databases used in web and other large-scale applications, to scale with minimal disruption to operations. Remember from Chapter 2, "Variety of NoSQL Databases," that scalability is the capability to add or remove servers from a cluster of servers as needed to accommodate the load on the system. When you scale databases, the capability to accommodate both reads and writes is an important property. Key-value databases take different approaches to scaling read and write operations. Let's consider two options:

- Master-slave replication
- Masterless replication

### Scaling with Master-Slave Replication

One way to keep up with a growing demand for read operations is to add servers that can respond to queries. It is easy to imagine applications that would have many more reads than writes. During the World Cup finals, football fans around the world (and soccer fans in the United States) who have to work instead of watch the game would be checking their favorite sport score website for the latest updates. News sites would similarly have a greater proportion of reads than writes. Even e-commerce sites can experience a higher ratio of page views than data writes because customers may browse many descriptions and reviews for each item they ultimately end up adding to their shopping carts.

In applications such as this, it is reasonable to have more servers that can respond to queries than accept writes. A master-slave replication model works well in this case.

The master is a server in the cluster that accepts write and read requests. It is responsible for maintaining the master record of all writes and replicating, or copying, updated data to all other servers in the cluster. These other servers only respond to read requests. As Figure 3.7 shows, master-slave architectures have a simple hierarchical structure.

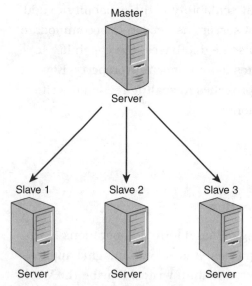

**Figure 3.7**   *Master-slave architectures have a simple communication pattern during normal operations.*

An advantage of master-slave models is simplicity. Except for the master, each node in the cluster only needs to communicate with one other server: the master. The master accepts all writes, so there is no need to coordinate write operations or resolve conflicts between multiple servers accepting writes.

A disadvantage of the master-slave replication model is that if the master fails, the cluster cannot accept writes. This can adversely impact the availability of the cluster  The master server is known as a single point of failure—that is, a single component in a system that if it fails, the entire system fails or at least loses a critical capacity, such as accepting writes.

Designers of distributed systems have developed protocols so active servers can detect when other servers in the cluster fail. For example, a server may send a simple message to ask a random server in the cluster if it is still active. If the randomly selected server replies, then the first server will know the other server is active.

In the case of master-slave configurations, if a number of slave servers do not receive a message from the master within some period of time, the slaves may determine the master has failed. At that point, the slaves initiate a protocol to promote one of the slaves to master (see Figure 3.8). Once active as the master, the new master server begins accepting write operations and the cluster would continue to function, accepting both read and write operations.

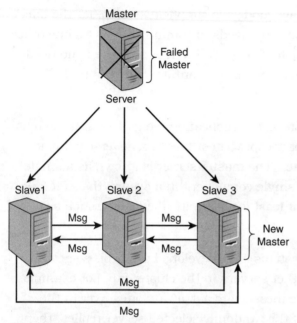

**Figure 3.8**   *Once a failed master server is detected, the slaves initiate a protocol to elect a new master.*

## Scaling with Masterless Replication

The master-slave replication model with a single server accepting writes does not work well when there are a large number of writes. Imagine the Rolling Stones decide to have one more world tour. Fans around the world flock to buy concert tickets. The fans would generate a large number of reads when they look up the cities that will be hosting concerts, but once they find one or two close cities, they are ready to purchase tickets.

The software engineers who write the concert ticket program have a lot to think about, including

- Storing concert locations and dates.
- Available seats in each venue.

- Cost of seats in various sections.

- Any limits on the number of tickets purchased by a single customer.

- Ensuring that seats that appear to be available to a user are still available when the user chooses to purchase the ticket. This assumes the customer opts to buy the ticket almost immediately after seeing the availability.

There are probably many more requirements, but these are sufficient to give you a basic idea of the challenges the software engineers are up against.

With the possibility of a surge in the number of customers trying to write to the database, a single server accepting writes will limit scalability. A better option for this application is a masterless replication model in which all nodes accept reads and writes. An immediate problem that comes to mind is: How do you handle writes so that two or more servers do not try to sell the same seat in a concert venue to multiple customers? (See Figure 3.9.)

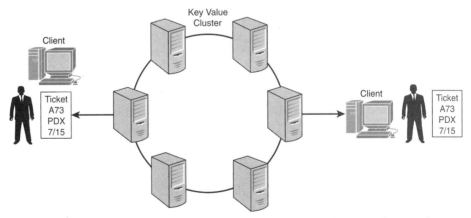

**Figure 3.9**  *A fan's worst nightmare: Multiple fans are able to purchase tickets for the same seat.*

There is an elegant solution to this problem that is described later in the "Keys: More Than Meaningless Identifiers" section. For now, let's assume that only one customer can purchase a seat at a concert venue at a particular date and time. There is still the problem of scaling reads.

In a masterless replication model, there is not a single server that has the master copy of updated data, so no single server can copy its data to all other servers. Instead, servers in a masterless replication model work in groups to help their neighbors.

Consider a set of eight servers configured in a masterless replication model and set up in a ring structure. For simplicity, assume that the servers are named 1, 2, 3, and so on up to Server 8. In the ring structure, Server 1 is logically linked to Servers 2 and 8, Server 2 is linked to Servers 1 and 3, Server 3 is linked to Servers 2 and 4, and so on. Figure 3.10 shows the full configuration.

> ❖ **Note**  The ring structure is a useful abstraction for discussing replication in a masterless model. In a data center, the eight servers would probably all be connected to a single network hub and able to directly communicate with each other.

Database administrators can configure a key-value database to keep a particular number of replicas. In this scenario, the administrator has decided that four replicas are sufficient. Each time there is a write operation to one of the servers, it replicates that change to the three other servers holding its replica. In this scenario, each server replicates to its two neighbors and to the server two links ahead. For example, Server 2 replicates to its neighbors Server 1 and Server 3 as well as Server 4, which is two links ahead. Figure 3.11 shows the full replication pattern.

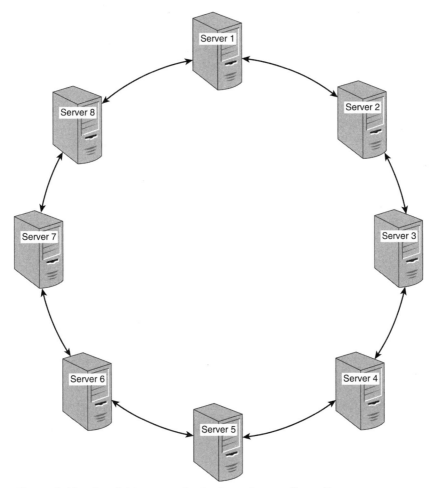

**Figure 3.10**   *An eight-server cluster in a ring configuration.*

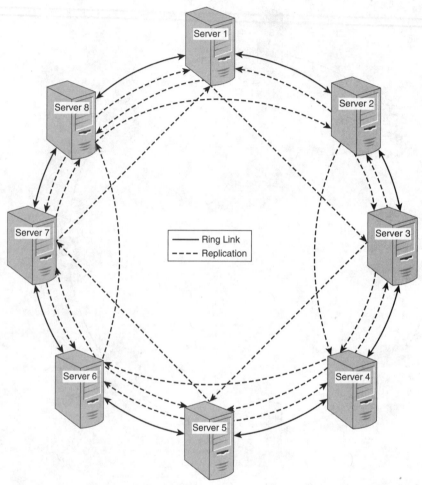

**Figure 3.11**    *An eight-server cluster in a ring configuration with a replication factor of 4.*

Now that you have had a basic introduction to the essential features of key-value data stores, it is time to drill down into some of the properties of two components: keys and values.

# Keys: More Than Meaningless Identifiers

As already stated, keys are used to identify, index, or otherwise reference a value in a key-value database. The one essential property of a key is that it must be unique within a namespace. This makes keys sound pretty simple, and they are—sometimes.

## How to Construct a Key

If you have worked with relational databases, you may have used counters or sequences to generate keys. Counters and sequences are functions that return a new unique number each time the function is called. Database application designers use these routinely to make keys for rows of data stored in a table. Each generated number is a unique identifier used by a row in a table.

Designers could use one counter to generate primary keys for all tables, or they could use a different counter or sequence for each table. Either way, each row in a table has a unique identifier. Just as keys in key-value databases must be unique in a namespace, the primary key of a row of data must be unique to the table.

> ❖ **Tip** It is considered good practice to use meaningless keys in relational database design.

The sole purpose of a primary key, the reasoning goes, is to uniquely identify a row. If you were to use a property of the data, such as the last name and first initial of a customer, you might run into problems with duplicates. Also, values stored in rows may change.

For example, consider how quickly the meaning of a primary key would change if you used the two-letter state abbreviation of the state in which a customer lives as part of a key for that customer. You could have a key such as 'SMITH_K_TX' for a Katherine Smith who lives in

Texas. If Katherine Smith moves to Illinois, then the primary key is no longer meaningful.

> ❖ **Caution** Primary keys should not be changed, so you could not simply change the key to 'SMITH_K_IL.' That would violate the principle that primary keys are immutable. You could conceivably change a primary key (if the database management system allowed such updates), but you would have to update all references to that key in other tables.

Storing a primary key to a row in another table is known as a foreign key. As you can see, the way relational databases work, it makes sense to have meaningless keys.

In NoSQL databases, and key-value databases in general, the rules are different. Key-value databases do not have a built-in table structure. With no tables, there are no columns. With no columns, there is no way to know what a value is for except for the key. Consider a shopping cart application using a key-value database with meaningless keys:

```
Cart[12387] = 'SKU AK8912j4'
```

This key is the type of identifier you would likely see in a relational database. This key-value pair only tells you that a cart identified by number 12387 has an item called 'SKU AK8912j4'. You might assume from the value that SKU stands for *stock keeping unit*, a standard term in retail to refer to a specific type of product. However, you don't know who this cart belongs to or where to ship the product.

One way to solve this problem is to create another namespace, such as custName. Then you could save a value such as

```
CustName[12387] = 'Katherine Smith'
```

This would solve the immediate problem of identifying who owns the cart, but you can see that this approach does not generalize well. Every attribute tracked in the application would need a separate namespace. Alternatively, you can use meaningful keys that entail information about attributes.

As discussed earlier, you can construct meaningful names that entail information about entity types, entity identifiers, and entity attributes. For example:

```
Cust:12387:firstName
```

could be a key to store the first name of the customer with `customerID` `12387`. This is not the only way to create meaningful names, but it is the one used throughout this book. Again, the basic formula is

```
Entity Name + ':' + Entity Identifier +':' + Entity
    Attribute
```

The delimiter does not have to be a `':'` but it is a common practice.

## Using Keys to Locate Values

Up to this point, there has been a fair amount of discussion about how to construct keys, why keys must be unique within a namespace, and why meaningful keys are more useful in key-value databases than relational databases. There has been some mention of the idea that keys are used to look up associated values, but there has been no explanation about how that happens. It is time to address that topic.

If key-value database designers were willing to restrict you to using integers as key values, then they would have an easy job of designing code to fetch or set values based on keys. They could load a database into memory or store it on disk and assume that the first value stored in a namespace is referenced by key 1, the next value by key 2, and so on. Fortunately, key-value designers are more concerned with designing useful data stores than simplifying data access code.

Using numbers to identify locations is a good idea, but it is not flexible enough. You should be able to use integers, character strings, and even lists of objects as keys if you want. The good news is that you can. The trick is to use a function that maps from integers, character strings, or lists of objects to a unique string or number. These functions that map from one type of value to a number are known as hash functions.

❖ **Note**  Not all key-value databases support lists and other complex structures. Some are more restricted in the types and lengths of keys than others.

### Hash Functions: From Keys to Locations

A hash function is a function that can take an arbitrary string of characters and produce a (usually) unique, fixed-length string of characters.

❖ **Note**  Actually, the value returned by the hash function is not always unique; sometimes two unrelated inputs can generate the same output. This is known as a *collision*.

▶ *Refer to Chapter 4, "Key-Value Database Terminology," for information on how to deal with collisions.*

For example, the keys mentioned earlier in the chapter to describe customer shipping information are mapped to hash values listed in Table 3.1.

**Table 3.1** *Key to Hash Value Mappings*

| Key | Hash Value |
| --- | --- |
| customer:1982737:<br>firstName | e135e850b892348a4e516cfcb385eba3bfb6d209 |
| customer:1982737:<br>lastName | f584667c5938571996379f256b8c82d2f5e0f62f |
| customer:1982737:<br>shippingAddress | d891f26dcdb3136ea76092b1a70bc324c424ae1e |
| customer:1982737:<br>shippingCity | 33522192da50ea66bfc05b74d1315778b6369ec5 |
| customer:1982737:<br>shippingState | 239ba0b4c437368ef2b16ecf58c62b5e6409722f |
| customer:1982737:<br>shippingZip | 814f3b2281e49941e1e7a03b223da28a8e0762ff |

Each hash value is quite different from the others, although they all have the same 'customer:1982737:' prefix. One of the properties of hash functions is that they map to what appear to be random outputs. In this example, the SHA-1 hash function is used to generate the hash values.

The values are all numbers in hexadecimal, a base-16 number system. The hexadecimal integers are 0–9 and a–f, which represent 10–15. This is about 1.4615016e+48 different values. Needless to say, this should be plenty for any key-value database application.

**Keys Help Avoid Write Problems**

Now, let's see how you can use the numbers returned by the hash function to map to a location. To keep things simple, the discussion focuses on using the number returned by a hash function to determine which server in a cluster should be used to store the value associated with the key. An actual key-value implementation would have to map to a location on disk or in memory, but that is beyond the scope of this discussion.

Assume you are working with the eight-server cluster that you saw in Figure 3.10. You can take advantage of the fact that the hash function returns a number. Because the write load should be evenly distributed across all eight servers, you can send one eighth of all writes to each server. You could send the first write to Server 1, the second to Server 2, the third to Server 3, and so on in a round-robin fashion, but this would not take advantage of the hash value.

One way to take advantage of the hash value is to start by dividing the hash value by the number of servers. Sometimes the hash value will divide evenly by the number of servers. (For this discussion, assume the hash function returns decimal numbers, not hexadecimal numbers, and that the number of digits in the number is not fixed.)

If the hash function returns the number 32 and that number is divided by 8, then the remainder is 0. If the hash function returns 41 and it is divided by 8, then the remainder is 1. If the hash function returns 67, division by 8 leaves a remainder of 3.

As you can see, any division by 8 will have a remainder between 0 and 7. Each of the eight servers can be assigned a number between 0 and 7.

In this discussion, the remainder will be called the modulus after the modulo arithmetic operation that returns a remainder. Figure 3.12 shows how to assign each modulus to a server.

Let's return to the concert ticket application. A challenge was to ensure that two servers did not sell tickets to the same seat, at the same venue, in the same city, on the same night to more than one person. Because key-value databases running in a masterless configuration can accept writes from all servers, such a mistake could happen. The solution is to make sure any requests for the same seat, at the same venue, in the same city, on the same night all go to the same server.

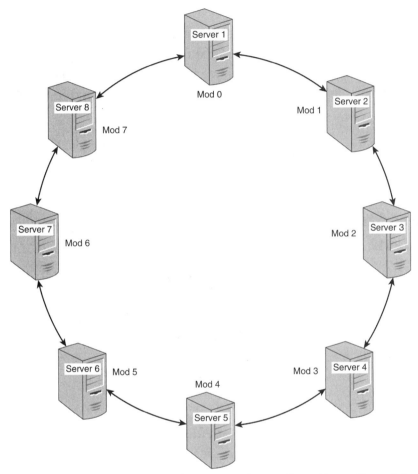

**Figure 3.12** *An eight-server cluster in a ring configuration with modulo number assigned.*

You can do this by making a key based on seat, venue, city, and date. For example, two fans want to purchase set A73 at the Civic Center in Portland, Oregon, on July 15. You could construct keys using the seat, an abbreviation for the venue (CIvCen in this case), the airport code for the city (PDX in this case), and a four-digit number for the date. In this example, the key would be

```
A73:CivCen:PDX:0715
```

Anyone trying to purchase that same seat on the same day would generate the same key. Because keys are mapped to servers using modulo operations, all requests for that seat, location, and date combination would go to the same server. There is no chance for another server to sell that seat, thus avoiding the problem with servers competing to sell the same ticket.

Keys, of course, are only half the story in key-value databases. It is time to discuss values.

# Values: Storing Just About Any Data You Want

This chapter started with the theme of simplicity. Key-value data stores are the simplest form of NoSQL database. That is in part because the foundational data structure of the associative array is so simple. NoSQL databases are also simple with respect to the way they store data.

## Values Do Not Require Strong Typing

Unlike strongly typed programming languages that require you to define variables and specify a type for those variables, key-value databases do not expect you to specify types for the values you store.

You could, for example, store a string along with a key for a customer's address:

```
'1232 NE River Ave, St. Louis, MO'
```

or you could store a list of the form:

```
('1232 NE River Ave', 'St. Louis', 'MO')
```

or you could store a more structured format using JavaScript Object Notation, such as

```
{ 'Street:' : '1232 NE River Ave', 'City' : 'St. Louis',:
  'State' : 'MO' }
```

Key-value databases make minimal assumptions about the structure of data stored in the database.

While in theory, key-value databases allow for arbitrary types of values, in practice database designers have to make implementation choices that lead to some restrictions. Different implementations of key-value databases have different restrictions on values. For example, some key-value databases will typically have some limit on the size of values. Some might allow multiple megabytes in each value, but others might have smaller size limitations.

Even in cases in which you can store extremely large values, you might run into performance problems that lead you to work with smaller data values.

> ❖ **Note** It is important to consider the design characteristics of the key-value database you choose to use. Consult the documentation for limitations on keys and values. Part of the process in choosing a key-value database is considering the trade-off of various features. One key-value database might offer ACID transactions but limit you to small keys and values. Another key-value data store might allow for large values but limit keys to numbers or strings. Your application requirements should be considered when weighing the advantages and disadvantages of different database systems.

## Limitations on Searching for Values

Keep in mind that in key-value databases, operations on values are all based on keys. You can retrieve a value by key, you can set a value by key, and you can delete values by key. That is pretty much the repertoire of operations. If you want to do more, such as search for an address in which the city is "St. Louis," you will have to do that with an application program. If you were using a relational database, you could issue a SQL query, such as the following:

```
SELECT
    address,
    city,
    state,
    zip
FROM
    Customer
WHERE
    city = 'St. Louis'
```

Key-value databases do not support query languages for searching over values. There are two ways to address this limitation.

You, as an application developer, could implement the required search operations in your application. For example, you could generate a series of keys, query for the value of each key, and test the returned value for the pattern you seek.

Let's assume you decided to store addresses as a string such as '1232 NE River Ave, St. Louis, MO' and you store it like this:

```
appData[cust:9877:address] = '1232 NE River Ave, St.
  Louis, MO'
```

A pseudocode function for searching for customers in a particular city is

```
define findCustomerWithCity(p_startID, p_endID, p_City):
    begin
    # first, create an empty list variable to hold all
    # addresses that match the city name
```

```
returnList = ();
# loop through a range of identifiers and build keys
# to look up address values then test each address
# using the inString function to see if the city name
# passed in the p_City parameter is in the address
# string. If it is, add it to the list of  addresses
# to return
for id in p_startID to p_endID:
    address = appData['cust:' + id + ':address'];
    if inString(p_City, Address):
        addToList(Address,returnList );
# after checking all addresses in the ranges specified
# by the start and end ID return the list of addresses
# with the specified city name.
return(returnList);
end;
```

This method enables you to search value strings, but it is inefficient. If you need to search large ranges of data, you might retrieve and test many values that do not have the city you are looking for.

Some key-value databases incorporate search functionality directly into the database. This is an additional service not typically found in key-value databases but can significantly add to the usefulness of the database. A built-in search system would index the string values stored in the database and create an index for rapid retrieval. Rather than search all values for a string, the search system keeps a list of words with the keys of each key-value pair in which that word appears. Figure 3.13 shows a graphical depiction of what such an index might look like.

| Word | Keys |
|------|------|
| 'IL' | 'cust:2149:state' , 'cust:4111:state' |
| 'OR' | 'cust:9134:state' |
| 'MA' | 'cust:7714:state' , 'cust:3412:state' |
| 'Boston' | 'cust:1839:address' |
| 'St. Louis' | 'cust:9877:address' , 'cust:1171:address' |
| | . . . . |
| 'Portland' | 'cust:9134:city' |
| 'Chicago' | 'cust:2149:city' , 'cust:4111:city' |

**Figure 3.13**   *A search index helps efficiently retrieve data when selecting by criteria based on values.*

## Summary

Key-value databases are simple and flexible. They are based on the associative array, which is a more generalized data structure than arrays. Associative arrays allow for generalized index values, or keys. Keys may be integers, strings, lists of values, or other types.

An important constraint on keys is that they must be unique within a namespace. Keys are used to look up values and those values can vary by type. There are some practical limitations on the size of values and those limitations can vary by implementation. Some of the limitations of key-value databases, such as lack of query language, are mitigated with additional features such as search tools.

Key-value databases lend themselves to scalable designs based on both master-slave and masterless replication models. Master-slave architectures typically have a single node that accepts writes and multiple nodes that support read operations. Masterless architectures allow for multiple nodes to accept write and support reads.

Chapter 4 includes additional terminology and concepts needed to understand both the design and the use of key-value databases. Then, Chapter 5, "Designing for Key-Value Databases," discusses the use of key-value databases in application design and describes a number of useful design patterns to help you develop robust applications based on key-value databases.

## Review Questions

1. How are associative arrays different from arrays?
2. How can you use a cache to improve relational database performance?
3. What is a namespace?
4. Describe a way of constructing keys that captures some information about entities and attribute types.
5. Name three common features of key-value databases.
6. What is a hash function? Include important characteristics of hash functions in your definition.
7. How can hash functions help distribute writes over multiple servers?
8. What is one type of practical limitation on values stored in key-value databases?
9. How does the lack of a query language affect application developers using key-value databases?
10. How can a search system help improve the performance of applications that use key-value databases?

# References

Basho Technologies, Inc. Riak Documentation: http://docs.basho.com/ riak/latest/

Carlson, Josiah L. *Redis in Action*. Shelter Island, NY: Manning Publications Co., 2013.

Meyer, Mathias. *Riak Handbook*. Seattle, WA: Amazon Digital Services, Inc., 2013.

FoundationDB, FoundationDB Documentation: https:// foundationdb.com/key-value-store/documentation/index.html

Macedo, Tiago, and Fred Oliveira. *Redis Cookbook*. Sebastopol, CA: O'Reilly Media, Inc., 2011.

Oracle Corporation. Oracle NoSQL Documentation: http:// www.oracle.com/technetwork/database/database-technologies/ nosqldb/documentation/index.html.

Redis. io Documentation: http://redis.io/documentation

# Bibliography

Hernandez, Michael J. *Database Design for Mere Mortals: A Hands-On Guide to Relational Database Design*. Reading, MA: Addison-Wesley, 2003.

Viescas, John L., and Michael J. Hernandez. *SQL Queries for Mere Mortals*. Reading, MA: Addison-Wesley, 2007.

# 4

# Key-Value Database Terminology

*"I always try to think of a vocabulary to match different musical situations."*
—Roscoe Mitchell
Jazz composer and saxophonist

## Topics Covered In This Chapter

Key-Value Database Data Modeling Terms

Key-Value Architecture Terms

Key-Value Implementation Terms

This chapter is different from the first three chapters of this book. The intent of this chapter is to provide an explanation of important terms used when discussing key-value databases. Introducing terminology of a new domain, like NoSQL databases, presents something of a chicken-and-egg problem.

Which should come first? Should you learn about the basic ideas of key-value databases and then delve into a more detailed understanding of the terms and concepts that underlie key-value databases? Or, should you first learn the definition of terms independent of the bigger picture of key-value databases? There are advantages and disadvantages to both approaches.

This book tries to have the best of both worlds by introducing basic concepts and then providing detailed descriptions of key terms followed by an advanced topics chapter that includes a discussion of design patterns, potential pitfalls and traps, and a case study describing a typical use case for key-value databases.

This chapter is organized into three broad, somewhat overlapping topics: data modeling terms, architecture terms, and implementation terms. This structure is somewhat arbitrary and you could make the case that some terms in the architecture section should be in the implementation section and vice versa. The placement of the terms in chapter sections is far less important than the terms themselves.

NoSQL databases do not share the same level of standardization you find in relational databases. There is, for example, no standard NoSQL query language comparable to relational databases' SQL. Different vendors and open source projects sometimes introduce terms or use data structures not found in other NoSQL databases.

The terminology chapters (there is one for each of the four major types of NoSQL database) offer an opportunity to introduce vendor- or project-specific terminology. Although the *For Mere Mortals* series of books tends to not focus on specific software, a familiarity with vendor and open source project-specific terms may help when you start implementing your own NoSQL database–based applications.

## Key-Value Database Data Modeling Terms

Data models are abstractions that help organize the information conveyed by the data in databases. They are different from data structures.

Data structures are well-defined data storage structures that are implemented using elements of underlying hardware, particularly random access memory and persistent data storage, such as hard drives and flash devices. For example, an integer variable in a programming language may be implemented as a set of four contiguous bytes, or 32 bits.

An array of 100 integers can be implemented as a contiguous set of 4-byte memory addresses. Data structures also have a set of operations that manipulate the data structure. Addition, subtraction, multiplication, and division are some of the operations defined on integers. Reading and writing values based on indices are operations defined on arrays.

Data structures offer a higher level of organization so you do not have to think in low-level terms of memory addresses and machine-level operations on those addresses. Data models serve a similar purpose. They provide a level of organization and abstraction above data structures (see Figure 4.1).

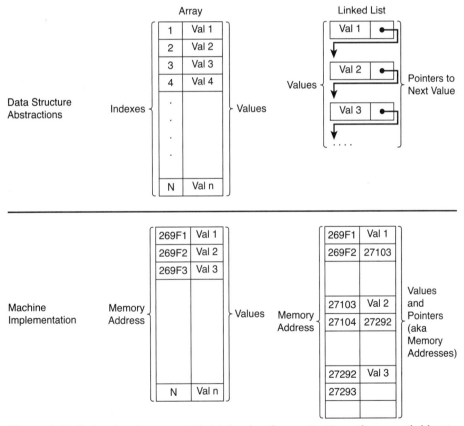

**Figure 4.1** *Data structures provide higher-level organizations than available at the machine level.*

Data models typically organize multiple kinds of related information. A customer management data model could model information about customers' names, addresses, orders, and payment histories. Clinical databases could include information such as patients' names, ages, genders, current prescriptions, past surgeries, allergies, and other medically relevant details.

In theory, you could write software that tracks all of these pieces of data in basic database structures like arrays and linked lists. In practice, such an approach would be an inefficient use of your time. Using data models and databases is a more effective and productive strategy (see Figure 4.2).

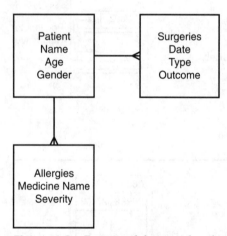

**Figure 4.2**   *Data models provide a layer of abstraction above data structures that allows database application developers to focus more on the information that must be managed and less on implementation issues.*

The elements of data models vary with the type of database. Relational databases are organized around tables. Tables are used to store information about entities, such as customers, patients, orders, and surgeries. Entities have attributes that capture information about particular entities. Attributes include names, ages, shipping addresses, and so forth.

In a relational database, a table is organized by a set of columns and each column corresponds to an attribute. Rows of the table correspond to a single instance of an entity, such as a particular customer or patient.

The software engineers who design databases choose data structures for implementing tables and other elements of a data model. This relieves application developers of needing to delve into such details. The price application developers must pay, however, is learning the terms and design patterns associated with data models used in their database.

❖ **Note** In relational database design, there is a distinction between logical data models and physical data models. Entities and attributes are used in logical data models. Tables and columns are the corresponding elements of physical data models. This book uses both *entity* and *table*. Because this is not a book about relational database design, a detailed explanation of the differences of logical and physical data models and when to use terms from each is beyond the scope of this book. For more on relational data modeling, see Michael J. Hernandez's *Database Design for Mere Mortals*, Second Edition (Addison-Wesley, 2003).

The following sections discuss some of the most important terms associated with data modeling in key-value databases, including key, value, namespace, partition, partition key, and schemaless.

## Key

A *key* is a reference to a value. It is analogous to an address. The address *1232 NE River St.* is a reference to a building located in a particular place. Among other things, it enables postal workers and delivery services to find a particular building and drop off or pick up letters and packages. The string "1232 NE River St." is obviously not a building, but it is a way to find the corresponding building. Keys in key-value databases are similarly not values but are ways of finding and manipulating values.

A key can take on different forms depending on the key-value database used. At a minimum, a key is specified as a string of characters, such as `"Cust9876"` or `"Patient:A384J:Allergies"`. Some key-value databases, such as Redis (www.redis.io), support more complex data structures as keys. The supported key data types in Redis version 2.8.13 include

- Strings

- Lists

- Sets

- Sorted sets

- Hashes

- Bit arrays

❖ **Note** Redis developers use the term *data structures server* instead of key-value data store. Visit http://redis.io/topics/data-types-intro for more information.

*Lists* are ordered collections of strings. *Sets* are collections of unique items in no particular order. *Sorted sets*, as the name implies, are collections of unique items in a particular order. *Hashes* are data structures that have key-value characteristics: They map from one string to another. Bit arrays are binary integer arrays in which each individual bit can be manipulated using various bit array operations.

▶ *Refer to the "Hash Functions" section later in this chapter for more detailed information on this topic.*

It helps to have a naming convention when creating keys, such as described in Chapter 3, "Introduction to Key-Value Databases." One convention is to use a combination of strings representing an entity type, a unique identifier for a particular entity, and an attribute.

> ❖ **Caution** Keep in mind that strings should not be too long. Long keys will use more memory and key-value databases tend to be memory-intensive systems already. At the same time, avoid keys that are too short. Short keys are more likely to lead to conflicts in key names. For example, the key
>
> ```
> CMP:1897:Name
> ```
>
> could refer to the name of a marketing campaign or the name of a component in a product. A better option would be
>
> ```
> CAMPN:1897:Name
> ```
>
> to refer to a marketing campaign and
>
> ```
> COMPT:1897:Name
> ```
>
> to refer to a component in a product.

Keys can also play an important role in implementing scalable architectures. Keys are not only used to reference values, but they are also used to organize data across multiple servers. The upcoming "Partition" section describes the use of keys for organizing data across servers.

## Value

The definition of value with respect to key-value databases is so amorphous that it is almost not useful. A *value* is an object, typically a set of bytes, that has been associated with a key. Values can be integers, floating-point numbers, strings of characters, binary large objects (BLOBs), semistructured constructs such as JSON objects, images, audio, and just about any other data type you can represent as a series of bytes.

> ❖ **Note** It is important to understand that different implementations of key-value databases have different restrictions on values. Most key-value databases will have a limit on the size of a value. Redis, for example, can have a string value up to 512MB in length.[1] FoundationDB (foundationdb.com), a key-value database known for its support of ACID transactions, limits the size of values to 100,000 bytes.[2]

Key-value implementations will vary in the types of operations supported on values. At the very least, a key-value database will support getting and setting values. Others support additional operations, such as appending a string to an existing value or randomly accessing a section of a string. This can be more efficient than retrieving a value, returning it to a client application, performing the append operation in the client application, and then performing a set operation to update the value.

> ❖ **Note** Another example of extended functionality is found in Riak (www.basho.com), which supports full text indexing of values so you can use an API to find keys and values using search queries.[3]

Keys and values are the basic building blocks of key-value databases, but they are only the beginning.

## Namespace

A *namespace* is a collection of key-value pairs. You can think of a namespace as a set, a collection, a list of key-value pairs without

---

1. http://redis.io/topics/data-types

2. https://foundationdb.com/key-value-store/documentation/beta1/ known-limitations.html

3. http://docs.basho.com/riak/latest/dev/using/search/

duplicates, or a bucket for holding key-value pairs. A namespace could be an entire key-value database. The essential characteristic of a namespace is it is a collection of key-value pairs that has no duplicate keys. It is permissible to have duplicate values in a namespace.

Namespaces are helpful when multiple applications use a key-value database. Developers of different applications should not have to coordinate their key-naming strategy unless they are sharing data (see Figure 4.3).

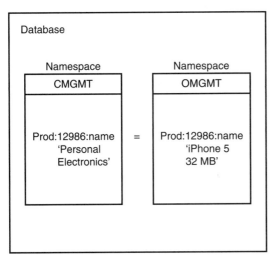

**Figure 4.3** *Namespaces enable duplicate keys to exist without causing conflicts by maintaining separate collections of keys.*

For example, one development team might work on a customer management system while another is working on an order-tracking system. Both will need to use customers' names and addresses. In this case, it makes sense to have a single set of customers used by both teams. It would avoid duplicate work to maintain two customer lists and eliminate the possibility of inconsistent data between the two databases.

When the two teams need to model data specific to their application, there is a potential for key-naming conflicts. The team working on the customer management system might want to track the top type of products each customer purchases, for example, personal electronics, clothing, sports, and so on. The team decides to use the prefix Prod for their product type keys. The team working on order tracking also needs to track products but at a more detailed level. Instead of tracking broad categories, like personal electronics, they track specific products, such as an iPhone 5 32MB. They also decide to use the prefix Prod.

You can probably see the problem this raises. Imagine both applications use the same customer data and, therefore, customer IDs. The customer management team might create a key such as 'Prod:12986:name' and assign the value 'personal electronic.' Meanwhile, the order management team wants to track the last product ordered by a customer and creates the key 'Prod:12986:name' and assigns it the value 'iPhone 5 32MB.'

In this situation, the value of the key is set to the last value written by one of the applications. When the other application reads the data, it will find not only an incorrect value, but also one that is out of the range of expected values.

Namespaces solve this problem by implicitly defining an additional prefix for keys. The customer management team could create a namespace called custMgmt, and the order management team could create a namespace called ordMgmt. They would then store all keys and values in their respective namespaces. The key that caused problems before effectively becomes two unique keys: custMgmt: Prod:12986:name and ordMgmt: Prod:12986:name.

## Partition

Just as it is helpful to organize data into subunits—that is, namespaces—it is also helpful to organize servers in a cluster into subunits. A partitioned cluster is a group of servers in which servers or instances of key-value database software running on servers are assigned to manage subsets of a database. Let's consider a simple example of a two-server cluster. Each server is running key-value database software. Ideally, each server should handle 50% of the workload. There are several ways to handle this.

You could simply decide that all keys starting with the letters *A* through *L* are handled by Server 1 and all keys starting with *M* through *Z* are managed by Server 2. (Assume for the moment that all keys start with a letter.) In this case, you are partitioning data based on the first letter of the key (see Figure 4.4).

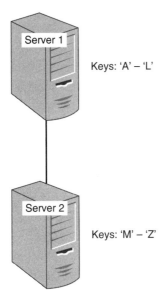

**Figure 4.4** *Servers in a cluster are assigned subsets of data to manage.*

Like so many simple strategies that sound reasonable at first, this one is vulnerable to significant problems. For example, most of the keys may start with the letter *C*, as in cust (customer), cmpg (campaign), comp (component), and so on, whereas very few keys start with letters from the latter half of the alphabet, for example, warh (warehouse). This imbalance in keys leads to an imbalance in the amount of work done by each server in the cluster.

Partition schemes should be chosen to distribute the workload as evenly as possible across the cluster. The "Partition Key" section describes a widely used method to help ensure a fairly even distribution of data and, therefore, workloads (see Figure 4.5).

> ❖ **Note** Note that a server may support more than one partition. This can happen if servers are running virtual machines and each virtual machine supports a single partition. Alternatively, key-value databases may run multiple instances of partition software on each server. This allows for a number of partitions larger than the number of servers.

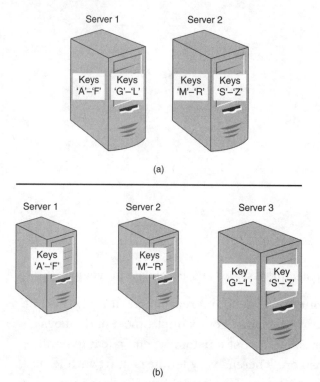

**Figure 4.5** *When multiple instances of key-value database software run on servers in a cluster, servers can be added to the cluster and instances reallocated to balance the workload.*

## Partition Key

A *partition key* is a key used to determine which partition should hold a data value. In key-value databases, all keys are used to determine where the associated value should be stored. Later, you see that other NoSQL database types, such as document databases, use one of several attributes in a document as a partition key.

In the previous example, the first letter of a key name is used to determine which partition manages it. Other simple strategies are partitioning by numeric value and string value. Any key in a key-value database is used as a partition key; good partition keys are ones that distribute workloads evenly.

In some cases, you may not have a key that by itself naturally distributes workloads evenly. In these cases, it helps to use a hash function. Hash functions map an input string to a fixed-sized string that is usually unique to the input string.

You can find out more about hash functions in the "Key-Value Architecture Terms" section later in this chapter. For now, it is sufficient to think of a hash function as a way to map from an imbalanced set of keys to a more equally distributed set of keys.

Key, value, namespace, partition, and partition key are all constructs that help you organize data within a key-value database. The key-value database software that you use makes use of particular architectures, or arrangements of hardware and software components. It is now time to describe important terms related to key-value database architecture.

## Schemaless

*Schemaless* is a term that describes the logical model of a database. In the case of key-value databases, you are not required to define all the keys and types of values you will use prior to adding them to the database. If you would like to store a customer name as a full name using a key such as

```
cust:8983:fullName = 'Jane Anderson'
```

you can do so without first specifying a description of the key or indicating the data type of the values is a string. Schemaless data models allow you to make changes as needed without changing a schema that catalogs all keys and value types (see Figure 4.6).

| Key-Value Database | |
|---|---|
| Keys | Values |
| cust:8983:firstName | 'Jane' |
| cust:8983:lastName | 'Anderson' |
| | |
| cust:8983:fullName | 'Jane Anderson' |
| | |

**Figure 4.6** *Schemaless data models allow for multiple types of representations of the same data to exist simultaneously.*

For example, you might decide that storing a customer's full name in a single value is a bad idea. You conclude that using separate first and last names would be better. You could simply change your code to save keys and values using statements such as the following:

```
cust:8983:firstName = 'Jane'
cust:8983:lastName = 'Anderson'
```

The full name and first/last name keys and values can coexist without a problem.

❖ **Tip** You would, of course, need to update your code to handle both ways of representing customer names or convert all instances of one form into the other.

Part III, "Document Databases," returns to the concept of schemaless databases and discusses the related concept of a polymorphic database, which is something of a middle ground between fixed schemas found in relational databases and schemaless models used in key-value databases.

## Key-Value Architecture Terms

The architecture of a key-value database is a set of characteristics about the servers, networking components, and related software that allows multiple servers to coordinate their work. Three terms frequently appear when discussing key-value architectures:

- Clusters

- Rings

- Replication

### Cluster

*Clusters* are sets to connected computers that coordinate their operations (see Figure 4.7). Clusters may be loosely or tightly coupled. Loosely coupled clusters consist of fairly independent servers that complete many functions on their own with minimal coordination with other servers in the cluster. Tightly coupled clusters tend to have high levels of communication between servers. This is needed to support more coordinated operations, or calculations, on the cluster. Key-value clusters tend to be loosely coupled.

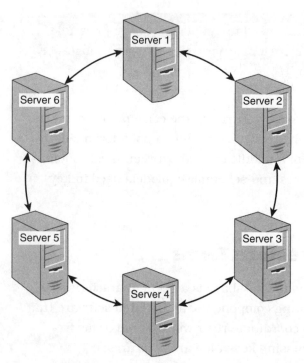

**Figure 4.7**   *A ring architecture of key-value databases links adjacent nodes in the cluster.*

Servers, also known as nodes, in a loosely coupled cluster share information about the range of data the server is responsible for and routinely send messages to each other to indicate they are still functioning. The latter message exchange is used to detect failed nodes. When a node fails, the other nodes in the cluster can respond by taking over the work of that node.

Some clusters have a master node. The master node in Redis, for example, is responsible for accepting read and write operations and copying, or replicating, copies of data to slave nodes that respond to read requests. If a master node fails, the remaining nodes in the cluster will elect a new master node. If a slave node fails, the other nodes in the cluster can continue to respond to read requests.

Masterless clusters, such as used by Riak, have nodes that all carry out operations to support read and write operations. If one of those nodes fails, other nodes will take on the read and write responsibilities of the failed node.

Because the failed node was also responsible for writes, the nodes that take over for the failed node must have copies of the failed node's data. Ensuring there are multiple copies of data on different nodes is the responsibility of the replication subsystem. This is described in the section "Replication," later in this chapter.

Each node in a masterless cluster is responsible for managing some set of partitions. One way to organize partitions is in a ring structure.

## Ring

A ring is a logical structure for organizing partitions. A *ring* is a circular pattern in which each server or instance of key-value database software running on a server is linked to two adjacent servers or instances. Each server or instance is responsible for managing a range of data based on a partition key.

Consider a simple hashlike function that maps a partition key from a string; for example, `'cust:8983:firstName'` to a number between 0 and 95. Now assume that you have an eight-node cluster and the servers are labeled Server 1, Server 2, Server 3, and so on. With eight servers and 96 possible hashlike values, you could map the partitions to servers, as shown in Table 4.1.

**Table 4.1**   *Server to Partition Mapping*

| Server Name | Partition Range |
| --- | --- |
| Server 1 | 0–11 |
| Server 2 | 12–23 |
| Server 3 | 24–35 |
| Server 4 | 36–47 |
| Server 5 | 48–59 |
| Server 6 | 60–71 |
| Server 7 | 72–83 |
| Server 8 | 84–95 |

In this model, Server 2 is linked to Server 1 and Server 3; Server 3 is linked to Server 2 and Server 4; and so on. Server 1 is linked to Server 8 and Server 2. Refer to Figure 4.7 to see a graphical depiction of a ring architecture.

A ring architecture helps to simplify some otherwise potentially complex operations. For example, whenever a piece of data is written to a server, it is also written to the two servers linked to the original server. This enables high availability of a key-value database. For example, if Server 4 fails, both Server 3 and Server 5 could respond to read requests for the data on Server 4. Servers 3 and 5 could also accept write operations destined for Server 4. When Server 4 is back online, Servers 3 and 5 can update Server 4 with the writes that occurred while it was down (see Figure 4.8).

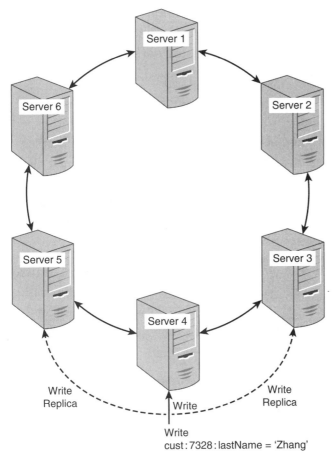

**Figure 4.8** *One way to replicate data is to write copies of data to adjacent nodes in the cluster ring.*

## Replication

Replication is the process of saving multiple copies of data in your cluster. This provides for high availability as described previously.

One parameter you will want to consider is the number of replicas to maintain. The more replicas you have, the less likely you will lose data; however, you might have lower performance with a large number of replicas. If your data is easily regenerated and reloaded into your key-value database, you might want to use a small number of replicas. If you have little tolerance for losing data, a higher replica number is recommended.

Some NoSQL databases enable you to specify how many replicas must be written before a write operation is considered complete from the perspective of the application sending the write request. For example, you may configure your database to store three replicas. You may also specify that as soon as two of the replicas are successfully written, a successful write return value can be sent to the application making the write request. The third replica will still be written, but it will be done while the application continues to do other work.

You should take replicas into consideration with reads as well. Because key-value databases do not typically enforce two-phase commits, it is possible that replicas have different versions of data. All the versions will eventually be consistent, but sometimes they may be out of sync for short periods.

To minimize the risk of reading old, out-of-date data, you can specify the number of nodes that must respond with the same answer to a read request before a response is returned to the calling application. If you are keeping three replicas of data, you may want to have at least two responses from replicas before issuing a response to the calling program.

The higher the number required, the more likely you are to send the latest response. This can add to the latency of the read because you might have to wait longer for the third server to respond.

Up to this point, most of the terms described have dealt with logical modeling and the organization of servers and related processes. Now it is time to address algorithms implemented in and processes that run within the key-value database software to implement higher-level functions.

# Key-Value Implementation Terms

The terms discussed in this last set of key-value vocabulary deal with topics you generally do not work with directly. These terms cover operations that happen behind the scenes of application programs but are nonetheless crucial to the functioning of a key-value database.

## Hash Function

*Hash functions* are algorithms that map from an input—for example, a string of characters—to an output string. The size of the input can vary, but the size of the output is always the same. For example, a simple string like 'Hello world' maps to

```
2aae6c35c94fcfb415dbe95f408b9ce91ee846ed
```

While longer text, such as the following:

> "There is a theory which states that if ever anyone discovers exactly what the Universe is for and why it is here, it will instantly disappear and be replaced by something even more bizarre and inexplicable. There is another theory which states that this has already happened."
>
> DOUGLAS ADAMS
> THE RESTAURANT AT THE END OF THE UNIVERSE, 1980

yields an equal-sized output string:

```
3f4d004fcb7c40b02deb393d34db9bd02b067f56
```

Clearly, the two output strings are quite different. This would be expected when the inputs are so different. One of the important characteristics of hash algorithms is that even small changes in the input can lead to large changes in the output. For example, if you hash 'Hello World' instead of 'Hello world', the output string is

```
0a4d55a8d778e5022fab701977c5d840bbc486d0
```

Hash functions are generally designed to distribute inputs evenly over the set of all possible outputs. The output space can be quite large. For example, the SHA-1 has $2^{160}$ possible output values. This is especially useful when hashing keys. No matter how similar your keys are, they are evenly distributed across the range of possible output values. The ranges of output values can be assigned to partitions and you can be reasonably assured that each partition will receive approximately the same amount of data.

For example, assume you have a cluster of 16 nodes and each node is responsible for one partition. You can use the first digit output by the SHA-1 function to determine which partition should receive the data.

> ❖ **Note** As you might recall, the SHA-1 function outputs a hexadecimal, or base-16, number. The hexadecimal digits are 0–9 and a–f for a total of 16 digits.

The key `'cust:8983:firstName'` has a hash value of

`4b2cf78c7ed41fe19625d5f4e5e3eab20b064c24`

and would be assigned to partition 4, while the key `'cust:8983:last-Name'` has a hash value of

`c0017bec2624f736b774efdc61c97f79446fc74f`

and would be assigned to node 12 (c is the hexadecimal digit for the base-10 number 12).

Although there are many possible outputs for hash functions, it is possible for two distinct input strings to map to the same output string.

## Collision

A *collision* occurs when two distinct inputs to a hash function produce the same output. When it is difficult to find two inputs that map to the same hash function output, the hash function is known as collision resistant. If a hash table is not collision resistant or if you encounter one of those rare cases in which two inputs map to the same output, you will need a collision resolution strategy.

Basically, a collision resolution strategy is a way to deal with the fact that you have two inputs that map to the same output. If the hash table only has room for one value, then one of the hashed values will be lost.

A simple method to deal with this is to implement a list in each cell of a hash table. Most entries will include a single value, but if there are collisions, the hash table cell will maintain a list of keys and values, as shown in Figure 4.9. This is a logical representation of a generic solution to the collision problem; actual implementations may vary.

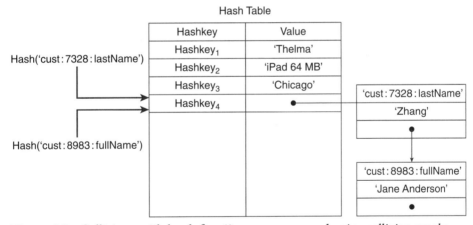

**Figure 4.9** *Collisions with hash functions are managed using collision resolution strategies, such as maintaining linked lists of values.*

## Compression

Key-value databases are memory intensive. Large numbers of large values can quickly consume substantial amounts of memory. Operating systems can address this problem with virtual memory management, but that entails writing data to disk or flash storage.

Reading from and writing to disk is significantly slower than reading from random access memory, so avoid it when possible. One option is to add more memory to your servers. There are both technical and cost limitations on this option. In the case of disk-based, key-value stores, such as the LevelDB library (code.google.com/p/leveldb/), there is still a motivation to optimize storage because the time required to read and write data is a function of the size of the data.

One way to optimize memory and persistent storage is to use compression techniques. A compression algorithm for key-value stores should perform compression and decompression operations as fast as possible. This often entails a trade-off between the speed of compression/decompression and the size of the compressed data.

Faster compression algorithms can lead to larger compressed data than other, slower algorithms (see Figure 4.10). For example, the Snappy compression algorithm compresses 250MB per second and decompresses 500MB per second on a Core i7, 64-bit mode processor but produces compressed data that is 20% to 100% larger than the same data compressed by other algorithms.[4]

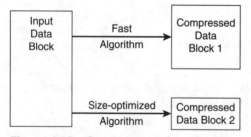

**Figure 4.10**   *Compression algorithms may be designed to optimize for speed or data size.*

---

4. https://code.google.com/p/snappy/

## Summary

Key-value databases come with their own terminology used to describe data models, architecture, and implementation components. Keys, values, partitions, and partition keys are important concepts related to data models. You will see some of the terms again when you learn about other types of NoSQL databases.

It is also important to understand the architecture employed with key-value databases. Clusters, rings, and replication are key topics with regard to architecture.

Database application developers do not need to work with implementation issues on a regular basis, but it helps to understand them, particularly when tuning parameters. Key concepts related to implementation include hash functions, collision, and compression.

Now that you understand key-value database terminology and were introduced to key-value databases in Chapter 3, it is time to examine more advanced applications of key-value databases and review established design patterns that can help you develop robust, scalable, key-value database applications.

## Review Questions

1. What are data models? How do they differ from data structures?
2. What is a partition?
3. Define two types of clusters. Which type is typically used with key-value data stores?
4. What are the advantages of having a large number of replicas? What are the disadvantages?
5. Why would you want to receive a response from more than one replica when reading a value from a key-value data store?

6.  Under what circumstances would you want to have a large number of replicas?

7.  Why are hash functions used with key-value databases?

8.  What is a collision?

9.  Describe one way to handle a collision so that no data is lost.

10. Discuss the relation between speed of compression and the size of compressed data.

# References

Adams, Douglas. *The Restaurant at the End of the Universe.* Reprint Edition, Del Rey. 1995.

Basho Technologies, Inc. Riak Documentation: http://docs.basho.com/riak/latest/

Google, Snappy Documentation: https://code.google.com/p/snappy/

Key-Value Store 2.0 Documentation: https://foundationdb.com/key-value-store/documentation/index.html

Redis Documentation: http://redis.io/documentation

Redman, Eric. "A Little Riak Book." http://littleriakbook.com/

Seeger, Marc. "Key-Value Stores: A Practical Overview": http://blog.marc-seeger.de/assets/papers/Ultra_Large_Sites_SS09-Seeger_Key_Value_Stores.pdf

# 5

# Designing for Key-Value Databases

*"Design is not just what it looks like and feels like.*
*Design is how it works."*
—STEVE JOBS
FORMER CEO, APPLE COMPUTER, INC.

## Topics Covered In This Chapter

Key Design and Partitioning

Designing Structured Values

Limitations of Key-Value Databases

Design Patterns for Key-Value Databases

Case Study: Key-Value Databases for Mobile Application Configuration

Through the first four chapters of this book, you have learned the basics of NoSQL databases and details of key-value databases in particular. It is now time to put those details to work. When you design an application that uses a key-value database, you should consider several factors, including

- How to structure keys

- What types of information you want to capture in values

- How to compensate for limitations of key-value databases

- How to introduce abstractions that help create higher-level organizational structures than simple key-value pairs

Well-designed keys can make your application code easier to read and streamline the maintenance of your application and your key-value database. Capturing the right data in your key-value pairs is important both for meeting functional requirements and for ensuring adequate performance of your application. As useful as key-value databases are, there are some significant limitations, such as poor support for retrieving a range of values. There are ways to work around these limitations, and this chapter describes design patterns you might want to use in your applications and key-value database designs.

---

### Design Pattern Definition

**The Wikipedia definition of a design pattern is "A general reusable solution to a commonly occurring problem within a given context in software design. A design pattern is not a finished design that can be transformed directly into source or machine code. It is a description or template for how to solve a problem that can be used in many different situations."[1]**

---

# Key Design and Partitioning

How you design your keys can impact the ease of working with your key-value database. At one end of the design spectrum, you could come up with random keys for every value you want to store. Obviously, a key like `'laklsjfdjjd'` is virtually useless unless you have an uncanny memory for strings or have a data structure that can map nonsense keys to something meaningful. Keys should have some logical structure to make code readable and extensible, but they should also be designed with storage efficiency in mind.

---

1. http://en.wikipedia.org/wiki/Software_design_pattern

## Keys Should Follow a Naming Convention

The naming convention you choose is less important than choosing one. A well-designed naming convention enables developers to easily devise keys for new entities, instances, and attributes.

Here are some general guidelines. These are not hard-and-fast rules; they are tips that can work well for you in various situations.

- Use meaningful and unambiguous naming components, such as `'cust'` for customer or `'inv'` for inventory.

- Use range-based components when you would like to retrieve ranges of values. Ranges include dates or integer counters.

- Use a common delimiter when appending components to make a key. The ':' is a commonly used delimiter, but any character that will not otherwise appear in the key will work.

- Keep keys as short as possible without sacrificing the other characteristics mentioned in this list.

❖ **Tip** Anticipating all possible entities' types can be difficult, so coming up with unambiguous name components isn't always possible. Try to use at least three or four letters to distinguish an entity type or attribute. `'Cst'` or `'cust'` are better than `'c'` for a customer abbreviation.

## Well-Designed Keys Save Code

A well-designed key pattern helps minimize the amount of code a developer needs to write to create functions that access and set values. For example, consider a key pattern that consists of an entity or object type (for example, `'customer'`), a unique identifier for that entity or object type (for example, `'198277'`), an attribute name (for example, 'fname'), and common delimiter (for example, ':'). A single function with two parameters can get any value:

```
define getCustAttr(p_id, p_attrName)
    v_key = 'cust' + ':' + p_id + ':' + p_attrName;
    return(AppNameSpace[v_key]);
```

In this pseudocode example, the function getCustAttr has parameters for the customer identifier and the name of the attribute that should have its value returned. The local variable, v_key, is a string created by concatenating the parts of the key. Because the key follows a standard naming convention, every attribute about a customer can be retrieved using this function. The last line of the pseudocode function returns the value associated with key specified by the string in variable v_key. AppNameSpace is the name of the namespace holding keys and values for this application.

❖ **Note** In practice, you should have a naming convention for namespaces, too. For example, a customer management namespace might be 'CstMgtNS'.

The associated set function is similar but uses three parameters. The third parameter is used to pass in the value to be saved:

```
define setCustAttr(p_id, p_attrName, p_value)
    v_key = 'cust' + ':' + p_id + ':' + p_attrName
    AppNameSpace[v_key] = p_value
```

❖ **Note** In production applications, you should include appropriate error checking and handling. Set functions should check the status of write operations to ensure the minimum number of replicas has been written. If the database could not save the minimum number of replicas, you might want to attempt the write operation again some number of times before returning an error.

Using generalized set and get functions helps improve the readability of code and reduces the repeated use of low-level operations, such as concatenating strings and looking up values.

## Dealing with Ranges of Values

Consider using values that indicate ranges when you want to retrieve groups of values. For example, you might want to include a six-digit date in a key if you want to retrieve all customers who made a purchase on a particular date. In this case, `'cust061514'` could be used as a prefix instead of `'cust'` to indicate customers who bought products on June 15, 2014. The customer ID would be stored as a value associated with each key.

For example, the following are keys associated with the first 10 customers who purchased products on June 15, 2014:

- cust061514:1:custId
- cust061514:2:custId
- cust061514:3:custId
- cust061514:4:custId
- ...
- cust061514:10:custId

This type of key is useful for querying ranges of keys because you can easily write a function to retrieve a range of values. For example, the following getCustPurchaseByDate function retrieves a list of customerIDs who made purchases on a particular date:

```
define getCustPurchByDate(p_date)
    v_custList = makeEmptyList();
    v_rangeCnt = 1;
```

```
v_key = 'cust:' + p_date + ':' + v_rangeCnt +
  ':custId';
while exists(v_key)
    v_custList.append(myAppNS[v_key]);
    v_rangeCnt = v_rangeCnt + 1;
    v_key = 'cust:' + p_date + ':' + v_rangeCnt +
      ':custId';

return(v_custList);
```

The function takes one parameter, the date of purchases, although this code could easily generalize to accept a range of dates. The function starts by initializing two local variables: v _ custList is set to an empty list, which will hold customer IDs, and v _ rangeCnt, which will hold the counters associated with the range of customers that made purchases on the date specified in the parameter p _ date.

Because there is no way to know the number of customers that made purchases, the code uses a while loop and checks a terminating condition. In this case, the while loop terminates when it checks for a key and finds it does not exist. If there were only 10 purchases on June 15, 2014, then when the loop checks the key 'cust:061514:11:custId', it does not find a corresponding key-value pair in the database and the while loop terminates.

In the while loop, the key stored in the local variable v _ key is used to look up the value in the myAppNS namespace. The key returns the customer ID, and the code appends the value to the local variable v _ custList. When the while loop terminates, the list of customer IDs in v _ custList is returned.

You might have realized that although using this type of function will standardize your code, it is no more efficient than retrieving each key-value pair individually. In some data stores, values can be ordered on disk in a specific sort order, making it more efficient to read a range of values because they are stored in contiguous blocks. If your key-value database offers ordered key values or allows for secondary indexes, you might find those are more efficient options for retrieving ranges of values than using a function like the one above.

## Keys Must Take into Account Implementation Limitations

Different key-value databases have different limitations. Consider those limitations when choosing your key-value database.

Some key-value databases restrict the size of keys. For example, FoundationDB limits the size of keys to 10,000 bytes.[2]

Others restrict the data types that can be used as keys. Riak treats keys as binary values or strings.[3] The Redis data store takes a liberal approach to keys and allows for more complex structures than string. Valid data types for Redis keys include[4]

- Binary safe strings

- Lists

- Sets

- Sorted sets

- Hashes

- Bit arrays

- HyperLogLogs (a probabilistic data structure for estimating number of entities in a set)

The variety of data types supported by Redis allows you more flexibility when creating keys. Instead of concatenating entity types, identifiers, and attributes as a string such as `'cust:19873:fname'`, you could

---

2. https://foundationdb.com/key-value-store/documentation/known-limitations.html

3. http://docs.basho.com/riak/1.3.0/references/appendices/concepts/Keys-and-Objects/

4. http://redis.io/topics/data-types-intro

use a list, such as ('cust', '19873', 'fname'). Redis keys can be up to 512MB in length.[5] It sounds unlikely that you would create a 512MB string by concatenating components, but large binary objects, such as images, are valid key types and can reach substantial sizes.

> ❖ **Tip**  Before using large keys in production, be sure to test the performance of key-value databases with large keys so you understand the level of performance you can expect.

## How Keys Are Used in Partitioning

*Partitioning* is the process of grouping sets of key-value pairs and assigning those groups to different nodes in a cluster. *Hashing* is a common method of partitioning that evenly distributes keys and values across all nodes. Another method that is sometimes used is called range partitioning.

*Range partitioning* works by grouping contiguous values and sending them to the same node in a cluster (see Figure 5.1). This assumes a sort order is defined over the key. For example, you could partition by customer number, date, or part identifier. Range partitioning requires some kind of table to map from keys to partitions, as shown in Table 5.1.

**Table 5.1**  *Sample Range Partition Table*

| Range of Values | Assigned Node |
| --- | --- |
| cust:00001-cust:00999 | Server 1 |
| cust:01000-cust:01999 | Server 2 |
| cust:02000-cust:02999 | Server 3 |
| cust:04000-cust:04999 | Server 4 |

-----

5. http://redis.io/topics/data-types

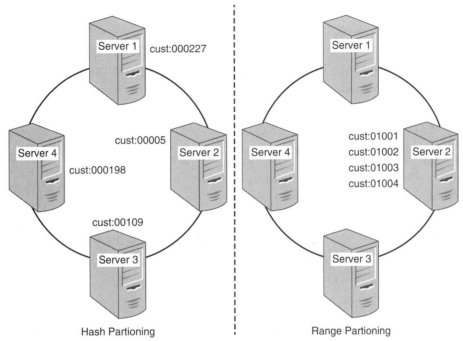

**Figure 5.1**    *Different hashing schemes will lead to different key-to-node assignments.*

If you decide to use range partitioning, carefully consider how your data volumes may grow. If you need to restructure your partitioning scheme, some keys may be reassigned to different nodes and data will have to migrate between nodes.

# Designing Structured Values

The term *values* can cover a wide range of data objects, from simple counts to hierarchical data structures with embedded complex structures. All can be assigned as values in a key-value database. But ask yourself, do you really want structured data types in your database? As usual in database design, the answer is "it depends."

Consider two possible cases. In the first, you have two attributes that are frequently used together. In the second, you have a set of attributes that are logically related, and some but not all of the attributes are frequently used together. As you shall see, each is best managed with a different approach.

## Structured Data Types Help Reduce Latency

You should consider the workload on your server as well as on developers when designing applications that use key-value data stores. Consider an application development project in which the customer address is needed about 80% of the time when the customer name is needed. This can occur when you frequently need to display the customer's name and mailing address, although occasionally you only need the name, for example, as part of a form header.

It makes sense to have a function that retrieves both the name and the address in one function call. Here is a sample get function for name and address:

```
define getCustNameAddr(p_id)
    v_fname = getCustAttr(p_id,'fname');
    v_lname = getCustAttr(p_id,'lname');
    v_addr  = getCustAttr(p_id,'addr');
    v_city = getCustAttr(p_id,'city');
    v_state = getCustAttr(p_id,'state');
    v_zip = getCustAttr(p_id,'zip');
    v_fullName = v_fname + ' ' + v_lname;
    v_fullAddr = v_city + ' ' + v_state + ' ' + v_zip;
    return(makeList(v_fullName, v_fullAddr);
```

This function retrieves six values, creates two local variable strings, creates a list to hold both the name and address, and returns that list. If customer name and address are frequently retrieved, it makes sense to use a function such as getCustNameAddr rather than duplicate the multiple getCustAttr calls each time the customer name and address are needed.

Assuming the developer needs to call `getCustNameAddr` frequently, it would help to optimize this code as much as possible. The `getCustAttr` function is called multiple times so it is a good candidate for optimizing. The code for that function is simple and does not lend itself to significant optimization.

The other operations in the `getCustNameAddr`, concatenating strings and making a list, are primitive operations that take little time. The best option for optimizing `getCustNameAddr` is to reduce the number of times the developer has to call `getCustAddr`.

Each time `getCustAddr` is called, it builds a key by concatenating strings. This primitive operation does not take much time. Fetching a value from the key-value database can take a long time, at least compared with primitive operations. The reason is that retrieving a value can require reading from a disk. This means that the read operation must wait for the read/write heads to get into position.

The latency, or time you have to wait for the disk read to complete, is significantly longer than the time needed to perform other operations in the function (see Figure 5.2).

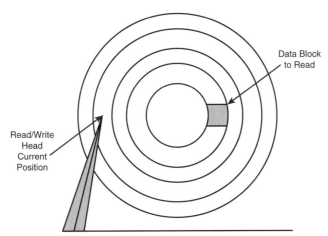

**Figure 5.2** *Reading a value from disk requires the read/write heads to move to the proper track and the platter to rotate to the proper block. This can lead to long latencies.*

One way to improve the speed of fetching values from the key-value database is to store frequently used values in memory. This works well in many cases but is limited by the amount of room in memory allocated to caching keys and values.

Another approach is to store commonly used attribute values together. In the case of a customer management database, you could store a list with both the customer's name and address together, for example:

```
cstMgtNS[cust: 198277:nameAddr] = '{ 'Jane Anderson' ,
  '39 NE River St. Portland, OR 97222'}
```

This is a more complex value structure than using several different keys but has significant advantages in some cases. By storing a customer name and address together, you might reduce the number of disk seeks that must be performed to read all the needed data (see Figure 5.3).

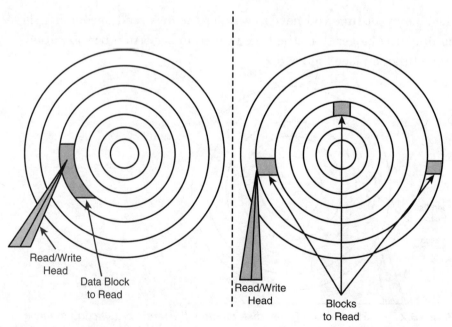

**Figure 5.3** *Reading a single block of data is faster than reading multiple blocks referenced by multiple keys.*

Key-value databases usually store the entire list together in a data block so there is no need to hash multiple keys and retrieve multiple data blocks. An exception to this rule occurs if the data value is larger than the disk data block size. This can occur if you store a large image or other sizeable object as a value.

If there are many times you need a customer name but not the address, you might want to store the name separately. This would duplicate the customer name in your key-value database, but that should not be considered a problem.

❖ **Note** Generally, you should avoid duplicating data in relational database design, although it is a common practice in NoSQL databases.

Duplicating data is also a common way to improve the performance of relational database queries. Known as denormalization, duplicating data can reduce the number of joins required to perform a query and substantially improve application performance.

The same pattern holds in NoSQL databases. You can use the name-only key to look up just the name when that is the only attribute needed, and you can use the name and address key when you need both.

There are advantages to storing structures as values, but there are also limits to those advantages. As you will see in the next section, storing too much data in a value can have adverse effects on application performance.

## Large Values Can Lead to Inefficient Read and Write Operations

Ancient Greek philosophers advocated *sophrosyne*, a state of mind that led to self-control and moderation. It is a practice that will serve you well when designing data structures for key-value databases.

Using structured data types, such as lists and sets, can improve the overall efficiency of some applications by minimizing the time required to retrieve data. It is important to also consider how increasing the size of a value can adversely impact read and write operations. Consider a data structure that maintains customer order information in a single value, such as the following:

```
{
    'custFname': 'Liona',
    'custLname':  'Williams',
    'custAddr' :  '987 Highland Rd',
    'custCity' :  'Springfield',
    'custState': 'NJ',
    'custZip'  :   21111,
    'ordItems' [
        {
            'itemID' : '85838A',
            'itemQty' : 2 ,
            'descr' : 'Intel Core i7-4790K Processor
             (8M Cache,
    4.40 GHz)',
        'price:' : $325.00
        } ,
        {
        'itemID' : '38371R',
        'itemQty' : 1 ,
      'descr' : 'Intel BOXDP67BGB3 Socket 1155, Intel
        P67',
          CrossFireX & SLI SATA3&USB3.0, A&GbE, ATX
          Motherboard',
      'price' : $140.00
        } ,
        {
      'itemID' : '10484K',
      'itemQty' : 1,
      'descr' : 'EVGA GeForce GT 740 Superclocked Single
        Slot 4GB
         DDR3 Graphics Card'
          'price': '$201.00'
        } ,
```

```
{
 'itemID' : '67594M',
'itemQty' : 1,
'descr': 'Rosewill Black Gaming ATX Mid Tower
  Computer Case',
'price' : $47.98
} ,
{
 'itemID' : '46328A',
'itemQty' : 2,
'descr': 'WD Blue 1 TB Desktop Hard Drive: 3.5
  Inch, 7200 RPM,
  SATA 6 Gb/s, 64 MB Cache - WD10EZEX',
   'price' : $63.50
   }
   ]
}
```

This data structure includes customer information as well as order information. The customer information is stored as a set of string values and corresponding attribute names. The order items are stored in an array in which each element is a list structure with item identifier, quantity, product description, and price. This entire list can be stored under an order key, such as `'ordID:781379'`.

The advantage of using a structure such as this is that much of the information about orders is available with a single key lookup. Let's consider how this data structure might be built.

When the customer adds her first item to her cart, the list is created and the customer name and address are copied from the customer database. An order array is created and a list with the item identifier, quantity, description, and price is added to the array. The key value is hashed and the entire data structure is written to disk. The customer then adds another item to the cart, and a new entry is added to the array of ordered items. Because the value is treated as an atomic unit, the entire list (for example, customer information and ordered items) is written to the disk again. This process continues for each of the additional items.

Assume the key-value database allocates enough storage for an average order size when the value is first created. Adding the fifth order item causes the size of the data structure to exceed the allocated space. When an additional item is added to the ordItems array, the new item will be written to a new block.

As values grow in size, the time required to read and write the data can increase. Data is generally read in blocks. If the size of a value exceeds the size of a block, then multiple blocks must be read. During write operations, an entire value has to be written, even if only a small part of the value has changed.

You might think that because a read operation must read an entire block, as long as the size of the value is less than the size of a data block on disk, there is no additional penalty. It is true the time to position the read/write heads and read the data block is the same. However, there is an indirect penalty. When values are smaller than the disk data block size, multiple values can be stored in a single block. When a block is read, all the values in the block can be added to the in-memory cache. This increases the likelihood that a future read will find the value it needs in the cache. This saves the time required to perform a disk read.

Of course, if an entire large-sized value is in the cache, then any of the embedded attributes are available for low-latency reads from the cache. This could help performance if there are multiple reads to multiple parts of the value data structure. If, however, you load a large value into the cache and only reference a small percentage of the data, you are essentially wasting valuable memory (see Figure 5.4).

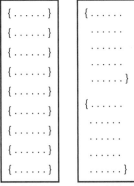

Small Values　　Large Values

**Figure 5.4**　*Data is read in blocks. Blocks may store a large number of small-sized values or few large-sized values. The former can lead to better performance if frequently used attributes are available in the cache.*

If you find yourself needing to frequently design large value structures, you might want to consider using a document database rather than a key-value database. Document databases are discussed in depth in Chapters 6 through 8.

# Limitations of Key-Value Databases

Key-value databases are the simplest of the NoSQL databases. This makes them easy to learn and use, but it also brings with them important limitations. You have just read about the disadvantages of using large data values. There are some others to keep in mind as well. In particular, it is important to remember the following:

- The only way to look up values is by key.

- Some key-value databases do not support range queries.

- There is no standard query language comparable to SQL for relational databases.

These are limitations with key-value databases in general. As you will no doubt learn as you work with different key-value database implementations, vendors and open source project developers take it upon themselves to devise ways to mitigate the disadvantages of these limitations.

## Look Up Values by Key Only

Imagine what it would be like if you had to look up every piece of information about someone using only an identifier, like a Social Security number or a student ID number. You might have no trouble remembering the identifier for a handful of friends and family, but after that, tracking down information will start to get difficult.

The same thing can occur with key-value databases. At times, you will want to look up information about an object without already knowing the key value. In the most basic versions of key-value databases, this is not possible. Fortunately, key-value database developers have added extended features to address this limitation.

One approach is to use text search capabilities. Riak, for example, provides a search mechanism and API that indexes data values as they are added to the database. The API supports common search features, such as wildcard searches, proximity searches, range searches, and Boolean operators. Search functions return a set of keys that have associated values that satisfy the search criteria. If you wanted to list all orders that included the purchase of a computer case and motherboard but not a CPU, you might use a statement such as the following:

```
field: { 'motherboard' AND 'computer case') AND NOT 'CPU'
```

This type of search is useful, for example, when you want to find all customers from Illinois who placed orders in the past two weeks.

❖ **Note** More on Riak search is available at http://docs.basho.com/ riak/latest/dev/using/search/.

Another way to get around key-only lookup is to use secondary indexes. If your key-value database supports secondary indexes directly, you will be able to specify an attribute in a value to index. For example, you could create an index on state or city in an address value to enable lookup by state or city name.

## Key-Value Databases Do Not Support Range Queries

Range queries, such as selecting records with dates between a start and end date or names in some range of the alphabet, are fairly common in database applications. The basic key-value database does not support these types of queries unless you use a specialized naming convention and lookup table described earlier in the section, "Dealing with Ranges of Values." A specialized type of key-value database, known as an ordered key-value database, keeps a sorted structure that allows for range queries.

If you use a key-value database that supports secondary indexes, you may have the ability to perform range queries on the indexed values. Some text search engines also support range searches over text.

## No Standard Query Language Comparable to SQL for Relational Databases

Key-value databases are designed for simple lookup operations. It should be no surprise that there is not a standard query language for key-value databases.

You will find, however, that some key-value databases understand commonly used structures, such as XML and JavaScript Object Notation (JSON). Many programming languages have libraries that support constructing and parsing XML and JSON. Search applications, such as Solr (http://lucene.apache.org/solr/) and Lucene (http://lucene.apache.org/), have mechanisms for parsing XML and JSON as well. This combination of structured formats and programming libraries is not equivalent to a standard query language, but they do start to provide some of the capabilities you would expect in such a query language.

There are limitations to the basic key-value data model, but today there are multiple implementations that offer enhanced features that enable developers to more easily implement frequently needed application features.

## Design Patterns for Key-Value Databases

Design patterns, or general software solutions, were popularized by Erich Gamma, Richard Helm, Ralph Jackson, and John Vlissides in their book *Design Patterns: Elements of Reusable Object-Oriented Software*. This book is popularly known as the Gang of Four, or the GoF, book.

The idea that you can reuse solutions in different applications is well understood and known to all but the most novice programmers. The value of the Gang of Four book is that it cataloged and described a number of useful software patterns that could be applied in a variety of languages. Design patterns appear in database applications as well.

It is now time to consider several design patterns that may prove useful when using key-value databases to develop your applications. These include

- Time to Live (TTL) keys

- Emulating tables

- Aggregates

- Atomic aggregates

- Enumerable keys

- Indexes

Design patterns can be useful as described or can require some modification to fit your needs. Think of design patterns as guides to solving common problems, not dogmatic solutions handed down by a cadre of design elders that must be followed precisely.

Just as importantly, pay attention to the solutions you repeatedly use when developing applications. You might find some of your most frequently used design patterns are ones you discover yourself.

## Time to Live (TTL) Keys

*Time to Live* is a term frequently used in computer science to describe a transient object. For example, a packet of data sent from one computer to another can have a Time to Live parameter that indicates the number of times it should be forwarded to another router or server while en route to its destination. If the packet is routed through more devices than specified by the TTL parameter, it is dropped and the packet is undelivered.

TTL is sometimes useful with keys in a key-value database, especially when caching data in limited memory servers or when keys are used to hold a resource for some specified period of time. A large e-commerce company selling tickets to sporting and music events might have thousands of users active at any time. When a customer indicates he wants to purchase tickets for several seats, the ticketing application may add key-value pairs to the database to hold those seats while the customer's payment is processed. The e-commerce company does not want one customer buying seats that another customer has already added to his or her cart. At the same time, the company does not want seats held for long periods of time, especially if customers abandon their carts. A TTL parameter associated with a key can help here (see Figure 5.5).

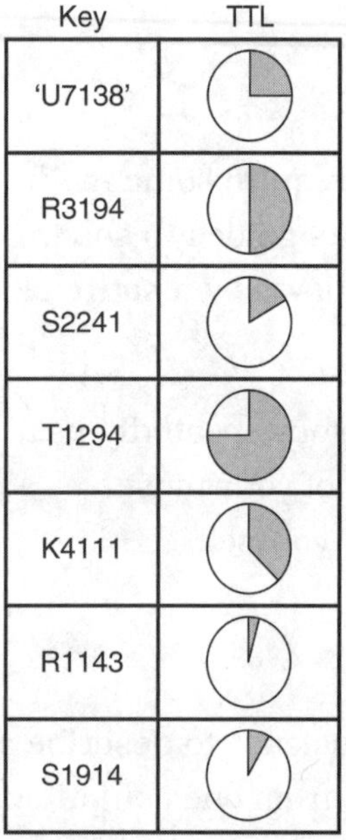

| Key | TTL |
|-----|-----|
| 'U7138' | |
| R3194 | |
| S2241 | |
| T1294 | |
| K4111 | |
| R1143 | |
| S1914 | |

**Figure 5.5**    *Time to Live keys are useful for allowing users to reserve a product or resource for a limited time while other operations, such as making a payment, complete.*

The application may create a key that references the seat being saved and the value could be the identifier of the customer purchasing the seat. Setting a five-minute Time to Live parameter would provide enough time for someone to enter his or her payment information without unduly delaying access to the ticket if the payment authorization fails or the customer abandons the cart. This also saves the application developer from needing to develop a custom method that might include keeping a time stamp with a key and checking multiple keys at regular intervals to determine whether any have expired.

❖ **Tip** Time to Live properties are database-specific, so check the documentation of your key-value database to see whether they are supported and how to specify an expiration.

## Emulating Tables

Although most key-value databases do not explicitly support a data structure like the relational table, it can be a useful construct.

> ❖ **Note** The Oracle NoSQL database is unlike most key-value databases and provides an API for manipulating data using a table metaphor.[6]

A method of emulating tables has been partially described in earlier chapters using a key-naming convention based on entity name, unique identifier, and attribute name. See the "Key Design and Partitioning" section found earlier in this chapter.

It is not practical to fully emulate the features of relational tables. For example, this design pattern does not include a SQL-like query capability. Instead, it focuses on implementing basic get and set operations.

The two functions defined earlier, getCustAttr and setCustAttr, are sample building blocks for building row-level-like functions, such as addCustRecord and getCustRecord. Assume a customer record consists of a name and address. The following is a pseudocode function of the addCustRecord:

```
define addCustRecord (p_id, p_fname, p_lname, p_addr,
  p_city, p_state, p_zip)
    begin
        setCustAttr(p_id,'fname', p_fname);
        setCustAttr(p_id,'lname',p_lname);
        setCustAttr(p_id,'addr',p_addr);
        setCustAttr(p_id,'city',p_city);
        setCustAttr(p_id,'state',p_state);
        setCustAttr(p_id,'zip', p_zip);
    end;
```

6. See Chapter 4 of "Getting Started with Oracle NoSQL Database Tables." http://docs.oracle.com/cd/NOSQL/html/GettingStartedGuideTables/tablesapi.html

The following is the corresponding get record function:

```
define getCustRecord (p_id)
    begin
        v_custRec = make_list (
            getCustAttr(p_id,'fname', p_fname),
            getCustAttr(p_id,'lname',p_lname),
            getCustAttr(p_id,'addr',p_addr),
            getCustAttr(p_id,'city',p_city),
            getCustAttr(p_id,'state',p_state),
            getCustAttr(p_id,'zip', p_zip)
        );
        return(v_custRec);
    end;
```

Emulating tables is helpful when you routinely get or set a related set of attributes. This pattern is useful when you are dealing with a small number of emulated tables.

If you find yourself emulating many tables or implementing complicated filtering conditions and range searches, you should consider alternative approaches. These can include using key-value databases that support

- Table constructs, such as Oracle's NoSQL database

- Advanced search features, such as Riak

- Relational databases, such as MySQL

## Aggregates

Aggregation is a pattern that supports different attributes for different subtypes of an entity. In a relational database, you can handle subtypes in a couple of different ways. You could create a single table with all attributes across all subtypes.

You could also create a table with the attributes common to all subtypes and then create an additional table for each of the subtypes.

Consider the concert ticket sales system. Many concerts are held in large stadiums with assigned seats, some are held in smaller venues with no assigned seating, and still others are multiday festivals with multiple stages and open seating. Table 5.2 shows a list of attributes that must be tracked for the various kinds of concerts.

**Table 5.2**  *Sample Attributes for Multiple Types of Concerts*

| Attribute | Concert Subtype |
|---|---|
| Concert date | Stadium and small venue |
| Festival start date | Festival |
| Festival end date | Festival |
| Location description | All |
| Assigned seat | Stadium |
| Start time | Stadium and small venue |
| Price | All |
| Performer name | Stadium and small venue |
| Festival name | Festival |

Two attributes are used by all concert types, three are used by stadium and small venue concerts, three are used by festivals only, and one is used by stadiums only.

In a relational database, you could create a single table with all the attributes listed in Table 5.2, or you could create a table with common attributes and subtype tables, as shown in Figure 5.6. The single table would have unused columns and could become unwieldy as the number of subtypes and attributes grows. Using a table with common attributes and subtype tables requires join operations to get all data about a concert ticket. Aggregation in key-value databases takes a different approach.

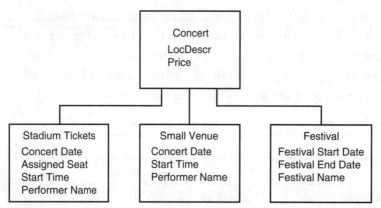

**Figure 5.6**    *Entity subtypes can be modeled in relational databases as a common table with tables to store attributes of each subtype.*

A single entity type, that is, 'concert', can be used for all types and the values can be lists of attribute value pairs specific to each type. In addition, a type indicator is used in the list to distinguish the concert type. For example, a value of a stadium ticket could be

```
{'type':'stadium', 'conDate':15-Mar-2015, 'locDescr':
   'Springfield Civic Center', 'assgnSeat': 'J38',
   'startTime':'17:30', 'price':'$50.00', 'perfName':
   'The National' }
```

The following is a sample small venue concert ticket:

```
{'type':'small venue', 'conDate': 12-Jun-2015,
   'locDescr': 'Plymoth Concert Hall', 'startTime':'17:30',
   'price':'$75.00', 'perfName':'Joshua Redman' }
```

Finally, a sample festival ticket is

```
{'type':'festival', 'festStartDate': 01-Feb-2015,
   'festEndDate': 01-Feb-2015, 'locDescr': 'Portland, OR',
   price:'$100.00', 'festName':'PDX Jazz Festival'}
```

Each of these lists can be assigned to a ticket key stored in a namespace called ConcertApp, such as

```
ConcertApp[ticket:18380] = {'type':'stadium',
    'conDate':15-Mar-2015, 'locDescr': 'Springfield
    Civic Center', 'assgnSeat': 'J38', 'startTime':'17:30',
    'price':'$50.00', 'perfName': 'The National' }
ConcertApp[ticket:18381] = {'type':'small venue',
    'conDate': 12-Jun-2015, 'locDescr': 'Plymoth Concert
    Hall', 'startTime':'17:30', 'price':'$75.00',
    'perfName':'Joshua Redman' }
ConcertApp[ticket:18382] = {'type':'festival',
    'festStartDate': 01-Feb-2015, 'festEndDate':
    01-Feb-2015, 'locDescr': 'Portland, OR',
    'price':'$100.00', 'festName':'PDX Jazz Festival'}
```

You can write set and get functions to check the type of ticket and then assign or retrieve the appropriate attribute values.

## Atomic Aggregates

Atomic aggregates contain all values that must be updated together or not at all. Recall that relational databases support the ACID properties, and the *A* in ACID stands for atomicity. Relational databases and some key-value databases provide transactions to ensure multiple statements are all completed successfully or not at all.

> ❖ **Tip** If you are using a key-value database that does not support transactions, you might want to use the atomic aggregate pattern in place of transactions.

The atomic aggregate pattern uses a single assignment statement to save multiple values. For example, if the concert ticket application logged a record each time a stadium ticket is purchased, it should record the date, location, and seat assignment. For example:

```
ConcertApp[ticketLog:9888] = {'conDate':15-Mar-2015,
    'locDescr':
'Springfield Civic Center', 'assgnSeat': 'J38'}
```

This will save all three values or none at all. If you tried to log each attribute separately, you would run the risk of completing some but not all of the operations.

Consider, if you used the following three statements instead of the one atomic aggregate statement above:

```
ConcertApp[ticketLog:9888:conDate]    = 15-Mar-2015
ConcertApp[ticketLog:9888:locDescr]   = 'Springfield Civic
  Center'
ConcertApp[ticketLog:9888:assgnSeat]  = 'J38'
```

If the server writing this data to disk failed after writing the `locDescr` attribute but before writing the `assgnSeat` attribute, then you would lose a critical piece of data. The atomic aggregate pattern is not a full substitute for transaction support, but it does help avoid partially writing a set of attributes.

## Enumerable Keys

Enumerable keys are keys that use counters or sequences to generate new keys. This on its own would not be too useful; however, when combined with other attributes, this can be helpful when working with groups of keys. Take logging, for example.

You saw in the "Atomic Aggregates" section that you could save information about each ticket sale using an assignment, such as the following:

```
ConcertApp[ticketLog:9888] = {'conDate':15-Mar-2015,
  'locDescr':
'Springfield Civic Center', 'assgnSeat': 'J38'}
```

The key is a combination of the entity name `'ticketLog'` and a counter. Presumably, the counter starts at 1 and increases by one each time a ticket is sold. This is suitable for recording information, but it does not help if you want to work with a range of logged values.

For example, if you wanted to retrieve log entries for all tickets sold on a particular day, a better key format would be `'ticketLog'` concatenated to a date concatenated with a counter, such as `'ticketLog:20140617:10'`, which is the key assigned to the tenth ticket sold on June 17, 2014.

You can retrieve a range of ticket keys by generating a series of keys, for example, `'ticketLog:20140617:1'`, `'ticketLog:20140617:2'`, `'ticketLog:20140617:3'`, and so on until you generate a key that does not exist or until you reach a number of keys you specify.

## Indexes

Inverted indexes are sets of key-value pairs that allow for looking up keys or values by other attribute values of the same entity. Let's revisit the ticket logging key-value example:

```
ConcertApp[ticketLog:9888] = {'conDate':15-Mar-2015,
  'locDescr':
'Springfield Civic Center', 'assgnSeat': 'J38'}
```

This is useful for recording all seats assigned across concerts, but it is not easy to list only seats assigned in a particular location unless your key-value database provides search capabilities. For those that do not, inverted indexes can help. If you want to track all seats assigned in the Springfield Civic Center, you could use a function such as the following:

```
define addLocAssgnSeat(p_locDescr, p_seat)
    begin
        v_seatList = ConcertApp[p_locDescr]
        v_seatList = append(v_seatList, p_seat)
        ConcertApp[p_locDescr] = v_seatList
    end;
```

This function accepts the location name and seat as parameters. `v_seatList` is a local variable to store a copy of the current list of sold seats at the location. The `append` statement adds the parameter `p _ list` to `v _ seatList`, and the following statement assigns the new set of sold seats to the value associated with the location specified by the parameter `p _ locDescr`.

If the function is initially called as the following, it would set the value of `ConcertApp['Springfield Civic Center']` to `{'J38'}`:

```
addLocAssgnSeat('Springfield Civic Center', 'J38')
```

If the application then sold the following seats 'J39', 'A17', 'A18', 'A19', and 'R22' and called the `addLocAssngSeat` function for each sale, the value of `ConcertApp[('Springfield Civic Center']` would be `{'J38', 'J39', 'A17', 'A18', 'A19', 'R22'}`.

The design patterns discussed here solve some common problems you may face when developing applications using key-value attributes. The Time to Live pattern is useful when you have operations that may be disrupted and can be safely ignored after some period of inactivity or inability to finish the operation.

Emulating tables streamlines the getting and setting of multiple attributes related to a single instance of an entity, but should not be overused. Frequent use of emulating tables can indicate a misuse of a key-value database.

A document database or relational database may be a better option. Aggregates provide a means for working with entities that need to manage subtypes and different attributes associated with each subtype. The atomic aggregate pattern is used when you have multiple attributes that should be set together. It is not a full substitute for transactions, but it serves some of the purposes of transactions. Enumerable keys provide a crude range functionality by allowing a program to generate and test for the existence of keys. Finally, indexes allow you to look up attribute values starting with something other than a key.

❖ **Tip** It is important to remember that these patterns are like templates: They are starting points for solving a problem, but you should feel free to modify and adjust as needed to meet your requirements.

Chapter 1, "Different Databases for Different Requirements," briefly introduced a case study about a fictional company called TransGlobal Transport and Shipping. Now that you have reviewed the structure, function, and design of key-value databases and related applications, it is time to consider how they can be applied in realistic use cases.

## Summary

Key-value databases are the simplest of the NoSQL databases, but they can satisfy the needs of application developers who need basic storage and retrieval services. Designing for key-value databases requires several steps. You should define a naming convention for keys that allows developers to easily create keys and document the types of values associated with the keys. Values can be basic data types or more complicated data structures. Data structures allow for storing multiple attributes together, but large values can have adverse performance consequences. Design patterns described in this chapter can provide starter solutions to common problems as well as help organize applications by introducing an additional level of abstraction. Some key-value database implementations provide additional features such as search and secondary indexes. Take advantage of these when possible. They are likely to be more efficient and require less code than a "do-it-yourself" version of the same functionality.

# Case Study: Key-Value Databases for Mobile Application Configuration

TransGlobal Transport and Shipping (TGTS) coordinates the movement of goods around the globe for businesses of all sizes. Customers of TGTS contact the shipper and provide detailed information about packages and cargo that need to be shipped. Simple orders can be a single package shipped across the country, and more complicated orders can entail hundreds of parcels or shipping containers that are transported internationally. To help their customers track their shipments, TGTS is developing a mobile app called TGTS Tracker.

TGTS Tracker will run on the most popular mobile device platforms. To allow customers to monitor their shipments from any of their mobile devices, application designers have decided to keep configuration information about each customer in a centralized database. This configuration information includes

- Customer name and account number

- Default currency for pricing information

- Shipment attributes to appear in the summary dashboard

- Alerts and notification preferences

- User interface options, such as preferred color scheme and font

In addition to configuration information, designers want the app to quickly display summary information in a dashboard. Slower response times are acceptable when customers need to look up more detailed information about shipments. The database supporting TGTS Tracker should support up to 10,000 simultaneous users, with reads making up 90% of all I/O operations.

The design team evaluated relational databases and key-value databases. Relational databases are well suited to manage complex relations between multiple tables, but the need for scalability and fast read operations convinced them that a key-value database was the better choice for TGTS Tracker.

The range of data that is required by the mobile app is fairly limited so the designers felt confident that a single namespace would be sufficient. They chose TrackerNS as the name of the app's namespace.

Each customer has an account number, so this was selected as a unique identifier for each customer.

The designers then moved on to decide on the structure of values. After reviewing preliminary designs of the user interface, they determined that name and account number appear frequently together, so it made sense to keep them together in a single list of values. The default currency is also frequently required, so it is included in the list of values along with customer name and account number. Because this app is designed to track the status of shipments, there is little need for administrative information, such as billing address, so it is not stored in the key-value database.

The app designers decided to use the following naming convention for keys: entity type:account number. Given the list of data types the tracker manages, the designers decided the database should support four entity types:

- Customer information, abbreviated 'cust'
- Dashboard configuration options, abbreviated 'dshb'
- Alerts and notification specifications, abbreviated 'alrt'
- User interface configurations, abbreviated 'ui'

The next step in the design process is determining attributes for each entity. The customer entity maintains the customer name and preferred currency. The account number is part of the key, so there is no need to store it again in the list of values. The following is a sample customer key-value pair:

```
TrackerNS['cust:4719364'] = {'name':'Prime Machine, Inc.',
  'currency':'USD'}
```

The dashboard configuration detail is a list of up to six attributes about a shipment that will appear on a summary screen. The following are options, with abbreviations in parentheses:

- Ship to company (shpComp)
- Ship to city (shpCity)
- Ship to state (shpState)
- Ship to country (shpCountry)
- Date shipped (shpDate)
- Expected date of delivery (shpDelivDate)
- Number of packages/containers shipped (shpCnt)
- Type of packages/containers shipped (shpType)
- Total weight of shipment (shpWght)
- Note on shipment (shpNotes)

The following is a sample dashboard configuration specification:

```
TrackerNS['dash:4719364'] =
  {'shpComp','shpState','shpDate','shpDelivDate'}
```

The alerts and notification data indicate when messages should be sent to a customer. An alert and notification can be sent when a shipment is picked up, delivered, or delayed. The message can be sent as either an email address or as a text message to a phone. Multiple people can receive messages, and each person receiving a message can be notified under different conditions.

This is modeled with a list of lists as a value. For example, the person with email address 'jane.washingon@primemachineinc.com' might get emails when packages are picked up and the person with phone number (202)555-9812 might get a text message when packages are delayed. The key-value pair for that would look like the following:

```
TrackerNS[alrt:4719364] =
    { altList :
    {'jane.washingon@primemachineinc.com','pickup'},
    {'(202)555-9812','delay'}
}
```

Finally, the user interface configuration options are a simple list of attribute value pairs, such as font name, font size, and color scheme. A key-value pair for a user interface specification could be

```
TrackerNS[alrt:4719364] = { 'fontName': 'Cambria',
        'fontSize': 9,
        'colorScheme' : 'default'
    }
```

Now that the designers have defined the entity types, key-naming conventions, and structure of values, developers can write supporting code to set and retrieve keys and their values.

## Review Questions

1. Describe four characteristics of a well-designed key-naming convention.

2. Name two types of restrictions key-value databases can place on keys.

3. Describe the difference between range partitioning and hash partitioning.

4. How can structured data types help reduce read latency (that is, the time needed to retrieve a block of data from a disk)?

5. Describe the Time to Live (TTL) key pattern.

6. Which design pattern provides some of the features of relational transactions?

7. When would you want to use the Aggregate pattern?

8. What are enumerable keys?

9. How can enumerable keys help with range queries?

10. How would you modify the design of TGTS Tracker to include a user's preferred language in the configuration?

# References

Basho Technologies, Inc., Riak Documentation:
http://docs.basho.com/riak/latest/.

FoundationDB. Key-Value Store 2.0 Documentation:
https://foundationdb.com/key-value-store/documentation/index.html.

Katsov, Ilya. "NoSQL Data Modeling Techniques." Highly Scalable Blog: http://highlyscalable.wordpress.com/2012/03/01/nosql-data-modeling-techniques/.

Oracle Corporation. "Oracle NoSQL Database, 12c Release 1":
http://docs.oracle.com/cd/NOSQL/html/index.html.

Redis Documentation: http://redis.io/documentation.

Wikipedia. "Software Design Patterns":
http://en.wikipedia.org/wiki/Software_design_pattern.

# Part III
## Document Databases

# 6

# Introduction to
# Document Databases

*"I am a man of fixed and unbending principles,
the first of which is to be flexible at all times."*
—EVERETT DIRKSEN
FORMER U.S. SENATOR

## Topics Covered In This Chapter

**What Is a Document?**

**Avoid Explicit Schema Definitions**

**Basic Operations on Document Databases**

Developers often turn to document databases when they need the flexibility of NoSQL databases but need to manage more complex data structures than those readily supported by key-value databases. Like key-value databases, and unlike relational databases, document databases do not require you to define a common structure for all records in the data store. Document databases, however, do have some similar features to relational databases. For example, it is possible to query and filter collections of documents much as you would rows in a relational table. Of course, the syntax, or structure, of queries is different between SQL and NoSQL databases, but the functionality is comparable.

This chapter begins the second section of the book dedicated to document databases. The discussion begins by defining a document with respect to document databases. The focus then moves to the structure of documents and the ability to vary the structure of documents within a collection. The later sections of the chapter address basic database operations, organizing data as well as indexing and retrieving documents.

# What Is a Document?

When you see the term *document*, you might think of a word processing or spreadsheet file or perhaps even a paper document. These are the types of things many people would probably think of when they see the word *document*. They have nothing to do with document databases, at least with respect to the NoSQL type of database.

> ❖ **Note** There are applications that do maintain databases that store word processing, spreadsheets, emails, and other electronic objects you might describe as a document. Attorneys, for example, might use a relational database to store documents related to their cases. These are reasonably and properly called document databases, but they are not the type referred to when discussing NoSQL document databases. From this point on, references in this book to document databases refer to NoSQL document databases, not databases that store electronic documents.

## Documents Are Not So Simple After All

Let's start with another common type of document: an HTML document. Figure 6.1 shows a simple HTML document rendered according to formatting commands in the file.

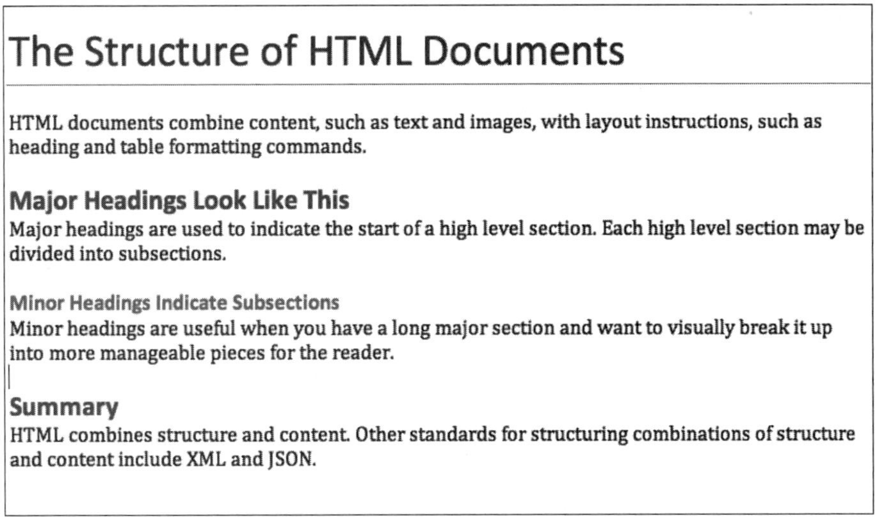

---

# The Structure of HTML Documents

HTML documents combine content, such as text and images, with layout instructions, such as heading and table formatting commands.

## Major Headings Look Like This

Major headings are used to indicate the start of a high level section. Each high level section may be divided into subsections.

### Minor Headings Indicate Subsections

Minor headings are useful when you have a long major section and want to visually break it up into more manageable pieces for the reader.

## Summary

HTML combines structure and content. Other standards for structuring combinations of structure and content include XML and JSON.

---

**Figure 6.1** *A simple example of an HTML document with basic formatting commands.*

HTML documents store two types of information:

- Content commands

- Formatting commands

Content includes text and references to image, audio, or other media files. This is information the viewer of the document will see and hear when the document is rendered. The document also contains formatting commands that specify how the layout and the format of content should look. For example, the title is rendered in a larger font than major headings or subheadings because of different formatting commands. A subset of the HTML code and content that generates Figure 6.1 is shown in Listing 6.1.

❖ **Note** Some HTML code has been removed from Listing 6.1 for clarity.

**Listing 6.1**   *Sample of HTML Code Used to Generate Figure 6.1*

```
<body bgcolor=white lang=EN-US style='tab-interval:.5in'>

<div class=Section1>

<div style='mso-element:para-border-div;border:none;
  border-bottom:solid #4F81BD;
mso-border-bottom-themecolor:accent1;border-bottom:1.0pt;
  padding:0in 0in 4.0pt 0in'>
<p class=MsoTitle>The Structure of HTML Documents</p>

</div>

<p class=MsoNormal><o:p> </o:p></p>

<p class=MsoNormal>HTML documents combine content, such as
text and images, with layout instructions, such as heading
and table formatting commands. </p>

<p class=MsoNormal><o:p> </o:p></p>

<h1>Major Headings Look Like This</h1>

<p class=MsoNormal>Major headings are used to indicate the
start of a high level section. Each high level section may
be divided into subsections.</p>

<p class=MsoNormal><o:p> </o:p></p>

<h2>Minor Headings Indicate Subsections</h2>

<p class=MsoNormal style='tab-stops:132.0pt'>Minor
headings are useful when you have a long major section and
want to visually break it up into more manageable pieces
for the reader.</p>

<p class=MsoNormal style='tab-stops:132.0pt'><o:p> 
  </o:p></p>
```

```
<h1>Summary</h1>

<p class=MsoNormal style='tab-stops:132.0pt'>HTML combines
structure and content. Other standards for structuring
combinations of structure and content include XML and
JSON.</p>

</div>
</body>
</html>
```

The formatting commands indicate which text should be displayed with a major heading (for example, surrounded by `<h1>` and `</h1>`), when to start a new paragraph (that is, the `<p>` and `</p>` tags), and other rendering instructions.

The details of the particular commands are not important for this discussion—the key point is that HTML combines formatting and content in a single document. In much the same way, documents in document databases combine structure and content.

HTML documents use predefined tags to indicate formatting commands. Documents in document databases are not constrained to a predefined set of tags for specifying structure. Instead, developers are free to choose the terms they need to structure their content just as data modelers choose table and column names for relational databases.

Let's consider a simple example of a customer record that tracks the customer ID, name, address, first order date, and last order date. Using JavaScript Object Notation (JSON), a sample customer record is

```
{
    "customer_id":187693,
   "name": "Kiera Brown",
   "address" : {
       "street" : "1232 Sandy Blvd.",
       "city" :   "Vancouver",
       "state" :  "Washington",
```

```
       "zip" :   "99121"
       },
   "first_order" : "01/15/2013",
   "last_order" : " 06/27/2014"
}
```

## The Structure of JSON Objects

JSON objects are constructed using several simple syntax rules:

- Data is organized in key-value pairs, similar to key-value databases.

- Documents consist of name-value pairs separated by commas.

- Documents start with a { and end with a }.

- Names are strings, such as "customer _ id" and "address".

- Values can be numbers, strings, Booleans (true or false), arrays, objects, or the NULL value.

- The values of arrays are listed within square brackets, that is [ and ].

- The values of objects are listed as key-value pairs within curly brackets, that is, { and }.

JSON is just one option for representing documents in a document database. The same information in the preceding example is represented in XML as follows:

```
<customer_record>
<customer_id>187693</customer_id>
 <name>"Kiera Brown"</name>
 <address>
    <street>"1232 Sandy Blvd."</street>
    <city>"Vancouver"</city>
    <state>"Washington"</state>
    <zip>"99121"</zip>
 </address>
```

```
<first_order>"01/15/2013"</first_order>
<last_order>"06/27/2014"</last_order>
</customer_record>
```

❖ **Note** Describing the full syntax of XML is beyond the scope of this chapter. See XMLFiles.com or W3Schools.com/xml for details.

To summarize, a document is a set of key-value pairs. Keys are represented as strings of characters. Values may be basic data types (such as numbers, strings, and Booleans) or structures (such as arrays and objects). Documents contain both structure information and data. The name in a name-value pair indicates an attribute and the value in a name-value pair is the data assigned to that attribute. JSON and XML are two formats commonly used to define documents.[1]

## Documents and Key-Value Pairs

An advantage of documents over key-value databases is that related attributes are managed within a single object. As you may recall, you can emulate some aspects of relational tables using a naming convention based on the name of the entity modeled, a unique identifier for an instance of that entity, and the name of the attribute.

Documents, like relational tables, organize multiple attributes in a single object. This allows database developers to more easily implement common requirements, such as returning all attributes of an entity based on a filter applied to one of the attributes. For example, in one step you could filter a list of customer documents to identify those whose last purchase was at least six months ago and return their IDs, names, and addresses. If you were using a key-value database, you would need to query all last purchase dates, generate a list of unique identifiers associated with those customers with a purchase

---

1. Binary JSON, or BSON, is a binary representation of JSON objects and is another method for specifying documents.

date greater than six months, and then query for names and addresses associated with each identifier in the list (see Figure 6.2).

<u>Document Database</u>

>  Last Purchase Date > (Today () – 180)

<u>Key Value</u>
>  Customer_List =  Return Customer_ID
>            Where Last Purchase Date >
>              (Today () – 180);
>
>  Customer_Name =  Return Customer Name
>            Value Where
>              Customer_ID in
>                Customer_List;
>
>  Customer_Address =  Return Customer Address
>            Value Where
>              Customer_ID in
>                Customer_List;

**Figure 6.2**   *Document databases require less code than key-value data stores to query multiple attributes.*

## Managing Multiple Documents in Collections

The full potential of document databases becomes apparent when you work with large numbers of documents. Documents are generally grouped into collections of similar documents. One of the key parts of modeling document databases is deciding how you will organize your documents into collections.

### Getting Started with Collections

Collections can be thought of as lists of documents. Document database designers optimize document databases to quickly add, remove, update, and search for documents. They are also designed for scalability, so as your document collection grows, you can add more servers to your cluster to keep up with demands for your database.

It is important to note that documents in the same collection do not need to have identical structures, but they should share some common structures. For example, Listing 6.2 shows a collection of four documents with similar structures.

**Listing 6.2**    *Documents with Similar Structures*

```
{
    {
     "customer_id":187693,
     "name": "Kiera Brown"
     "address" : {
                   "street" : "1232 Sandy Blvd.",
                   "city" :   "Vancouver",
                   "state" :  "WA",
                   "zip" :   "99121"
                   },
    "first_order" : "01/15/2013",
    "last_order" : " 06/27/2014"
}
    {
     "customer_id":187694,
     "name": "Bob Brown",
     "address" : {
                   "street" : "1232 Sandy Blvd.",
                   "city" :   "Vancouver",
                   "state" :  "WA",
                   "zip" :   "99121"
                   },
    "first_order" : "02/25/2013",
    "last_order" : " 05/12/2014"
    }

    {
     "customer_id":179336,
     "name": "Hui Li",
     "address" : {
                   "street" : "4904 Main St.",
                   "city" :   "St Louis",
                   "state" :  "MO",
                   "zip" :   "99121"
                   },
    "first_order" : "05/29/2012",
```

```
    "last_order" : " 08/31/2014",
    "loyalty_level" : "Gold",
    "large_purchase_discount" : 0.05,
    "large_purchase_amount" : 250.00
    }

{
    "customer_id":290981,
    "name": "Lucas Lambert",
    "address" : {
                "street" : "974 Circle Dr.",
                "city" :   "Boston",
                "state" :  "MA",
                "zip" :   "02150"
                },
    "first_order" : "02/14/2014",
    "last_order" : " 02/14/2014",
    "number_of_orders" : 1,
    "number_of_returns" : 1
    }
}
```

Notice that the first two documents have the same structure while the third and fourth documents have additional attributes. The third document contains three new fields: loyalty _ level, large _ purchase _ discount, and large _ purchase _ amount. These are used to indicate this person is considered a valued customer who should receive a 5% discount on all orders over $250. (The currency type is implicit.) The fourth document has two other new fields, number _ of _ orders and number _ of _ returns. In this case, it appears that the customer made one purchase on February 14, 2014, and returned it.

One of the advantages of document databases is that they provide flexibility when it comes to the structure of documents. If only 10% of your documents need to record loyalty and discount information, why should you have to clutter the other 90% with unused fields? You do not have to when using document databases. The next section addresses this issue in more detail.

## Tips on Designing Collections

Collections are sets of documents. Because collections do not impose a consistent structure on documents in the collection, it is possible to store different types of documents in a single collection. You could, for example, store customer, web clickstream data, and server log data in the same collection. In practice, this is not advisable.

In general, collections should store documents about the same type of entity. The concept of an entity is fairly abstract and leaves a lot of room for interpretation. You might consider both web clickstream data and server log data as a "system event" entity and, therefore, they should be stored in the same collection.

### *Avoid Highly Abstract Entity Types*

A system event entity such as this is probably too abstract for practical modeling. This is because web clickstream data and server log data will have few common fields. They may share an ID field and a time stamp but few other attributes. The web clickstream data will have fields capturing information about web pages, users, and transitions from one page to another. The server log documents will contain details about the server, event types, severity levels, and perhaps some descriptive text. Notice how dissimilar web clickstream data is from server log data:

```
{ "id" : 12334578,
    "datetime" :  "201409182210",
    "session_num" : 987943,
    "client_IP_addr" : "192.168.10.10",
    "user_agent" : "Mozilla / 5.0",
    "referring_page" : "http://www.example.com/page1"
}

{ "id" : 31244578,
    "datetime" :  "201409172140",
    "event_type" : "add_user",
```

```
    "server_IP_addr" : "192.168.11.11",
    "descr" :  "User jones added with sudo privileges"
}
```

If you were to store these two document types in a single collection, you would likely need to add a type indicator so your code could easily distinguish between a web clickstream document and a server log event document.

In the preceding example, the documents would be modified to include a type indicator:

```
{ "id" : 12334578,
    "datetime" :  "201409182210",
    "doc_type": "click_stream",
    "session_num" : 987943,
    "client_IP_addr" : "192.168.10.10",
    "user_agent" : "Mozilla / 5.0",
    "referring_page" : "http://www.example.com/page1"
}

{ "id" : 31244578,
    "datetime" :  "201409172140"
    "doc_type" : "server_log"
    "event_type" : "add_user"
    "server_IP_addr" : "192.168.11.11"
    "descr" :  "User jones added with sudo privileges"
}
```

> ❖ **Tip** If you find yourself using a 'doc _ type' field and frequently filtering your collection to select a single document type, carefully review your documents. You might have a mix of entity types.

Filtering collections is often slower than working directly with multiple collections, each of which contains a single document type. Consider if you had a system event collection with 1 million documents: 650,000 clickstream documents and 350,000 server log events. Because both types of events are added over time, the document collection will likely store a mix of clickstream and server log documents in close proximity to each other.

If you are using disk storage, you will likely retrieve blocks of data that contain both clickstream and server log documents. This will adversely impact performance (see Figure 6.3).

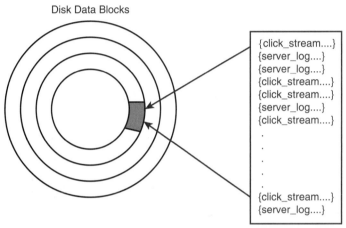

**Figure 6.3**  *Mixing document types can lead to multiple document types in a disk data block. This can lead to inefficiencies because data is read from disk but not used by the application that filters documents based on type.*

You might argue that indexes could be used to improve performance. Indexes certainly improve data access performance in some cases. However, indexes may be cached in memory or stored on disk. Retrieving indexes from disk will add time to processing. Also, if indexes reference a data block that contains both clickstream and server log data, the disk will read both types of records even though one will be filtered out in your application.

Depending on the size of the collection, the index, and the number of distinct document types (this is known as cardinality in relational database terminology), it may be faster to scan the full document collection rather than use an index. Finally, consider the overhead of writing indexes as new documents are added to the collection.

## Watch for Separate Functions for Manipulating Different Document Types

Another clue that a collection should be broken into multiple collections is your application code. The application code that manipulates a collection should have substantial amounts of code that apply to all documents and some amount of code that accommodates specialized fields in some documents.

For example, most of the code you would write to insert, update, and delete documents in the customer collection would apply to all documents. You would probably have additional code to handle loyalty and discount fields that would apply to only a subset of all documents.

❖ **Tip** If your code at the highest levels consists of `if` statements conditionally checking document types that branch to separate functions to manipulate separate document types, it is a good indication you probably have mixed document types that should go in separate collections (see Figure 6.4).

High-Level Branching
```
    doc.
If (doc_type = 'click_stream'):
    process_click_stream (doc)
Else
    process_server_log (doc)
```

Lower-Level Branching
```
book.title = doc.title
book.author = doc.author
book.year = doc.publication_year
book.publisher = doc.publisher
book.descr = book.title + book.author + book.year + book.publisher
if (doc.ebook = true);
   book.descr = book.descr + doc.ebook_size
```

**Figure 6.4**  *High-level branching in functions manipulating documents can indicate a need to create separate collections. Branching at lower levels is common when some documents have optional attributes.*

### Use Document Subtypes When Entities Are Frequently Aggregated or Share Substantial Code

The document collection design tips have so far focused on ensuring you do not mix dissimilar documents in a single collection. If there were no more design tips, you might think that you should never use type indicators in documents. That would be wrong—very wrong.

There are times when it makes sense to use document type indicators and have separate code to handle the different types.

❖ **Note** When it comes to designing NoSQL databases, remember design principles but apply them flexibly. Always consider the benefits and drawbacks of a design principle in a particular situation. That is what the designers of NoSQL databases did when they considered the benefits and drawbacks of relational databases and decided to devise their own data model that broke many of the design principles of relational databases.

It is probably best to start this tip with an example. In addition to tracking customers and their clickstream data, you would like to track the products customers have ordered. You have decided the first step in this process is to create a document collection containing all products, which for our purposes, includes books, CDs, and small kitchen appliances. There are only three types of products now, but your client is growing and will likely expand into other product types as well.

All of the products have the following information associated with them:

- Product name
- Short description
- SKU (stock keeping unit)
- Product dimensions
- Shipping weight

- Average customer review score

- Standard price to customer

- Cost of product from supplier

Each of the product types will have specific fields. Books will have fields with information about

- Author name

- Publisher

- Year of publication

- Page count

The CDs will have the following fields:

- Artist name

- Producer name

- Number of tracks

- Total playing time

The small kitchen appliances will have the following fields:

- Color

- Voltage

- Style

How should you go about deciding how to organize this data into one or more document collections? Start with how the data will be used. Your client might tell you that she needs to be able to answer the following queries:

- What is the average number of products bought by each customer?

- What is the range of number of products purchased by customers (that is, the lowest number to the highest number of products purchased)?

- What are the top 20 most popular products by customer state?

- What is the average value of sales by customer state (that is, Standard price to customer – Cost of product from supplier)?

- How many of each type of product were sold in the last 30 days?

All the queries use data from all product types, and only the last query subtotals the number of products sold by type. This is a good indication that all the products should be in a single document collection (see Figure 6.5). Unlike the example of the collection with clickstream and server log data, the product document types are frequently used together to respond to queries and calculate derived values.

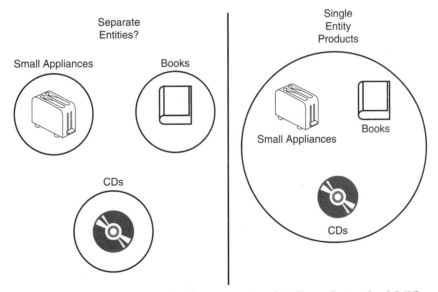

**Figure 6.5** *When is a toaster the same as a database design book? When they are treated the same by application queries. Queries can help guide the organization of documents and collections.*

Another reason to favor a single document collection is that the client is growing and will likely add new product types. If the number of product types grows into the tens or even hundreds, the number of collections would become unwieldy.

> ❖ **Note** Relational databases are often used to support a broad range of query types. NoSQL databases complement relational databases by providing functionality optimized for particular aspects of application support. Rather than start with data and try to figure out how to organize your collections, it can help to start with queries to understand how your data will be used. This can help inform your decisions about how to structure collections and documents.

To summarize, avoid overly abstract document types. If you find yourself writing separate code to process different document subtypes, you should consider separating the types into different collections. Poor collection design can adversely affect performance and slow your application. There are cases where it makes sense to group somewhat dissimilar objects (for example, small kitchen appliances and books) if they are treated as similar (for example, they are all products) in your application.

Documents and collections are the organizing structures of document database storage. You might be wondering when and where you define the specification describing documents. Programmers define structures and record types before using them in their programs. Relational database designers spend a substantial amount of time crafting and tuning data models that define tables, columns, and other data structures.

Now it is time to consider how such specifications, known as schemas, are used in document databases.

## Avoid Explicit Schema Definitions

If you have worked with relational databases, you are probably familiar with defining database schemas. A *schema* is a specification that describes the structure of an object, such as a table. A pseudoschema specification for the customer record discussed above is

```
CREATE TABLE customer (
    customer_ID   integer,
    name varchar(100),
    street  varchar(100),
    city varchar(100),
    state varchar(2),
    zip varchar(5),
    first_purchase_date  date,
    last_purchase_date  date
)
```

This schema defines a table to hold customer and address information. All customer records have the same eight columns: customer _ id, name, street, city, state, zip, first _ purchase _ date, and last _ purchase _ date. Each column is assigned a specific data type, either integer, date, or varchar. Varchar is a variable character string. The number in parentheses following varchar is the maximum length of the value stored in that attribute.

Data modelers have to define tables in a relational database before developers can execute code to add, remove, or update rows in the table. Document databases do not require this formal definition step. Instead, developers can create collections and documents in collections by simply inserting them into the database (see Figure 6.6).

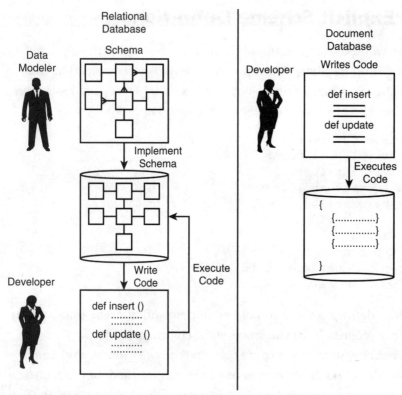

**Figure 6.6**   *Relational databases require an explicitly defined schema, but document databases do not.*

Document databases are designed to accommodate variations in documents within a collection. Because any document could be different from all previously inserted documents, it does not make sense to require data modelers to specify all possible document fields prior to building and populating the database. This freedom from the need to predefine the database structure is captured in the term often used to describe document databases: schemaless.

Although it is true that you do not have to define a schema prior to adding documents, there is an organization implicit in the set of documents you insert into the database. The organization is apparent in the code that manipulates the documents from the database.

For example, if you were building the product database described previously, you would have code that sets the value of artist, producer, number of tracks, and total play time for each CD inserted. Similarly, you would have code to set small appliance fields and book fields as well. Presumably, you would use the same code to set common fields, such as product name and SKU.

Polymorphic schema is another term that describes document databases. Polymorphic is derived from Latin and literally means "many shapes." This makes it an apt description for a document database that supports multiple types of documents in a single collection.

## Basic Operations on Document Databases

The basic operations on document databases are the same as other types of databases and include the following:

- Inserting

- Deleting

- Updating

- Retrieving

There is no standard data manipulation language used across document databases to perform these operations. The examples that follow use a command structure similar to that of MongoDB, currently the most commonly used document database.[2]

Before introducing the basic operations, there is one additional data structure to introduce and that is the database. The database is the container for collections and containers are for documents. The logical relationship between these three data structures is shown in Figure 6.7.

---

2. DB-Engines Rankings. http://db-engines.com/en/ranking.

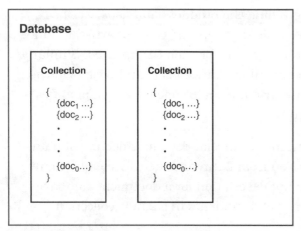

**Figure 6.7** *The database is the highest-level logical structure in a document database and contains collections of documents.*

❖ **Note** By convention, the database container is referred to as 'db' in sample code. To refer to a collection, you prefix the collection name with 'db'. For example, the collection customer is indicated by 'db.customer.' The basic operations are performed on collections specified in this way.

## Inserting Documents into a Collection

Collections are objects that can perform a number of different operations. The insert method adds documents to a collection. For example, the following adds a single document describing a book by Kurt Vonnegut to the books collection:

```
db.books.insert( {"title":" Mother Night", "author": "Kurt
    Vonnegut, Jr."} )
```

❖ **Tip** It is a good practice to include a unique identifier with each document when it is inserted.

Instead of simply adding a book document with the title and author name, a better option would be to include a unique identifier as in

```
db.books.insert( {book_id: 1298747,
                "title":"Mother Night",
                "author": "Kurt Vonnegut, Jr."} )
```

❖ **Note** Different document databases have different recommendations for unique identifiers. MongoDB adds a unique identifier if one is not provided. CouchDB supports any string as a unique identifier but recommends using a Universally Unique Identifier (UUID). Check your document database documentation for details on unique identifiers.

In many cases, it is more efficient to perform bulk inserts instead of a series of individual inserts. For example, the following three insert commands could be used to add three books to the book collection:

```
db.books.insert( {"book_id": 1298747,
                "title":"Mother Night",
                "author": "Kurt Vonnegut, Jr."} )

db.books.insert( {"book_id": 639397,
                "title":"Science and the Modern World",
                "author": "Alfred North Whitehead"} )

db.books.insert( {"book_id": 1456701,
                "title":"Foundation and Empire",
                "author": "Isaac Asimov"} )
```

Each of these commands would incur the overhead of the write operation. A single bulk insert would incur that overhead only once, so it is especially useful for loading a large number of documents at once. The same three documents listed above could be added with the following command:

```
db.books.insert(
     [
                  {"book_id": 1298747,
                   "title":"Mother Night",
                   "author": "Kurt Vonnegut, Jr."},

                  {"book_id": 639397,
                   "title":"Science and the Modern World",
                   "author": "Alfred North Whitehead"},

                  {"book_id": 1456701,
                   "title":"Foundation and Empire",
                   "author": "Isaac Asimov"}
     ]
}
```

The [ and ] in the parameter list delimit an array of documents to insert.

> ❖ **Tip** Check your document database documentation for limits on the size of bulk inserts. If you have many large documents, you may need to perform multiple bulk inserts to ensure that your array of documents does not exceed the bulk insert size limit.

## Deleting Documents from a Collection

You can delete documents from a collection using the remove methods. The following command deletes all documents in the books collection:

```
db.books.remove()
```

Note that the collection still exists, but it is empty.

The remove command is probably more frequently used for selective deleting rather than removing all documents from a collection. To delete a single document, you can specify a query document that matches the document you would like to delete. A query document is a list of keys and values that are matched against documents. The query document

```
{"book_id": 639397}
```

uniquely identifies the book titled *Science and the Modern World*. (For those familiar with SQL, this is analogous to specifying a WHERE clause.) To delete the book titled *Science and the Modern World*, you would issue the following command:

```
db.books.remove({"book_id": 639397})
```

The remove command deletes all documents that match the query document. This example used the unique identifier for a book, so only one book is deleted. Suppose you have removed all books from the books collection and then execute the following command:

```
db.books.insert(
    [
        {"book_id": 1298747,
                    "title":"Mother Night",
                    "author": "Kurt Vonnegut, Jr."},

        {"book_id": 1298770,
                    "title":"Cat's Cradle",
                    "author": "Kurt Vonnegut, Jr."},

        {"book_id": 639397,
                    "title":"Science and the Modern
                      World",
                    "author": "Alfred North
                      Whitehead"},

        {"book_id": 1456701,
                    "title":"Foundation and Empire",
                    "author": "Isaac Asimov"}
    ]
```

The books collection now has four books. Executing the following `remove` command will delete the two books by Kurt Vonnegut, Jr.:

```
db.books.remove({"author": "Kurt Vonnegut, Jr."})
```

You should be especially careful when deleting documents that may be referenced in other documents. For example, assume you have a simple orders collection that contains customers and books they ordered:

```
{
    {"customer_id" : 183747, "book_id": 639397},
    {"customer_id" : 165301, "book_id": 639397},
    {"customer_id" : 183747, "book_id":1298770},
    ...
}
```

If you execute the following command, you will remove two books with IDs 1298747 and 1298770:

```
db.books.remove({"author": "Kurt Vonnegut, Jr."})
```

The orders collection, however, will still have references to these IDs. If your application code were to try to look up the book with ID 1298770, it would fail.

> ❖ **Note** Relational databases can be designed to prevent this type of problem, but document databases depend on application code to manage this type of data integrity.

## Updating Documents in a Collection

Once a document has been inserted into a collection, it can be modified with the `update` method. The `update` method requires two parameters to update:

- Document query
- Set of keys and values to update

> ❖ **Note** Because we are using MongoDB syntax, it should be noted that the MongoDB update method takes three optional parameters in addition to the two described here. They are out of the scope of this chapter.

Like the `remove` method, the document query of the `update` command is a set of keys and values identifying the documents to update. To indicate you want to update Kurt Vonnegut Jr.'s *Mother Night*, you would use the following query document:

```
{"book_id": 1298747}
```

> ❖ **Note** When using MongoDB syntax, you should note that the MongoDB `update` method takes three optional parameters in addition to the two described here. However, the other options are out of the scope of this chapter.

MongoDB uses the `$set` operator to specify which keys and values should be updated. For example, the following command adds the quantity key with the value of 10 to the collection:

```
db.books.update ({"book_id": 1298747},
                {$set  {"quantity" : 10 }})
```

The full document would then be

```
{"book_id": 1298747,
    "title":"Mother Night",
    "author": "Kurt Vonnegut, Jr.",
    "quantity" : 10}
```

The `update` command adds a key if it does not exist and sets the value as indicated. If the key already exists, the `update` command changes the value associated with it.

Document databases sometimes provide other operators in addition to set commands. For example, MongoDB has an increment operator ($inc), which is used to increase the value of a key by the specified amount. The following command would change the quantity of *Mother Night* from 10 to 15:

```
db.books.update ({"book_id": 1298747},
               {$inc  {"quantity" : 5 }})
```

Check your document database documentation for details on update operators.

## Retrieving Documents from a Collection

The find method is used to retrieve documents from a collection. As you might expect, the find method takes an optional query document that specifies which documents to return. The following command matches all documents in a collection:

```
db.books.find()
```

This is useful if you want to perform an operation on all documents in a collection.

If, however, you only want a subset of documents in the database, you would specify selection criteria using a document. For example, the following returns all books by Kurt Vonnegut, Jr.:

```
db.books.find({"author": "Kurt Vonnegut, Jr."})
```

These two find examples both return all the keys and values in the documents. There are times when it is not necessary to return all key-value pairs. In those cases, you can specify an optional second argument that is a list of keys to return along with a "1" to indicate the key should be returned.

```
db.books.find({"author": "Kurt Vonnegut, Jr."},
             {"title" : 1} )
```

This returns only the titles of books by Kurt Vonnegut, Jr.

> ❖ **Tip** By default, MongoDB returns the unique identifier as well, even if it is not explicitly listed in the set of keys to return.

More complex queries are built using conditionals and Boolean operators. To retrieve all books with a quantity greater than or equal to 10 and less than 50, you could use the following command:

```
Db.books.find( {"quantity" : {"$gte" : 10, "$lt" : 50 }} )
```

Notice that even more complex criteria are still constructed as query documents.

The conditionals and Booleans supported in MongoDB include the following:

- $lt—Less than
- $let—Less than or equal to
- $gt—Greater than
- $gte—Greater than or equal to
- $in—Query for values of a single key
- $or—Query for values in multiple keys
- $not—Negation

Document databases can provide more extensive query capabilities, including the ability to match regular expressions or apply full-text search. Check the documentation for your document database for additional information.

> ▶ *In addition to these basic operations, document databases support advanced functions such as indexing. These more advanced features are covered in Chapter 8, "Designing for Document Databases."*

# Summary

Documents are flexible data structures. They do not require predefined schemas and they readily accommodate variations in the structure of documents. Documents are organized into related sets called collections. Collections are analogous to a relational table, and documents are analogous to rows in a relational table.

The flexibility of document databases enables you to make poor design decisions with regard to organizing collections. Collections should contain similar types of entities, although the keys and values may differ across documents.

There are times when modeling documents using highly abstract entities, such as the system event entity discussed previously, can adversely affect performance and lead to more complicated application code than necessary. There are other times, however, when abstract entities, such as products, are appropriate. Analyze the types of queries your database will support to guide your design decisions.

Unlike relational databases, there is not a standard query language for document databases. The examples in this chapter, and subsequent chapters, are based on the syntax of a commonly used document database. The principles and concepts described here should apply across document databases, although implementation details will vary.

# Review Questions

1. Define a document with respect to document databases.
2. Name two types of formats for storing data in a document database.
3. List at least three syntax rules for JSON objects.
4. Create a sample document for a small appliance with the following attributes: appliance ID, name, description, height, width, length, and shipping weight. Use the JSON format.

5. Why are highly abstract entities often avoided when modeling document collections?

6. When is it reasonable to use highly abstract entities?

7. Using the db.books collection described in this chapter, write a command to insert a book to the collection. Use MongoDB syntax.

8. Using the db.books collection described in this chapter, write a command to remove books by Isaac Asimov. Use MongoDB syntax.

9. Using the db.books collection described in this chapter, write a command to retrieve all books with quantity greater than or equal to 20. Use MongoDB syntax.

10. Which query operator is used to search for values in a single key?

## References

Chodorow, Kristina. *50 Tips and Tricks for MongoDB Developers.* Sebastopol, CA: O'Reilly Media, Inc., 2011.

Chodorow, Kristina. *MongoDB: The Definitive Guide.* Sebastopol, CA: O'Reilly Media, Inc., 2013.

Copeland, Rick. *MongoDB Applied Design Patterns.* Sebastopol, CA: O'Reilly Media, Inc., 2013.

Couchbase Documentation: http://docs.couchbase.com/

MongoDB 2.6 Manual: http://docs.mongodb.org/manual/

O'Higgins, Niall. *MongoDB and Python: Patterns and Processes for the Popular Document-Oriented Database.* Sebastopol, CA: O'Reilly Media, Inc., 2011.

■ ■ ■ ■ ■ ■ ■ ■ ■ ■

# **7**

# **Document Database Terminology**

*"We must dare to think 'unthinkable' thoughts. We must
learn to explore all the options and possibilities that
confront us in a complex and rapidly changing world."*
—J. William Fulbright
Former U.S. Senator

## **Topics Covered In This Chapter**

Document and Collection Terms

Types of Partitions

Data Modeling and Query Processing

The previous chapter introduced the basic concepts of document
databases. This chapter focuses on defining commonly used terms in
document database theory and practice.

> ❖ **Note** As with the other terminology chapters in this book, the
> goal is to provide in-depth descriptions of key terms used in doc-
> ument databases. Some of the terminology is generally applicable
> to other distributed databases as well, whereas some is specific to
> document databases.

The first set of terms is related to the basic data structures of document
databases. You should be familiar with these from the last chapter, but
they are presented here as well in somewhat more formal terms.

The second section defines terms you will come across as you learn
about document database architecture. The terms defined in this section are used to describe distributed databases in general, especially

with regard to how to scale large databases. You will see these terms frequently as you work with NoSQL technologies.

The final section is the most heterogeneous. It contains a mix of document modeling terms and operations. The document modeling terms are high-level broad concepts. The next chapter introduces more specific design patterns. The section concludes with several somewhat miscellaneous but important terms you should be familiar with when working with document databases.

## Document and Collection Terms

Documents and collections are the basic data structures of a document database. They are somewhat analogous to rows and tables in relational databases. The informal introduction to these terms in Chapter 6, "Introduction to Document Databases," was sufficient to introduce the basic concepts of document databases. Now it is time for more formal definitions that allow for more precise descriptions and reasoning about these structures.

The following terms are defined:

- Document
- Collection
- Embedded document
- Schemaless
- Polymorphic schema

At the end of this section, you should have an understanding of how documents are organized into collections. You should also understand important properties of document database organization that allow for flexible database design. This is one of the primary reasons document databases have gained popularity among developers.

## Document

A *document* is a set of ordered key-value pairs. A *key value* is a data structure that consists of two parts called, not surprisingly, the key and the value.

> ❖ **Note** For those who may have skipped the section of this book on key-value databases, a *key* is a unique identifier used to look up a value. A *value* is an instance of any supported data type, such as a string, number, array, or list.

### Documents: Ordered Sets of Key-Value Pairs

Because a document is a set, it has one instance of each member. Members are key-value pairs. For example, the following is a set with three members: 'foo': 'a', 'bar': 'b', and 'baz': 'c':

```
{ 'foo': 'a', 'bar': 'b', 'baz': 'c'}
```

A slight change turns this set into a nonset (also known as a *bag*):

```
{'foo': 'a', 'bar': 'b', 'baz': 'c', 'foo': 'a'}
```

This list of key values is not a set because there are two instances of the key-value pair 'foo': 'a'.

Sets do not distinguish by order. The following set

```
{ 'foo': 'a', 'bar': 'b', 'baz': 'c'}
```

is equivalent to

```
{'baz': 'c', 'foo': 'a', 'bar': 'b'}
```

However, for the purposes of designing document databases, these are different documents. The order of key-value pairs matters in determining the identity of a document. The document { 'foo': 'a', 'bar':

'b', 'baz': 'c'} is not the same document as {'baz': 'c', 'foo': 'a', 'bar': 'b'}.

### Key and Value Data Types

Keys are generally strings. Some key-value databases support a more extensive set of key data types, so document databases could, in principle, support multiple data types as well.

Values can be a variety of data types. As you might expect, document databases support values of numbers and strings. They also support more structured data types, such as arrays and other documents.

Arrays are useful when you want to track multiple instances of a value and the values are all of one type. For example, if you need to model an employee and a list of her projects, you could use a document such as

```
{   'employeeName' :  'Janice Collins',
    'department' : 'Software engineering'
     'startDate' : '10-Feb-2010',
    'pastProjectCodes' : [ 189847, 187731, 176533, 154812]
}
```

The key pastProjectCodes is a list of project code numbers. All project codes are numbers, so it is appropriate to use an array.

Alternatively, if you want to store, or embed, more information about projects along with the employee information, you could include another document within the employee document. One such version is

```
{   'employeeName' :   'Janice Collins',
    'department' : 'Software engineering',
    'startDate' : '10-Feb-2010',
    'pastProjects' : {
{'projectCode' : 189847,
     'projectName' : 'Product Recommendation System',
     'projectManager' : 'Jennifer Delwiney' },
{'projectCode' : 187731,
  'projectName' :  'Finance Data Mart version 3',
  'projectManager' : 'James Ross'},
```

```
{'projectCode': 176533,
 'projectName' : 'Customer Authentication',
    'projectManager' : 'Nick Clacksworth'},
{'projectCode': 154812,
 'projectName' : 'Monthly Sales Report',
 'projectManager': 'Bonnie Rendell'}
}
```

To summarize, documents are ordered sets of key-value pairs. Keys are used to reference particular values. Values can be either basic or structured data types.

## Collection

A *collection* is a group of documents. The documents within a collection are usually related to the same subject entity, such as employees, products, logged events, or customer profiles. It is possible to store unrelated documents in a collection, but this is not advised.

At the most basic level, collections allow you to operate on groups of related documents. If you maintain a collection of employee records, you can iterate over all employee records in the collection looking for particular employees, such as all employees with startDates earlier than January 1, 2011. If you have a large number of employees, this can be inefficient because you would have to compare every employee record to your search criteria.

In addition to allowing you to easily operate on groups of documents, collections support additional data structures that make such operations more efficient. For example, a more-efficient approach to scanning all documents in a collection is to use an index. Indexes on collections are like indexes in the back of book: a structured set of information that maps from one attribute, such as a key term, to related information, such as a list of page numbers (see Figure 7.1).

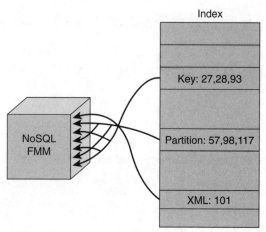

**Figure 7.1**   *Indexes map attributes, such as key terms, to related information, such as page numbers. Using an index is faster than scanning an entire book for key terms.*

Collections are groups of similar documents that allow you to easily access or operate on all documents in the group. Collections support additional data structures, such as indexes, to improve the efficiency of operations on those groups of documents.

## Embedded Document

One of the advantages of document databases is that they allow developers to store related data in more flexible ways than typically done in relational databases. If you were to model employees and the projects they work on in a relational database, you would probably create two tables: one for employee information and one for project information (see Figure 7.2).

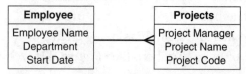

**Figure 7.2**   *Relational data models separate data about different entities into separate tables. This requires looking up information in both tables using a process known as joining.*

An embedded document enables document database users to store related data in a single document. This allows the document database to avoid a process called joining in which data from one table, called the foreign key, is used to look up data in another table.

Joining two large tables can be potentially time consuming and require a significant number of read operations from disk. Embedded documents allow related data to be stored together. When the document is read from disk, both the primary and the related information are read without the need for a join operation. Figure 7.3 shows embedded documents within a document.

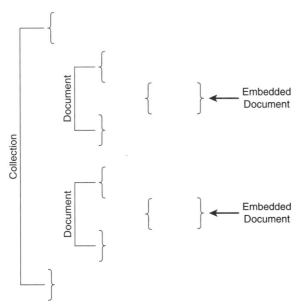

**Figure 7.3** *Embedded documents are documents within a document. Embedding is used to efficiently store and retrieve data that is frequently used together.*

Embedded documents are documents within documents. They are used to improve database performance by storing together data that is frequently used together.

Schemaless

Document databases do not require data modelers to formally specify the structure of documents. A formal structure specification is known as a *schema*. Relational databases do require schemas. They typically include specifications for

- Tables
- Columns
- Primary keys
- Foreign keys
- Constraints

These all help the relational database management system manage the data in the database. It also helps the database catch errors when data is added to the database. If, for example, someone tries to enter a string when a number is expected, the database management system will issue a warning.

Constraints are rules that describe what kind of data or relation between data is allowed. You could indicate in a schema that a column must always have a value and can never be empty.

❖ **Tip** An empty column in a relational database is referred to as having a NULL value.

Document databases do not require this specification step prior to adding documents to a collection. For this reason, document databases are called schemaless. Schemaless databases have two important differences compared with relational databases:

- More flexibility
- More responsibility

### Schemaless Means More Flexibility

In a schemaless database, developers and applications can add new key-value pairs to documents at any time. Once a collection is created, you can add documents to it. There is no need to tell the document database about the structure of the document. In fact, the structures will often vary between documents in a collection. The two documents

```
{  'employeeName' :  'Janice Collins',
   'department' : 'Software engineering'
   'startDate' : '10-Feb-2010',
   'pastProjectCodes' : [ 189847, 187731, 176533, 154812]
}
```

and

```
{  'employeeName' :  'Robert Lucas,
   'department' : 'Finance'
   'startDate' : '21-May-2009',
   'certifications' : 'CPA'
}
```

both describe employees, but the first is tailored to someone in the software engineering department and the second is designed for someone in the finance department.

These and variations on these documents are simply added to the collection as needed. There is no need to specify that some documents will have 'pastProjectCodes' and some will have 'certifications' keys. There is also no need to indicate that some values will be strings while others will be arrays.

> ❖ **Note** The document database management system infers the information it needs from the structure of the documents in the collection, not from a separate structure specification.

**Schemaless Means More Responsibility**

Schemaless databases are something of a double-edged sword. On the one hand, the flexibility of working without a schema makes it easy to accommodate differences in document structures. On the other hand, the document database management cannot enforce rules based on structure. Because there is no way to indicate that a key-value pair should always exist in a document, the document database management system will not check for it.

If the database management system does not enforce rules about data, what will? The answer is your application code.

> ❖ **Tip** An exception to this rule is the use of unique identifiers. If you specify a document without a unique identifier, the document database will probably add one for you. Check your document database's documentation for details.

Some of your application code should be dedicated to verifying rules about the structure of data. If you always require a name in an employee document, then your code that adds employees should check for that when new employees are added. This is a simple case of a data validation rule, but not all are so simple.

Over time, the keys and values you track in documents in a collection may change. You may have started collecting information about employees' certifications last year. Employees added since last year may all have a certification key. Employees whose documents have been updated may have a certification key and value as well. The remaining employee documents do not have a certification key.

In this situation, it is your code that uses and processes employee documents, not the code that adds employee documents, which must check for valid data structures or at least handle a case where an expected key does not exist (see Figure 7.4).

Application Code

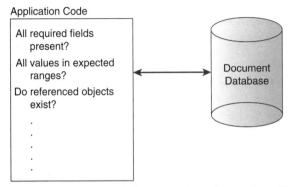

**Figure 7.4**  *Data validation code and error-handling code is used throughout applications to compensate for the lack of automatic, schema-based validation checks.*

Schemaless databases do not require formal structure specifications. Necessary information is inferred from documents within collections. This allows for more flexibility than in databases that require schemas, but there is less opportunity to automatically enforce data and document integrity rules.

## Polymorphic Schema

Another term you might encounter about document databases is polymorphic schema. It might seem odd that a database can be without a schema (*schemaless*) while at the same time having many schemas (*polymorphic schema*). It is actually quite logical when you consider the distinction between a formal specification of a structure and the structure that is implied by the documents in a collection.

> ❖ **Tip** Again, document databases are schemaless because you do not have to specify a formal definition of the structure of documents, keys, and values.

A document database is polymorphic because the documents that exist in collections can have many different forms (see Figure 7.5).

Polymorphic

```
{

    {'a' : 1,
     'b' : 2,
     'c' : 3

    }

    {'a' : 7,
     'b' : 8
     'd' : 10

    }

    {'a' : 20,
     'e' : 30,
     'f' : 40,
     'g' : 50

    }
}
```

**Figure 7.5**   *Schemaless means there is no formal definition of structure. Polymorphic schema means there are many document structures implied in the set of documents that occur in a collection.*

# Types of Partitions

*Partitioning* is a word that gets a lot of use in the NoSQL world—perhaps too much.

Chapter 2, "Variety of NoSQL Databases," introduced the CAP theorem, which you might remember describes limits on consistency, availability, and partition tolerance. In this context, the word *partition* refers to partitioning or separating a network into separate parts that are unreachable from each other.

This is an important concept for all distributed databases, but it is not the focus of partitioning with respect to document databases. Instead, when people use the term *partitioning* when discussing document databases, they are probably referring to splitting a document database and distributing different parts of the database to different servers.

There are two types of database partitioning: vertical partitioning and horizontal partitioning.

It is important to distinguish the meaning of the term *partitioning* based on the context in which it is used (see Figure 7.6).

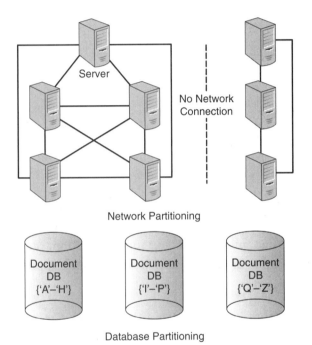

**Figure 7.6**   *The term* partitioning *has multiple meanings that are distinguished by the context, such as in the context of networks versus in the context of databases.*

## Vertical Partitioning

*Vertical partitioning* is a  technique for improving database performance by separating columns of a relational table into multiple separate tables (see Figure 7.7).

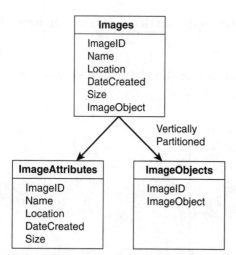

**Figure 7.7**    *Vertical partitioning is typically used with relational tables because they have a fixed structure.*

This technique is particularly useful when you have some columns that are frequently accessed and others that are not. Consider a table with images and attributes about those images, such as name, location, date image created, and so on. The table of images may be used in an application that allows users to look up images by characteristics.

Someone might want pictures from Paris, France, taken within the last three months. The database management system would probably use an index to find the rows of the table that meet the search criteria. If the application only lists the attributes in the resultset and waits for a user to pick a particular record before showing the image, then there is no reason to retrieve the image from the database along with the attributes.

If the image attributes and the image object were stored in the same table, reading the attributes could also force a reading of the image because of layout of data on the disk. By separating the image table into a table of image attributes and the image object, the database can more efficiently retrieve data for the application (see Figure 7.8).

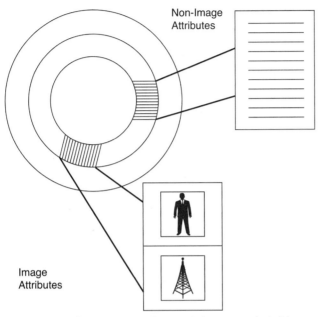

**Figure 7.8** *Separating columns into separate tables can improve the efficiency of reads because data that is not needed (for example, an image object) is not retrieved along with data that is likely needed (for example, image attributes).*

Vertical partitioning is more frequently used with relational database management systems than with document management systems. There are methods for implementing vertical partitioning in nonrelational databases, but horizontal partitioning, or sharding, is more common.

❖ **Note** For an example of sharding, see J. Kaur, et al. "A New and Improved Vertical Partitioning Scheme for Non-Relational Databases Using Greedy Method," *International Journal of Advanced Research in Computer and Communication Engineering* 2, no. 8 (August 2013).

## Horizontal Partitioning or Sharding

*Horizontal partitioning* is the process of dividing a database by documents in a document database or by rows in a relational database.

These parts of the database, known as shards, are stored on separate servers. (Horizontal partitioning of a document database is often referred to as *sharding.*) A single shard may be stored on multiple servers when a database is configured to replicate data. If data is replicated or not, a server within a document database cluster will have only one shard per server (see Figure 7.9).

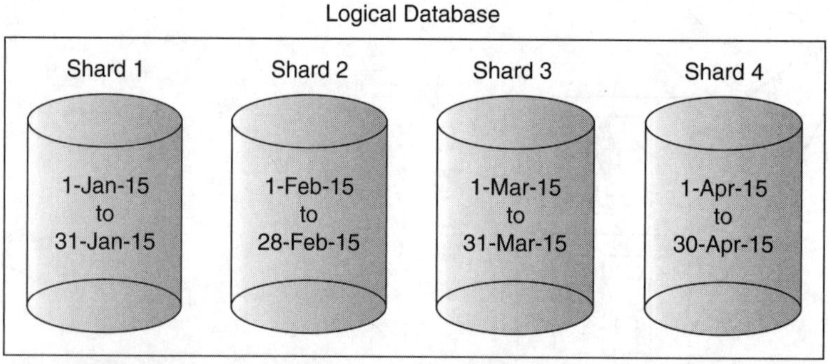

Logical Database

**Figure 7.9**  *Horizontal sharding splits a database by document or row and distributes sections of the database, known as shards, to different servers. When a cluster implements replication, a single shard will be available on multiple servers.*

Sharding offers a number of advantages when implementing large document databases. A large number of users or other heavy loads on a single server can tax the available CPU, memory, and bandwidth. One way to address this is to deploy a larger server with more CPU cores, more memory, and more bandwidth.

This solution, referred to as vertical scaling, can require significantly more money and time than sharding. Additional servers can be added to a cluster as demand for a document database grows. Existing servers are not replaced but continue to be used.

To implement sharding, database designers have to select a shard key and a partitioning method. These topics are discussed in the next sections.

**Separating Data with Shard Keys**

A *shard key* is one or more keys or fields that exist in all documents in a collection that is used to separate documents. A shard key could be virtually any atomic field in a document:

- Unique document ID

- Name

- Date, such as creation date

- Category or type

- Geographical region

❖ **Note** In spite of the discussion that document databases are schemaless, some elements of document databases parallel the schema of relational databases. The use of indexes is one such parallel. Indexes are part of the physical data model of a relational database, which means there is a data structure in the database that implements the index. Indexes are part of the schema of relational databases. Schemaless databases, such as document databases, can have schemalike objects such as indexes as well. Indexes help improve the speed of read operations and are useful when implementing sharding. Because all documents in a collection need to be placed into a shard, it is important for all documents to have the shard key.

The shard key specifies the values to use when grouping documents into different shards. The partitioning algorithm uses the shard key as input and determines the appropriate shard for that key (see Figure 7.10).

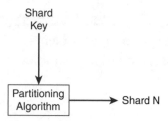

**Figure 7.10**    *Shard keys are input to the partitioning algorithm that outputs a shard.*

## Distributing Data with a Partitioning Algorithm

There are a number of different ways to horizontally partition data, including

- Range

- Hash

- List

A range partition is useful when you have an ordered set of values for shard keys, such as dates and numbers. For example, if all documents in a collection had a creation date field, it could be used to partition documents into monthly shards. Documents created between January 1, 2015, and January 31, 2015, would go into one shard, whereas documents created between February 1, 2015, and February 28, 2015, would go into another.

> ❖ **Note**  Business intelligence and other analytic systems that produce time-based reports—for example, a report comparing this month's sales with last month's sales—often use time-based range partitioning.

A hash partition uses a hash function to determine where to place a document. Hash functions are designed to generate values evenly across the range of values of the hash function. If, for example, you have an eight-server cluster, and your hash function generated values between 1 and 8, you should have roughly equal numbers of documents placed on all eight servers.

List-based partitioning uses a set of values to determine where to place data. You can imagine a product database with several types, including electronics, appliances, household goods, books, and clothes. These product types could be used as a shard key to allocate documents across five different servers.

If you needed even more partitions, you could combine product types with some other field, such as sales region, which could have values such as northeast, southeast, midwest, northwest, and southwest. Each of the five product types could be used with each of the five sales regions to create 25 possible shards, including

- Electronic—northeast
- Electronics—southeast
- Electronics—midwest
- Electronics—southwest
- Electronics—northwest
- Appliances—northeast
- Appliances—southeast
- Appliances—midwest
- And so forth...

Sharding is a fundamental process that enables many document databases to scale to meet demands of applications with a large number of users or other heavy loads. Vertical partitioning is possible with document databases. Horizontal partitioning, or sharding, is widely used.

Developers using document databases can choose keys to use for sharding. However, the developers of document database management systems are the ones who choose the sharding algorithms provided in the database.

The final section of this chapter introduces a few terms that do not fit well into any of the previous sections, but are important to understand before moving on to the document database modeling discussion in Chapter 8, "Designing for Document Databases."

# Data Modeling and Query Processing

Document databases are flexible. They can accommodate a wide range of document types and variations within document collections. If you were to sit down right now and start designing a document database, you would probably start with a list of queries you would like to run against your database. (At least that is one good way to start.) If you were designing a relational database, you would probably start by thinking about the entities you have to model and their relationship to each other.

After you have a basic understanding of the entities and their relations, you would probably engage in an exercise known as normalization. If you experience performance problems with your database, you might engage in a process known as denormalization. This process would be guided, to some degree, about what you learn about poorly performing queries by reviewing the output of the query processor.

You should be familiar with normalization and denormalization because you will likely encounter these terms when modeling document databases. The processes are less formal with document databases than relational databases so the explanations here will be much simpler than you would find in a book on relational databases.

Document databases also implement query processors to attempt to find the optimal sequence of steps to retrieve data specified by a query.

## Normalization

*Database normalization* is the process of organizing data into tables in such a way as to reduce the potential for data anomalies. An *anomaly* is an inconsistency in the data. For example, consider if your database had a table like the one shown in Table 7.1. A user queries the database for the address of a customer named Janice Washington. What address(es) should be returned?

**Table 7.1**   *User Address Queries*

| Order Number | Customer Name | Customer Address |
|---|---|---|
| 9837373 | Janice Washington | 873 Morton Dr, Houston, TX |
| 9837374 | Robert Denison | 1984 NE 34th Ave Apt 23, Portland, OR |
| 9837375 | Hu Zhang | 415 Commonwealth Ave, Boston, MA |
| 9837376 | Janice Washington | 187 River St, Seattle, WA |

The query could return 873 Morton Dr, Houston, TX; 187 River St, Seattle, WA; or both. It is possible that Janice Washington resides at both addresses, but it is also possible that one is a current address and one is a prior address. There is no indication in Table 7.1.

Normalization reduces the amount of redundant data in the database. Rather than repeat customer names and addresses with each order, those attributes would be placed in their own tables. Additional attributes could be associated with both customers and addresses. In particular, the address table could have an active address indicator to identify which of multiple addresses are current.

There are several rules for normalizing databases. Databases are said to be in different normal form depending on how many of the normalization rules are followed. It is common for data modelers to design to something called Third Normal Form, which means the first three rules of normalization are followed.[1]

Normalization is sometimes used to describe the way you design documents. When designers use multiple collections to store related data, it is considered normalized.

Normalized documents imply that you will have references to other documents so you can look up additional information. For example, a server log document might have a field with the identifier of the server that generates log event data. A collection of server documents would have additional information about each server so it does not have to be repeated in each log event document (see Figure 7.11).

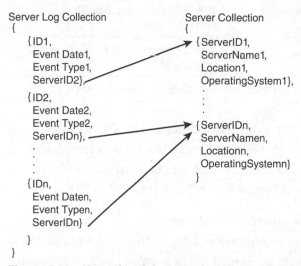

**Figure 7.11**    *Normalized documents reduce redundant data by referencing a single copy of data rather than repeating it in each document.*

---

1. For a basic introduction to normalization, see William Kent "A Simple Guide to Five Normal Forms in Relational Database Theory." September, 1982. http://www.bkent.net/Doc/simple5.htm

## Denormalization

Normalization helps avoid data anomalies, but it can cause performance problems. This is especially true if you have to look up data in two or more large tables. This process is called *joining*, and it is a basic operation in relational databases. A great deal of effort has gone into developing efficient ways to join data. Database administrators and data modelers can spend substantial amounts of time trying to improve the performance of join operations. It does not always lead to improvement.

Designing databases entails trade-offs. You could design a highly normalized database with no redundant data but suffer poor performance. When that happens, many designers turn to denormalization.

As the name implies, denormalization undoes normalization—specifically, it introduces redundant data. You might wonder, why introduce redundant data? It can cause data anomalies like that in Table 7.1. It obviously requires more storage to keep redundant copies of data. The reason to risk data anomalies and use additional storage is that denormalization can significantly improve performance.

When data is denormalized, there is no need to read data from multiple tables and perform joins on the data from the multiple collections. Instead, data is retrieved from a single collection or document. This can be much faster than retrieving from multiple collections, especially when indexes are available.

## Query Processor

Getting data from a document database is more complicated than getting it from key-value databases. Remember, if you have a key, you can retrieve an associated value from a key-value database.

Document databases offer more options for retrieving data. For example, you could retrieve documents created before a particular date, or documents that are a specific type, documents that contain the string "long distance running" in a product description, or some combination of all of these.

The query processor is an important part of a database management system. It takes as input queries and data about the documents and collections in the database and produces a sequence of operations that retrieve the selected data.

Key-value databases do not need query processors; they function by looking up values by keys. There is no need to analyze logical statements such as the following:

```
(createDate > '1-Jan-2015') AND (productType =
  'electronics')
```

When there can be multiple conditions on selecting documents, the query processor must make decisions, such as which criteria it should apply first. Should it find all documents with a creation date greater than January 1, 2015, or should it retrieve all documents about electronics products?

If there are fewer documents with a creation date after January 1, 2015, than there are documents with an electronics type, then it would make sense to retrieve documents based on creation date because it will return fewer documents than the other criteria. This means the second criterion is applied to a smaller number of documents.

This is a simple example of the kinds of options a query processor evaluates as it builds its plan to retrieve data.

# Summary

Document databases have some terminology specific to their type of NoSQL database, but they also share vocabulary with other NoSQL databases as well as relational databases. Documents parallel rows in relational tables, whereas collections are comparable to tables in relational tables. Partitioning, especially sharding, is used in document databases to split large databases over multiple servers to improve performance. Normalization, denormalization, and query processors also play crucial roles in the overall performance of document databases.

Chapter 8 delves into design issues particular to document databases.

# Review Questions

1. Describe how documents are analogous to rows in relational databases.

2. Describe how collections are analogous to tables in relational databases.

3. Define a schema.

4. Why are document databases considered schemaless?

5. Why are document databases considered polymorphic?

6. How does vertical partitioning differ from horizontal partitioning, or sharding?

7. What is a shard key?

8. What is the purpose of the partitioning algorithm in sharding?

9. What is normalization?

10. Why would you want to denormalize collections in a document database?

# References

Brewer, Eric. "CAP Twelve Years Later: How the 'Rules' Have Changed." Computer vol. 45, no. 2 (Feb 2012): 23–29.

Brewer, Eric A. "Towards Robust Distributed Systems." *PODC*. vol. 7. 2000.

Chodorow, Kristina. *50 Tips and Tricks for MongoDB Developers*. Sebastopol, CA: O'Reilly Media, Inc., 2011.

Chodorow, Kristina. *MongoDB: The Definitive Guide*. Sebastopol, CA: O'Reilly Media, Inc., 2013.

Copeland, Rick. *MongoDB Applied Design Patterns*. Sebastopol, CA: O'Reilly Media, Inc., 2013.

Couchbase. Couchbase Documentation: http://docs.couchbase.com/.

Han, Jing, et al. "Survey on NoSQL Database." Pervasive computing and applications (ICPCA), 2011 6th International Conference on IEEE, 2011.

MongoDB. MongoDB 2.6 Manual: http://docs.mongodb.org/manual/.

O'Higgins, Niall. *MongoDB and Python: Patterns and Processes for the Popular Document-Oriented Database*. Sebastopol, CA: O'Reilly Media, Inc., 2011.

# Designing for Document Databases

*"Making good decisions is a crucial skill at every level."*
—Peter Drucker
Author and Management Consultant

## Topics Covered In This Chapter

Normalization, Denormalization, and the Search for Proper Balance

Planning for Mutable Documents

The Goldilocks Zone of Indexes

Modeling Common Relations

Case Study: Customer Manifests

Designers have many options when it comes to designing document databases. The flexible structure of JSON and XML documents is a key factor in this—flexibility. If a designer wants to embed lists within lists within a document, she can. If another designer wants to create separate collections to separate types of data, then he can. This freedom should not be construed to mean all data models are equally good—they are not.

The goal of this chapter is to help you understand ways of assessing document database models and choosing the best techniques for your needs.

Relational database designers can reference rules of normalization to help them assess data models. A typical relational data model is designed to avoid data anomalies when inserts, updates, or deletes are performed. For example, if a database maintained multiple copies of a customer's current address, it is possible that one or more of those addresses are updated but others are not. In that case, which of the current databases is actually the current one?

In another case, if you do not store customer information separately from the customer's orders, then all records of the customer could be deleted if all her orders are deleted. The rules for avoiding these anomalies are logical and easy to learn from example.

> ❖ **Note** Document database modelers depend more on heuristics, or rules of thumb, when designing databases. The rules are not formal, logical rules like normalization rules. You cannot, for example, tell by looking at a description of a document database model whether or not it will perform efficiently. You must consider how users will query the database, how much inserting will be done, and how often and in what ways documents will be updated.

In this chapter, you learn about normalization and denormalization and how it applies to document database modeling. You also learn about the impact of updating documents, especially when the size of documents changes. Indexes can significantly improve query response times, but this must be balanced against the extra time that is needed to update indexes when documents are inserted or updated. Several design patterns have emerged in the practice of document database design. These are introduced and discussed toward the end of the chapter.

This chapter concludes with a case study covering the use of a document database for tracking the contents of shipments made by the fictitious transportation company introduced in earlier chapters.

# Normalization, Denormalization, and the Search for Proper Balance

Unless you have worked with relational databases, you probably would not guess that normalization has to do with eliminating redundancy. Redundant data is considered a bad, or at least undesirable, thing in the theory of relational database design. Redundant data is the root of anomalies, such as two current addresses when only one is allowed.

In theory, a data modeler will want to eliminate redundancy to minimize the chance of introducing anomalies. As Albert Einstein observed, "In theory, theory and practice are the same. In practice, they are not." There are times where performance in relational databases is poor because of the normalized model. Consider the data model shown in Figure 8.1.

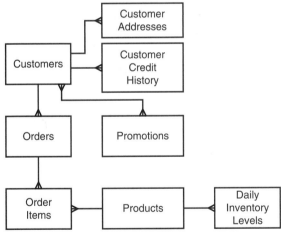

**Figure 8.1** *Normalized databases have separate tables for entities. Data about entities is isolated and redundant data is avoided.*

Figure 8.1 depicts a simple normalized model of customers, orders, and products. Even this simple model requires eight tables to capture a basic set of data about the entities. These include the following:

- Customers table with fields such as name, customer ID, and so on

- Loyalty Program Members, with fields such as date joined, amount spent since joining, and customer ID

- Customer Addresses, with fields such as street, city, state, start date, end date, and customer ID

- Customer Credit Histories report with fields such as credit category, start date, end date, and customer ID

- Orders, with fields such as order ID, customer ID, ship date, and so on

- Order Items, with fields such as order ID, order item ID, product ID, quantity, cost, and so on

- Products, with fields such as product ID, product name, product description, and so on

- Daily Inventory Levels, with fields such as product ID, date, quantity available, and so on

- Promotions, with fields such as promotion ID, promotion description, start date, and so on

- Promotion to Customers, with fields such as promotion ID and customer ID

Each box in Figure 8.1 represents an entity in the data model. The lines between entities indicate the kind of relationship between the entities.

## One-to-Many Relations

When a single line ends at an entity, then one of those rows participates in a single relation. When there are three branching lines ending at an entity, then there are one or more rows in that relationship. For example, the relation between Customer and Orders indicates that a customer can have one or more orders, but there is only one customer associated with each order.

This kind of relation is called a one-to-many relationship.

## Many-to-Many Relations

Now consider the relation between Customers and Promotions. There are branching lines at both ends of the relationship. This indicates that customers can have many promotions associated with them. It also means that promotions can have many customers related to them. For example, a customer might receive promotions that are targeted to all customers in their geographic area as well as promotions targeted to the types of products the customer buys most frequently.

Similarly, a promotion will likely target many customers. The sales and marketing team might create promotions designed to improve the sale of headphones by targeting all customers who bought new phones or tablets in the past three months. The team might have a special offer on Bluetooth speakers for anyone who bought a laptop or desktop computer in the last year. Again, there will be many customers in this category (at least the sales team hopes so), so there will be many customers associated with this promotion.

These types of relations are known as many-to-many relationships.

## The Need for Joins

Developers of applications using relational databases often have to work with data from multiple tables. Consider the Order Items and Products entities shown in Figure 8.2.

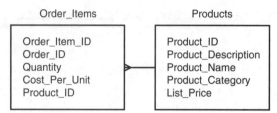

**Figure 8.2**   *Products and Order Items are in a one-to-many relationship. To retrieve Product data about an Order item, they need to share an attribute that serves as a common reference. In this case, Product_ID is the shared attribute.*

If you were designing a report that lists an order with all the items on the order, you would probably need to include attributes such as the name of the product, the cost per unit, and the quantity. The name of the product is in the Product table, and the other two attributes are in the Order Items table (see Figure 8.3).

❖ **Note** If you are familiar with the difference in logical and physical data models, you will notice a mix of terminology. Figures 8.1 and 8.2 depict logical models, and parts of these models are referred to as *entities* and *attributes*. If you were to write a report using the database, you would work with an implementation of the physical model.

For physical models, the terms *tables* and *columns* are used to refer to the same structures that are called *entities* and *attributes* in the logical data model. There are differences between entities and tables; for example, tables have locations on disks or in other data structures called table spaces. Entities do not have such properties.

For the purpose of this chapter, *entities* should be considered synonymous with *tables* and *attributes* should be considered synonymous with *columns*.

| Order Items | | | | |
|---|---|---|---|---|
| Order_Item_ID | Order_ID | Quantity | Cost_Per_Unit | Product_ID |
| 1298 | 789 | 1 | $25.99 | 345 |
| 1299 | 789 | 2 | $20.00 | 372 |
| 1300 | 790 | 1 | $12.50 | 591 |
| 1301 | 790 | 1 | $20.00 | 372 |
| 1302 | 790 | 3 | $12.99 | 413 |

| Products | | | | |
|---|---|---|---|---|
| Product_ID | Product_Description | Product_Name | Product_Category | List_Price |
| 345 | Easy clean tablet cover that fits most 10" Android tablets. | Easy Clean Cover | Electronic Accessories | 25.99 |
| 372 | Lightweight blue ear buds with comfort fit. | Acme Ear Buds | Electronic Accessories | 20 |
| 413 | Set of 10 dry erase markers. | 10-Pack Markers | Office Supplies | 15 |
| 420 | 60"×48" whiteboard with marker and eraser holder. | Large Whiteboard | Office Supplies | 56.99 |
| 591 | Pack of 100 individually wrapped screen wipes. | Screen Clean Wipes | Office Supplies | 12.99 |

**Figure 8.3** *To be joined, tables must share a common value known as a foreign key.*

In relational databases, modelers often start with designs like the one you saw earlier in Figure 8.1. Normalized models such as this minimize redundant data and avoid the potential for data anomalies. Document database designers, however, often try to store related data together in the same document. This would be equivalent to storing related data in one table of a relational database. You might wonder why data modelers choose different approaches to their design. It has to do with the trade-offs between performance and potential data anomalies.

To understand why normalizing data models can adversely affect performance, let's look at an example with multiple joins.

## Executing Joins: The Heavy Lifting of Relational Databases

Imagine you are an analyst and you have decided to develop a promotion for customers who have bought electronic accessories in the past 12 months. The first thing you want to do is understand who those customers are, where they live, and how often they buy from your business. You can do this by querying the Customer table.

You do not want all customers, though—just those who have bought electronic accessories. That information is not stored in the Customer table, so you look to the Orders table. The Orders table has some information you need, such as the date of purchase. This enables you to filter for only orders made in the past 12 months.

The Orders table, however, does not have information on electronic accessories, so you look to the Order Items table. This does not have the information you are looking for, so you turn to the Products table. Here, you find the information you need. The Products table has a column called Product_Category, which indicates if a product is an electronic accessory or some other product category. You can use this column to filter for electronic accessory items.

At this point, you have all the data you need. The Customer table has information about customers, such as their names and customer IDs. The Orders table has order date information, so you can select only orders from the past 12 months. It also allows you to join to the Order_Items table, which can tell you which orders contained products in the electronic accessories category. The category information is not directly available in the Order_Items table, but you can join the Order_Items table to the Products table to get the product category (see Figure 8.4).

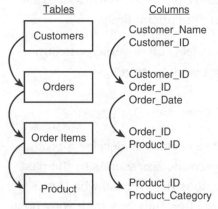

**Figure 8.4**   *Analyzing customers who bought a particular type of product requires three joins between four tables.*

To get a sense of how much work is involved in joining tables, let's consider pseudocode for printing the name of customers who have purchased electronic accessories in the last 12 months:

```
for cust in get_customers():
   for order in get_customer_orders(cust.customer_id):
      if today() - 365 <= order.order_date:
         for order_item in get_order_items
            (order.order_id):
            if 'electronic accessories' =
               get_product_category(order_item.product_id):
                  customer_set = add_item
                     (customer_set,cust.name);

for customer_name in customer_set:
   print customer_name;
```

In this example, the functions get _ customers, get _ customer _ orders, and get _ order _ items return a list of rows. In the case of get _ customers(), all customers are returned.

Each time get _ customer _ orders is called, it is given a customer _ id. Only orders with that customer ID are returned. Each time get _ order _ items is called, it is given an order _ id. Only order items with that order _ id are returned.

The dot notation indicates a field in the row returned. For example, order.order _ date returns the order _ date on a particular order. Similarly, cust.name returns the name of the customer currently referenced by the cust variable.

### Executing Joins Example

Now to really see how much work is involved, let's walk through an example. Let's assume there are 10,000 customers in the database. The first for loop will execute 10,000 times. Each time it executes, it will look up all orders for the customer. If each of the 10,000 customers has, on average, 10 orders, then the `for order` loop will execute 100,000 times. Each time it executes, it will check the order date.

Let's say there are 20,000 orders that have been placed in the last year. The `for order _ item` loop will execute 20,000 times. It will perform a check and add a customer name to a set of customer names if at least one of the order items was an electronic accessory.

Looping through rows of tables and looking for matches is one—rather inefficient—way of performing joins. The performance of this join could be improved. For example, indexes could be used to more quickly find all orders placed within the last year. Similarly, indexes could be used to find the products that are in the electronic accessory category.

Databases implement query optimizers to come up with the best way of fetching and joining data. In addition to using indexes to narrow down the number of rows they have to work with, they may use other techniques to match rows. They could, for example, calculate hash values of foreign keys to quickly determine which rows have matching values.

The query optimizer may also sort rows first and then merge rows from multiple tables more efficiently than if the rows were not sorted. These techniques can work well in some cases and not in others. Database researchers and vendors have made advances in query optimization techniques, but executing joins on large data sets can still be time consuming and resource intensive.

## What Would a Document Database Modeler Do?

Document data modelers have a different approach to data modeling than most relational database modelers. Document database modelers and application developers are probably using a document database for its scalability, its flexibility, or both. For those using document databases, avoiding data anomalies is still important, but they are willing to assume more responsibility to prevent them in return for scalability and flexibility.

For example, if there are redundant copies of customer addresses in the database, an application developer could implement a customer address update function that updates all copies of an address. She would always use that function to update an address to avoid introducing a data anomaly. As you can see, developers will write more code to avoid anomalies in a document database, but will have less need for database tuning and query optimization in the future.

So how do document data modelers and application developers get better performance? They minimize the need for joins. This process is known as denormalization. The basic idea is that data models should store data that is used together in a single data structure, such as a table in a relational database or a document in a document database.

**The Joy of Denormalization**

To see the benefits of denormalization, let's start with a simple example: order items and products. Recall that the `Order _ Items` entity had the following attributes:

- `order _ item _ ID`
- `order _ id`
- `quantity`
- `cost _ per _ unit`
- `product _ id`

The Products entity has the following attributes:

- `product _ ID`
- `product _ description`
- `product _ name`
- `product _ category`
- `list _ price`

An example of an order items document is

```
{
order_item_ID : 834838,
    order_ID: 8827,
    quantity: 3,
    cost_per_unit: 8.50,
    product_ID: 3648
}
```

An example of a product document is

```
{
    product_ID: 3648,
    product_description: "1 package laser printer paper.
      100% recycled.",
    product_name : "Eco-friendly Printer Paper",
    product_category : "office supplies",
    list_price : 9.00
}
```

If you implemented two collections and maintained these separate documents, then you would have to query the order items collection for the order item you were interested in and then query the products document for information about the product with `product _ ID 3648`. You would perform two lookups to get the information you need about one order item.

By denormalizing the design, you could create a collection of documents that would require only one lookup operation. A denormalized version of the order item collection would have, for example:

```
  {
order_item_ID : 834838,
    order_ID: 8827,
    quantity: 3,
    cost_per_unit: 8.50,
    product :
         {
```

```
            product_description: "1 package laser printer
               paper. 100% recycled.",
            product_name : "Eco-friendly Printer Paper",
            product_category : "office supplies",
            list_price : 9.00
        }
}
```

❖ **Note** Notice that you no longer need to maintain `product _ ID`
fields. Those were used as database references (or foreign keys in
relational database parlance) in the `Order _ Items` document.

### Avoid Overusing Denormalization

Denormalization, like all good things, can be used in excess. The goal
is to keep data that is frequently used together in the document. This
allows the document database to minimize the number of times it
must read from persistent storage, a relatively slow process even when
using solid state devices (SSDs). At the same time, you do not want to
allow extraneous information to creep into your denormalized collection (see Figure 8.5).

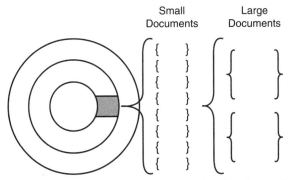

**Figure 8.5** *Large documents can lead to fewer documents retrieved when a
block of data is read from persistent storage. This can increase the total number
of data block reads to retrieve a collection or subset of collections.*

To answer the question "how much denormalization is too much?" you should consider the queries your application will issue to the document database.

Let's assume you will use two types of queries: one to generate invoices and packing slips for customers and one to generate management reports. Also, assume that 95% of the queries will be in the invoice and packing slip category and 5% of the queries will be for management reports.

Invoices and packing slips should include, among other fields, the following:

- order_ID

- quantity

- cost_per_unit

- product_name

Management reports tend to aggregate information across groups or categories. For these reports, queries would include product category information along with aggregate measures, such as total number sold. A management report showing the top 25 selling products would likely include a product description.

Based on these query requirements, you might decide it is better to not store product description, list price, and product category in the Order _ Items collection. The next version of the Order _ Items document would then look like this:

```
{
    order_item_ID : 834838,
    order_ID: 8827,
    quantity: 3,
    cost_per_unit: 8.50,
    product_name : "Eco-friendly Printer Paper"
}
```

and we would maintain a `Products` collection with all the relevant product details; for example:

```
{
    product_description: "1 package laser printer paper.
      100% recycled.",
    product_name : "Eco-friendly Printer Paper",
    product_category : 'office supplies',
    list_price : 9.00
}
```

Product _ name is stored redundantly in both the `Order _ Items` collection and in the `Products` collection. This model uses slightly more storage but allows application developers to retrieve information for the bulk of their queries in a single lookup operation.

### Just Say No to Joins, Sometimes

Never say never when designing NoSQL models. There are best practices, guidelines, and design patterns that will help you build scalable and maintainable applications. None of them should be followed dogmatically, especially in the presence of evidence that breaking those best practices, guidelines, or design patterns will give your application better performance, more functionality, or greater maintainability.

If your application requirements are such that storing related information in two or more collections is an optimal design choice, then make that choice. You can implement joins in your application code. A worst-case scenario is joining two large collections with two `for` loops, such as

```
for doc1 in collection1:
    for doc2 in collection2:
        <do something with both documents>
```

If there are *N* documents in collection1 and *M* documents in collection2, this statement would execute N × M times. The execution time for such loops can grow quickly. If the first collection has 100,000 documents and the second has 500,000, then the statement would execute 50,000,000,000 ($5 \times 10^5$) times. If you are dealing with collections this large, you will want to use indexes, filtering, and, in some cases, sorting to optimize your join by reducing the number of overall operations performed (see Figure 8.6).

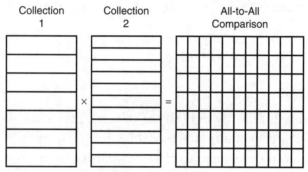

Collection 1 × Collection 2 = All-to-All Comparison

**Figure 8.6** *Simple join operations that compare all documents in one collection to all documents in another collection can lead to poor performance on large collections. Joins such as this can be improved by using indexes, filtering, and, in some cases, sorting.*

Normalization is a useful technique for reducing the chances of introducing data anomalies. Denormalization is also useful, but for (obviously) different reasons. Specifically, denormalization is employed to improve query performance. When using document databases, data modelers and developers often employ denormalization as readily as relational data modelers employ normalization.

> ❖ **Tip** Remember to use your queries as a guide to help strike the right balance of normalization and denormalization. Too much of either can adversely affect performance. Too much normalization leads to queries requiring joins. Too much denormalization leads to large documents that will likely lead to unnecessary data reads from persistent storage and other adverse effects.

There is another less-obvious consideration to keep in mind when designing documents and collections: the potential for documents to change size. Documents that are likely to change size are known as mutable documents.

# Planning for Mutable Documents

Things change. Things have been changing since the Big Bang. Things will most likely continue to change. It helps to keep these facts in mind when designing databases.

Some documents will change frequently, and others will change infrequently. A document that keeps a counter of the number of times a web page is viewed could change hundreds of times per minute. A table that stores server event log data may only change when there is an error in the load process that copies event data from a server to the document database. When designing a document database, consider not just how frequently a document will change, but also how the size of the document may change.

Incrementing a counter or correcting an error in a field will not significantly change the size of a document. However, consider the following scenarios:

- Trucks in a company fleet transmit location, fuel consumption, and other operating metrics every three minutes to a fleet management database.

- The price of every stock traded on every exchange in the world is checked every minute. If there is a change since the last check, the new price information is written to the database.

- A stream of social networking posts is streamed to an application, which summarizes the number of posts; overall sentiment of the post; and the names of any companies, celebrities, public officials, or organizations. The database is continuously updated with this information.

Over time, the number of data sets written to the database increases. How should an application designer structure the documents to handle such input streams? One option is to create a new document for each new set of data. In the case of the trucks transmitting operational data, this would include a truck ID, time, location data, and so on:

```
{
    truck_id: 'T87V12',
    time: '08:10:00',
    date :  '27-May-2015',
    driver_name: 'Jane Washington',
    fuel_consumption_rate: '14.8 mpg',
    ...
}
```

Each truck would transmit 20 data sets per hour, or assuming a 10-hour operations day, 200 data sets per day. The truck _ id, date, and driver _ name would be the same for all 200 documents. This looks like an obvious candidate for embedding a document with the operational data in a document about the truck used on a particular day. This could be done with an array holding the operational data documents:

```
{
    truck_id: 'T87V12',
    date :  '27-May-2015',
    driver_name: 'Jane Washington',
    operational_data:
            [
                {time : '00:01',
                 fuel_consumption_rate: '14.8 mpg',
                 ...},
                 {time : '00:04',
                 fuel_consumption_rate: '12.2 mpg',
                 ...},
                 {time : '00:07',
                 fuel_consumption_rate: '15.1 mpg',
                 ...},
            ...]
}
```

The document would start with a single operational record in the array, and at the end of the 10-hour shift, it would have 200 entries in the array.

From a logical modeling perspective, this is a perfectly fine way to structure the document, assuming this approach fits your query requirements. From a physical model perspective, however, there is a potential performance problem.

When a document is created, the database management system allocates a certain amount of space for the document. This is usually enough to fit the document as it exists plus some room for growth. If the document grows larger than the size allocated for it, the document may be moved to another location. This will require the database management system to read the existing document and copy it to another location, and free the previously used storage space (see Figure 8.7).

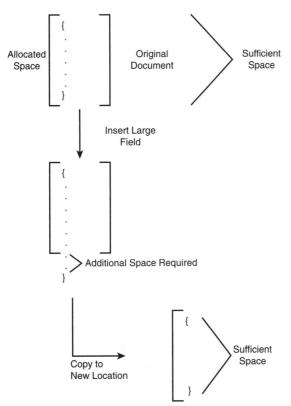

**Figure 8.7**   *When documents grow larger than the amount of space allocated for them, they may be moved to another location. This puts additional load on the storage systems and can adversely affect performance.*

## Avoid Moving Oversized Documents

One way to avoid this problem of moving oversized documents is to allocate sufficient space for the document at the time the document is created. In the case of the truck operations document, you could create the document with an array of 200 embedded documents with the time and other fields specified with default values. When the actual data is transmitted to the database, the corresponding array entry is updated with the actual values (see Figure 8.8).

```
                         {truck_id: 'T8V12'
                          date: '27-May-2015'
                          operational_data:
                              [{time: '00 : 00',
                                fuel_consumption_rate: 0.0}
                               {time: '00 : 00',
                                fuel_consumption_rate: 0.0}
     200 Embedded                   .
     Documents with                 .
     Default Values                 .
                                    .
                               {time: '00 : 00',
                                fuel_consumption_rate: 0.0}
                               ]
```

**Figure 8.8**    *Creating documents with sufficient space for anticipated growth reduces the need to relocate documents.*

Consider the life cycle of a document and when possible plan for anticipated growth. Creating a document with sufficient space for the full life of the document can help to avoid I/O overhead.

# The Goldilocks Zone of Indexes

Astronomers have coined the term *Goldilocks Zone* to describe the zone around a star that could sustain a habitable planet. In essence, the zone that is not too close to the sun (too hot) or too far away (too cold) is just right. When you design a document database, you also want to try to identify the right number of indexes. You do not want too few, which could lead to poor read performance, and you do not want too many, which could lead to poor write performance.

## Read-Heavy Applications

Some applications have a high percentage of read operations relative to the number of write operations. Business intelligence and other analytic applications can fall into this category. Read-heavy applications should have indexes on virtually all fields used to help filter results. For example, if it was common for users to query documents from a particular sales region or with order items in a certain product category, then the sales region and product category fields should be indexed.

It is sometimes difficult to know which fields will be used to filter results. This can occur in business intelligence applications. An analyst may explore data sets and choose a variety of different fields as filters. Each time he runs a new query, he may learn something new that leads him to issue another query with a different set of filter fields. This iterative process can continue as long as the analyst gains insight from queries.

Read-heavy applications can have a large number of indexes, especially when the query patterns are unknown. It is not unusual to index most fields that could be used to filter results in an analytic application (see Figure 8.9).

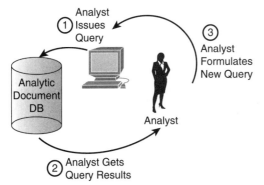

**Figure 8.9** *Querying analytic databases is an iterative process. Virtually any field could potentially be used to filter results. In such cases, indexes may be created on most fields.*

## Write-Heavy Applications

Write-heavy applications are those with relatively high percentages of write operations relative to read operations. The document database that receives the truck sensor data described previously would likely be a write-heavy database. Because indexes are data structures that must be created and updated, their use will consume CPU, persistent storage, and memory resources and increase the time needed to insert or update a document in the database.

Data modelers tend to try to minimize the number of indexes in write-heavy applications. Essential indexes, such as those created for fields storing the identifiers of related documents, should be in place. As with other design choices, deciding on the number of indexes in a write-heavy application is a matter of balancing competing interests.

Fewer indexes typically correlate with faster updates but potentially slower reads. If users performing read operations can tolerate some delay in receiving results, then minimizing indexes should be considered. If, however, it is important for users to have low-latency queries against a write-heavy database, consider implementing a second database that aggregates the data according to the time-intensive read queries. This is the basic model used in business intelligence.

Transaction processing systems are designed for fast writes and targeted reads. Data is copied from that database using an extraction, transformation, and load (ETL) process and placed in a data mart or data warehouse. The latter two types of databases are usually heavily indexed to improve query response time (see Figure 8.10).

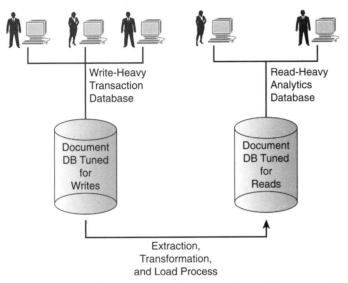

**Figure 8.10** *When both write-heavy and read-heavy applications must be supported, a two-database solution may be the best option.*

❖ **Tip** Identifying the right set of indexes for your application can take some experimentation. Start with the queries you expect to support and implement indexes to reduce the time needed to execute the most important and the most frequently executed. If you find the need for both read-heavy and write-heavy applications, consider a two-database solution with one database tuned for each type.

## Modeling Common Relations

As you gather requirements and design a document database, you will likely find the need for one or more of three common relations:

- One-to-many relations

- Many-to-many relations

- Hierarchies

The first two involve relations between two collections, whereas the third can entail an arbitrary number of related documents within a collection. You learned about one-to-one and one-to-many relations previously in the discussion of normalization. At that point, the focus was on the need for joins when normalizing data models. Here, the focus is on how to efficiently implement such relationships in document databases. The following sections discuss design patterns for modeling these three kinds of relations.

## One-to-Many Relations in Document Databases

One-to-many relations are the simplest of the three relations. This relation occurs when an instance of an entity has one or more related instances of another entity. The following are some examples:

- One order can have many order items.

- One apartment building can have many apartments.

- One organization can have many departments.

- One product can have many parts.

This is an example in which the typical model of document database differs from that of a relational database. In the case of a one-to-many relation, both entities are modeled using a document embedded within another document. For example:

```
{
    customer_id: 76123,
    name: 'Acme Data Modeling Services',
    person_or_business: 'business',
    address : [
                    { street: '276 North Amber St',
                        city: 'Vancouver',
                        state: 'WA',
                        zip: 99076} ,
```

```
{ street: '89 Morton St',
  city: 'Salem',
  state: 'NH',
  zip: 01097}
]
}
```

The basic pattern is that the *one* entity in a one-to-many relation is the primary document, and the *many* entities are represented as an array of embedded documents. The primary document has fields about the *one* entity, and the embedded documents have fields about the *many* entities.

## Many-to-Many Relations in Document Databases

A many-to-many relation occurs when instances of two entities can both be related to multiple instances of another entity. The following are some examples:

- Doctors can have many patients and patients can have many doctors.

- Operating system user groups can have many users and users can be in many operating system user groups.

- Students can be enrolled in many courses and courses can have many students enrolled.

- People can join many clubs and clubs can have many members.

Many-to-many relations are modeled using two collections—one for each type of entity. Each collection maintains a list of identifiers that reference related entities. For example, a document with course data would include an array of student IDs, and a student document would include a list of course IDs, as in the following:

**Courses:**

```
{
  { courseID: 'C1667',
    title: 'Introduction to Anthropology',
    instructor: 'Dr. Margret Austin',
    credits: 3,
    enrolledStudents: ['S1837', 'S3737', 'S9825' …
      'S1847'] },
  { courseID: 'C2873',
    title: 'Algorithms and Data Structures',
    instructor: 'Dr. Susan Johnson',
    credits: 3,
    enrolledStudents: ['S1837','S3737', 'S4321', 'S9825'
      … 'S1847'] },
  { courseID: C3876,
    title: 'Macroeconomics',
    instructor: 'Dr. James Schulen',
    credits: 3,
    enrolledStudents: ['S1837', 'S4321', 'S1470', 'S9825'
      … 'S1847'] },
  . . .
```

**Students:**

```
{
  {studentID:'S1837',
    name: 'Brian Nelson',
    gradYear: 2018,
    courses: ['C1667', C2873,'C3876']},
  {studentID: 'S3737',
    name: 'Yolanda Deltor',
        gradYear: 2017,
        courses: [ 'C1667','C2873']},
    …
}
```

The pattern minimizes duplicate data by referencing related documents with identifiers instead of embedded documents.

Care must be taken when updating many-to-many relationships so that both entities are correctly updated. Also remember that document databases will not catch referential integrity errors as a relational database will. Document databases will allow you to insert a student document with a courseID that does not correspond to an existing course.

## Modeling Hierarchies in Document Databases

Hierarchies describe instances of entities in some kind of parent-child or part-subpart relation. The product _ category attribute introduced earlier is an example where a hierarchy could help represent relations between different product categories (see Figure 8.11).

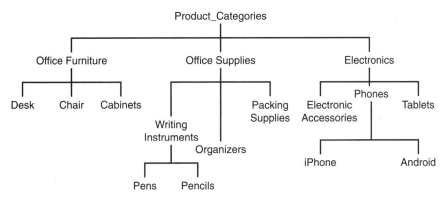

**Figure 8.11** *Hierarchies describe parent-child or part-subpart relations.*

There are a few different ways to model hierarchical relations. Each works well with particular types of queries.

### Parent or Child References

A simple technique is to keep a reference to either the parent or the children of an entity. Using the data depicted in Figure 8.11, you could model product categories with references to their parents:

```
{
    {productCategoryID: 'PC233', name:'Pencils',
       parentID:'PC72'},
    {productCategoryID: 'PC72', name:'Writing Instruments',
       parentID: 'PC37''},
```

```
    {productCategoryID: 'PC37', name:'Office Supplies',
       parentID: 'P01'},
    {productCategoryID: 'P01', name:'Product Categories' }
}
```

Notice that the root of the hierarchy, 'Product Categories', does not have a parent and so has no parent field in its document.

This pattern is useful if you frequently have to show a specific instance and then display the more general type of that category.

A similar pattern works with child references:

```
{
   {productCategoryID: 'P01', name:'Product Categories',
      childrenIDs: ['P37','P39','P41']},
   {productCategoryID: 'PC37', name:'Office Supplies',
      childrenIDs: ['PC72','PC73','PC74'']},
   {productCategoryID: 'PC72', name:'Writing
      Instruments', childrenIDs: ['PC233','PC234']'},
   {productCategoryID: 'PC233', name:'Pencils'}
}
```

The bottom nodes of the hierarchy, such as 'Pencils', do not have children and therefore do not have a childrenIDs field.

This pattern is useful if you routinely need to retrieve the children or subparts of the instance modeled in the document. For example, if you had to support a user interface that allowed users to drill down, you could use this pattern to fetch all the children or subparts of the current level of the hierarchy displayed in the interface.

### Listing All Ancestors

Instead of just listing the parent in a child document, you could keep a list of all ancestors. For example, the 'Pencils' category could be structured in a document as

```
{productCategoryID: 'PC233', name:'Pencils',
   ancestors:['PC72', 'PC37', 'P01']}
```

This pattern is useful when you have to know the full path from any point in the hierarchy back to the root.

An advantage of this pattern is that you can retrieve the full path to the root in a single read operation. Using a parent or child reference requires multiple reads, one for each additional level of the hierarchy.

A disadvantage of this approach is that changes to the hierarchy may require many write operations. The higher up in the hierarchy the change is, the more documents will have to be updated. For example, if a new level was introduced between 'Product Category' and 'Office Supplies', all documents below the new entry would have to be updated. If you added a new level to the bottom of the hierarchy—for example, below 'Pencils' you add 'Mechanical Pencils' and 'Non-mechanical Pencils'—then no existing documents would have to change.

> ❖ **Note** One-to-many, many-to-many, and hierarchies are common patterns in document databases. The patterns described here are useful in many situations, but you should always evaluate the utility of a pattern with reference to the kinds of queries you will execute and the expected changes that will occur over the lives of the documents. Patterns should support the way you will query and maintain documents by making those operations faster or less complicated than other options.

## Summary

This chapter concludes the examination of document databases by considering several key issues you should consider when modeling for document databases.

Normalization and denormalization are both useful practices. Normalization helps to reduce the chance of data anomalies while denormalization is introduced to improve performance. Denormalization is a common practice in document database modeling. One of the advantages of denormalization is that it reduces or eliminates the need for joins. Joins can be complex and/or resource-intensive operations. It helps to avoid them when you can, but there will likely be times you will have to implement joins in your applications. Document databases, as a rule, do not support joins.

In addition to considering the logical aspects of modeling, you should consider the physical implementation of your design. Mutable documents, in particular, can adversely affect performance. Mutable documents that grow in size beyond the storage allocated for them may have to be moved in persistent storage, such as on disks. This need for additional writing of data can slow down your applications' update operations.

Indexes are another important implementation topic. The goal is to have the right number of indexes for your application. All instances should help improve query performance. Indexes that would help with query performance may be avoided if they would adversely impact write performance in a noticeable way. You will have to balance benefits of faster query response with the cost of slower inserts and updates when indexes are in place.

Finally, it helps to use design patterns when modeling common relations such as one-to-many, many-to-many, and hierarchies. Sometimes embedded documents are called for, whereas in other cases, references to other document identifiers are a better option when modeling these relations.

Part IV, "Column Family Databases," introduces wide column databases. These are another important type of NoSQL database and are especially important for managing large data sets with potentially billions of rows and millions of columns.

# Case Study: Customer Manifests

Chapter 1, "Different Databases for Different Requirements," introduced TransGlobal Transport and Shipping (TGTS), a fictitious transportation company that coordinates the movement of goods around the globe for businesses of all sizes. As business has grown, TGTS is transporting and tracking more complicated and varied shipments. Analysts have gathered requirements and some basic estimates about the number of containers that will be shipped. They found a mix of common fields for all containers and specialized fields for different types of containers.

All containers will require a core set of fields such as customer name, origination facility, destination facility, summary of contents, number of items in container, a hazardous material indicator, an expiration date for perishable items such as fruit, a destination facility, and a delivery point of contact and contact information.

In addition, some containers will require specialized information. Hazardous materials must be accompanied by a material safety data sheet (MSDS), which includes information for emergency responders who may have to handle the hazardous materials. Perishable foods must also have details about food inspections, such as the name of the person who performed the inspection, the agency responsible for the inspection, and contact information of the agency.

The analyst found that 70%–80% of the queries would return a single manifest record. These are typically searched for by a manifest identifier or by customer name, date of shipment, and originating facility. The remaining 20%–30% would be mostly summary reports by customers showing a subset of common information. Occasionally, managers will run summary reports by type of shipment (for example, hazardous materials, perishable foods), but this is rarely needed.

Executives inform the analysts that the company has plans to substantially grow the business in the next 12 to 18 months. The analysts realize that they may have many different types of cargo in the future with specialized information, just as hazardous materials and perishable foods have specialized fields. They also realize they must plan for future scaling up and the need to support new fields in the database. They concluded that a document database that supports horizontal scaling and a flexible schema is required.

The analysts start the document and collection design process by considering fields that are common to most manifests. They decided on a collection called Manifests with the following fields:

- Customer name
- Customer contact person's name
- Customer address
- Customer phone number
- Customer fax
- Customer email
- Origination facility
- Destination facility
- Shipping date
- Expected delivery date
- Number of items in container

They also determine fields they should track for perishable foods and hazardous materials. They decide that both sets of specialized fields should be grouped into their own documents. The next question they have to decide is, should those documents be embedded with manifest documents or should they be in a separate collection?

## Embed or Not Embed?

The analysts review sample reports that managers have asked for and realize that the perishable foods fields are routinely reported along with the common fields in the manifest. They decide to embed the perishable foods within the manifest document.

They review sample reports and find no reference to the MSDS for hazardous materials. They ask a number of managers and executives about this apparent oversight. They are eventually directed to a compliance officer. She explains that the MSDS is required for all hazardous materials shipments. The company must demonstrate to regulators that their database includes MSDSs and must make the information available in the event of an emergency. The compliance officer and analyst conclude they need to define an additional report for facility managers who will run the report and print MSDS information in the event of an emergency.

Because the MSDS information is infrequently used, they decide to store it in a separate collection. The Manifest collection will include a field called msdsID that will reference the corresponding MSDS document. This approach has the added benefit that the compliance officer can easily run a report listing any hazardous material shipments that do not have an msdsID. This allows her to catch any missing MSDSs and continue to comply with regulations.

## Choosing Indexes

The analysts anticipate a mix of read and write operations with approximately 60%–65% reads and 35%–40% writes. They would like to maximize the speed of both reads and writes, so they carefully weigh the set of indexes to create.

Because most of the reads will be looks for single manifests, they decide to focus on that report first. The manifest identifier is a logical choice for index field because it is used to retrieve manifest doccuments.

Analysts can also look up manifests by customer name, shipment date, and origination facility. The analysts consider creating three indexes: one for each field. They realize, however, that they will rarely need to list all shipments by date or by origination facility, so they decide against separate indexes for those fields.

Instead, they create a single index on all three fields: customer name, shipment date, and origination facility. With this index, the database can determine if a manifest exists for a particular customer, shipping date, and origination facility by checking the index only; there is no need to check the actual collection of documents, thus reducing the number of read operations that have to be performed.

## Separate Collections by Type?

The analysts realize that they are working with a small number of manifest types, but there may be many more in the future. For example, the company does not ship frozen goods now, but there has been discussion about providing that service. The analysts know that if you frequently filter documents by type, it can be an indicator that they should use separate collections for each type.

They soon realize they are the exception to that rule because they do not know all the types they may have. The number of types can grow quite large, and managing a large number of collections is less preferable to managing types within a single collection.

By using requirements for reports and keeping in mind some basic design principles, the analysts are able to quickly create an initial schema for tracking a complex set of shipment manifests.

# Review Questions

1. What are the advantages of normalization?

2. What are the advantages of denormalization?

3. Why are joins such costly operations?

4. How do document database modelers avoid costly joins?

5. How can adding data to a document cause more work for the I/O subsystem in addition to adding the data to a document?

6. How can you, as a document database modeler, help avoid that extra work mentioned in Question 5?

7. Describe a situation where it would make sense to have many indexes on your document collections.

8. What would cause you to minimize the number of indexes on your document collection?

9. Describe how to model a many-to-many relationship.

10. Describe three ways to model hierarchies in a document database.

# References

Apache Foundation. Apache CouchDB 1.6 Documentation: http://docs.couchdb.org/en/1.6.1/.

Brewer, Eric. "CAP Twelve Years Later: How the 'Rules' Have Changed." Computer vol. 45, no. 2 (Feb 2012): 23–29.

Brewer, Eric A. "Towards Robust Distributed Systems." *PODC*. vol. 7. 2000.

Chodorow, Kristina. *50 Tips and Tricks for MongoDB Developers*. Sebastopol, CA: O'Reilly Media, Inc., 2011.

Chodorow, Kristina. *MongoDB: The Definitive Guide*. Sebastopol, CA: O'Reilly Media, Inc., 2013.

Copeland, Rick. *MongoDB Applied Design Patterns*. Sebastopol, CA: O'Reilly Media, Inc., 2013.

Couchbase. Couchbase Documentation: http://docs.couchbase.com/.

Han, Jing, et al. "Survey on NoSQL Database." Pervasive computing and applications (ICPCA), 2011 6th International Conference on IEEE, 2011.

MongoDB. MongoDB 2.6 Manual: http://docs.mongodb.org/manual/.

O'Higgins, Niall. *MongoDB and Python: Patterns and Processes for the Popular Document-Oriented Database*. Sebastopol, CA: O'Reilly Media, Inc., 2011.

OrientDB. OrientDB Manual, version 2.0: http://www.orientechnologies.com/docs/last/.

# ■■■■■■■■■■■ Part IV
# Column Family Databases

# Introduction to Column Family Databases

*"The family is one of nature's masterpieces."*
—GEORGE SANTAYANA
PHILOSOPHER

## Topics Covered In This Chapter

In the Beginning, There Was Google BigTable

Differences and Similarities to Key-Value and Document Databases

Architectures Used in Column Family Databases

When to Use Column Family Databases

Deciding what is Big Data or a large database is somewhat subjective. Are a million rows in a MySQL table a large database? To some it is, to others it is just an average, perhaps even small, table. There is little room for debate, however, when you start to get into the realm of billions of rows and tens of thousands of columns in a table. That is a very large database (VLDB) by any standard.

Relational databases might scale to VLDBs with a small set of large servers, but the cost would be prohibitive for most. Key-value databases have useful features for this scale of database, but lack support for organizing many columns and keeping frequently used data together. Document databases might scale[1] to this level but may not

---

1. Chris Biow, and Miles Ward. "PetaMongo: A Petabyte Database for as Little as $200." AWS re:Invent Conference, 2013. http://www.slideshare.net/mongodb/petamongo-a-petabyte-database-for-as-little-as-200.

have some of the features you might expect at this scale, such as a SQL-like query language.

Companies such as Google, Facebook, Amazon, and Yahoo! must contend with demands for very large database management solutions. In 2006, Google published a paper entitled "BigTable: A Distributed Storage System for Structured Data."[2] The paper described a new type of database, the column family database. Google designed this database for several of its large services, including web indexing, Google Earth, and Google Finance. BigTable became the model for implementing very large-scale NoSQL databases. Other column family databases include Cassandra, HBase, and Accumulo.

❖ **Note** Although the database community has standardized on the terms key value, document, and graph database, there is some variety in the terminology used with column family databases. The latter NoSQL databases are sometimes called wide column databases to emphasize their ability to manage tens of thousands (or more) of columns. They are also sometimes called *data stores* rather than *databases* because they lack some of the features of relational databases. This book uses the term *column family database* to (1) emphasize the importance of the column grouping function performed by column families and to (2) reinforce the idea that NoSQL databases are truly database management systems even when they lack some features of relational databases. Relational databases are popular and highly functional, but they do not define what constitutes a database or a database management system.

---

2. Fay Chang, et al. "BigTable: A Distributed Storage System for Structured Data." OSDI'06: Seventh Symposium on Operating System Design and Implementation, Seattle, WA, November, 2006. http://research.google.com/archive/bigtable.html.

# In the Beginning, There Was Google BigTable

The following are core features of Google BigTable:

- Developers have dynamic control over columns.

- Data values are indexed by row identifier, column name, and a time stamp.

- Data modelers and developers have control over location of data.

- Reads and writes of a row are atomic.

- Rows are maintained in a sorted order.

As Figure 9.1 shows, rows are composed of several column families. Each family consists of a set of related columns. For example, an address column family might contain

- Street address

- City

- State or province

- Postal code

- Country

Column families are organized into groups of data items that are frequently used together. Column families for a single row may or may not be near each other when stored on disk, but columns within a column family are kept together.

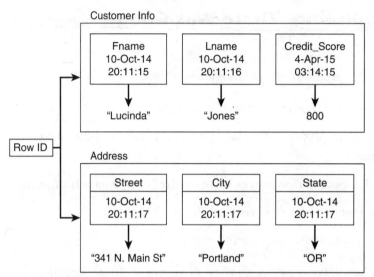

**Figure 9.1**    *A row in a column family database is organized as a set of column families. Column families consist of related columns; a data value is indexed by a row, a column name, and a time stamp.*

BigTable takes the middle ground with respect to defining data structures. A data modeler defines column families prior to implementing the database, but developers can dynamically add columns to a column family. There is no need to update a schema definition. From a developer's point of view, column families are analogous to relational tables and columns function like key-value pairs.

## Utilizing Dynamic Control over Columns

The use of column families and dynamic columns enables database modelers to define broad, course-grained structures (that is, column families) without anticipating all possible fine-grained variations in attributes. Consider the address column family described earlier.

Let's assume a company builds a column family database to store information about customers in the United States. The data modeler defines the address column family but no column names. The developer, who elicits detailed requirements from colleagues, determines that all customers are located in the United States. The developer adds a "State" column to the address column family. Several months later, the company expands its customer base into Canada, where regional governmental entities are known as provinces. The developer simply adds another column called "Province" to the database without having to wait for a data modeler to refine a database schema and update the database.

## Indexing by Row, Column Name, and Time Stamp

In BigTable, a data value is indexed by its row identifier, column name, and time stamp (see Figure 9.2). The row identifier is analogous to a primary key in a relational database. It uniquely identifies a row. Remember, a single row can have multiple column families. Unlike row-oriented relational databases that store all of a row's data values together, column family databases store only portions of rows together.

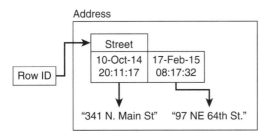

**Figure 9.2** *Data values are indexed by row identifier, column name, and time stamp. Multiple versions of a column value can exist. The latest version is returned by default when the column value is queried.*

The column name uniquely identifies a column. The time stamp orders versions of the column value. When a new value is written to a Big-Table database, the old value is not overwritten. Instead, a new value is added along with a time stamp. The time stamp allows applications to determine the latest version of a column value.

## Controlling Location of Data

You might recall discussions from earlier chapters about the speed with which data is retrieved based on where is it located on a disk. Database queries can cause the database management system to retrieve blocks of data from different parts of a disk. This can cause the database management system to wait while the disk spins to the proper position and the read/write head of the drive moves to the proper position as well.

One way to avoid the need to read multiple blocks of data located on different parts of the disk is to keep data close together when it is frequently used together. Turning back to the address example again, there are few cases in which you would want the street address of a customer but not want the city or state. It is logical to keep this data together. Column families serve this purpose. Columns families store columns together in persistent storage, making it more likely that reading a single data block can satisfy a query.

> ❖ **Caution** It might seem logical to keep streets, cities, and states close together on disks at all times, but that is not the case. Business intelligence systems, for example, often query for data by one of these attributes but not others. For example, a sales manager might issue a query to determine the number of tablets sold in the last month in the state of Colorado. There is no need to reference the city or street address of stores selling tablets. For applications such as these, data is more efficiently stored by columns. Columnar databases do just that. Instead of storing all data in a row together as row-oriented databases do or storing related groups of columns together, as column family databases do, columnar databases store columns of data together. Choosing a database management system with the appropriate storage model for your application is an important and early decision in application design (see Figure 9.3).

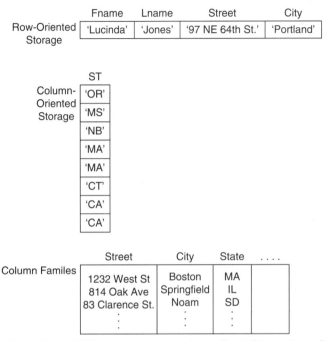

**Figure 9.3** *Different storage models offer different benefits. Choose a storage model that meets your query needs.*

## Reading and Writing Atomic Rows

The designers of BigTable decided to make all read and write operations atomic regardless of the number of columns read or written. This means that as you read a set of columns, you will be able to read all the columns needed or none of them. There are no partial results allowed with atomic operations (see Figure 9.4).

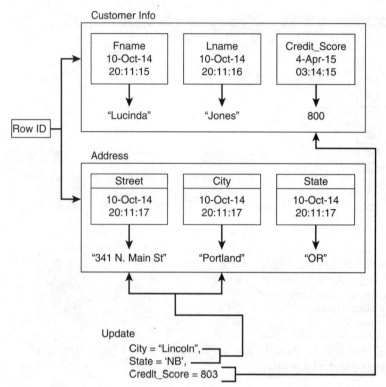

**Figure 9.4** *Read and write operations are atomic. All columns are read or written or none are.*

Similarly, if you update several columns in different column values, atomic writes guarantee that the write to all columns will succeed or they will all fail. You will never be left with partially written data. For example, if a customer moves from Portland, Oregon, to Lincoln, Nebraska, and you update the customer's address, you would never find a case in which the city changes from Portland to Lincoln but the state does not change from Oregon to Nebraska.

## Maintaining Rows in Sorted Order

BigTable maintains rows in sorted order. This makes it straightforward to perform range queries. Sales transactions, for example, may be ordered by date. When a user needs to retrieve a list of sales transactions for the past week, the data can be retrieved without sorting a large transaction table or using a secondary index that maintains date order.

Of course, you can only order a table in one way, so you must choose carefully when defining a sort order. The original BigTable implementation did not include support for multiple indexes on tables. You could define tables with the same information as a secondary index and manage that table yourself.

Google BigTable introduced a data management system designed to scale to petabytes of data using commodity hardware. The design balanced data modeling features with the need to scale. The designers of Google BigTable anticipated the need for hundreds of column families, tens of thousands (or more) columns, and billions of rows. As a result, the column family database has some features of key-value databases, document databases, and relational databases.

❖ **Note** Google BigTable is a good reference point for understanding column family databases. It is, however, only used by Google and is not publicly available. The two most widely used and publicly available column family databases are Cassandra (http://cassandra.apache.org/) and HBase (http://hbase.apache.org/).

HBase runs within the Hadoop ecosystem, whereas Cassandra is designed to function without Hadoop or other Big Data systems. Because Cassandra is the more independent of the two most popular column family databases, it will be used as the reference model for the remainder of the column family discussion.

# Differences and Similarities to Key-Value and Document Databases

Column family databases have characteristics similar to other NoSQL databases—key-value and document databases in particular. This is not surprising because all NoSQL databases were designed to address problems that challenged traditional relational databases. In addition, many NoSQL databases employ distributed database techniques to address scalability and availability concerns.

## Column Family Database Features

Key-value databases are the simplest of all NoSQL architectures. They consist of a keyspace, which is essentially a logical structure for isolating keys and values maintained for a particular purpose. You may implement a keyspace for each application, or you may have a single keyspace that is used by multiple applications. Whichever approach you choose, a keyspace is used to store related keys and their values.

Column families are analogous to keyspaces in key-value databases. Developers are free to add keys and values in key-value databases just as they are free to add columns and values to column families. In Cassandra terminology, a keyspace is analogous to a database in relational databases. In both key-value databases and Cassandra, a keyspace is the outermost logical structure used by data modelers and developers.

Unlike key-value databases, the values in columns are indexed by a row identifier as well as by a column name (and time stamp). (See Figure 9.5.)

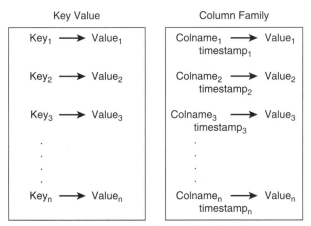

**Figure 9.5** *Keyspaces in key-value databases are analogous to column families in the way they maintain collections of attributes. Indexing, however, is different between the two database types.*

## Column Family Database Similarities to and Differences from Document Databases

Document databases extend the functionality found in key-value databases by allowing for highly structured and accessible data structures. Documents are analogous to rows in a relational database and store multiple fields of data, typically in a JSON or XML structure. You could also store JSON or XML strings in key-value databases, but those databases do not support querying based on contents of the JSON or XML string.

> ❖ **Note** Some key-value databases provide search engines to index the contents of JSON or XML documents stored as values, but this is not a standard component of key-value databases.

If you stored the following document in a key-value database, you could set or retrieve the entire document, but you could not query and extract a subset of the data, such as the address.

```
{
    "customer_id":187693,
    "name": "Kiera Brown",
    "address" : {
        "street" : "1232 Sandy Blvd.",
        "city" :   "Vancouver",
        "state" :   "Washington",
        "zip" :    "99121"
               }
    "first_order" : "01/15/2013",
    "last_order" : "06/27/2014"
}
```

Document databases enable you to query and filter based on elements in the document. For example, you could retrieve the address of customer Kiera Brown with the following command (using MongoDB syntax):

```
db.customers.find( { "customer_id":187693 }, { "address":
  1 } )
```

Column family databases support similar types of querying that allow you to select subsets of data available in a row. Cassandra uses a SQL-like language called Cassandra Query Language (CQL) that uses the familiar SELECT statement to retrieve data.

Column family databases, like document databases, do not require all columns in all rows. Some rows in a column family database may have values for all columns, whereas others will have values for only some columns in some column families (see Figure 9.6).

**Document Database:**

{fname: 'Lucinda',
lname: 'Jones',
Credit_Rating: 800,

Address:
      {Street : '341 N. Main St.',
      City: 'Portland',
      State: 'OR'
      }
{fname: 'Frank',
lname: 'Antonio',
Credit_Rating: 768
}

**Column Family Database:**

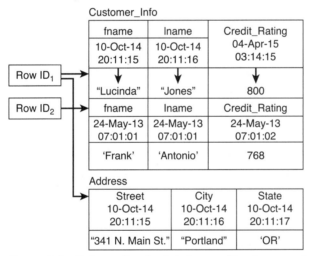

**Figure 9.6** *Column family databases, like document databases, may have values for some or all columns. Columns can be added programmatically as needed in both document and column family databases.*

In both column family and document databases, columns or fields can be added as needed by developers.

## Column Family Database Versus Relational Databases

Column family databases have some features that are similar to features in relational databases and others that are superficially similar but different in implementation.

Both column family databases and relational databases use unique identifiers for rows of data. These are known as row keys in column family databases and as primary keys in relational databases. Both row keys and primary keys are indexed for rapid retrieval.

Both types of databases can be thought of as storing tabular data, at least at some level of abstraction. The actual storage model varies, even between relational databases. Column family databases use the concept of maps (also known as dictionaries or associative arrays). A column key maps from a column name to a column value. A column family is a map/dictionary/associative array that points to a map/dictionary/associative array of columns (see Figure 9.7). In a sense, you have a map of map.

| Row Key A | Column 1 Key | Column 2 Key | Column 3 Key | ... | Column N Key |
|---|---|---|---|---|---|
| | Column 1 Value | Column 2 Value | Column 3 Value | ... | Column N Value |

**Figure 9.7**   *Column family databases store data using maps of maps to column values.*

Other important differences between column family databases and relational databases pertain to typed columns, transactions, joins, and subqueries.

Column family databases do not support the concept of a typed column. Column values can be seen as a series of bytes that are interpreted by an application, not the database. This provides developers with a great deal of flexibility because they can choose to interpret a string of bytes in different ways, depending on other values in a row. It also leaves developers with the responsibility to validate data before it is stored in the database.

**Avoiding Multirow Transactions**

Although you can expect to find atomic reads and writes with respect to a single row, column family databases such as Cassandra do not support multirow transactions. If you need to have two or more operations performed as a transaction, it is best to find a way to implement that operation using a single row of data. This may require some changes to your data model and is one of the considerations you should take into account when designing and implementing column families.

> ❖ **Note** Cassandra 2.0 introduced "lightweight transactions." These enable developers to specify conditions on INSERT and UPDATE operations. If the condition is satisfied, the operation is performed; otherwise, it is not performed. This feature is useful, but does not implement the full-blown ACID type of transaction found in relational databases and some NoSQL databases.

### Avoiding Subqueries

There should be minimal need for joins and subqueries in a column family database. Column families promote denormalization and that eliminates, or at least reduces, the need for joins.

In relational databses, a subquery is an inner query that runs, typically, as part of the WHERE clause of an outer query. For example, you might need to select all sales transactions performed by a salesperson with a last name of Smith. A SQL query such as the following could be used:

```
SELECT
    *
FROM
    sales_transactions
WHERE
SELECT
    sales_person_id
FROM
    sales_persons
WHERE
    last_name = 'Smith'
```

The part of the statement that begins with SELECT sales _ person _ id FROM ... is a subquery and executes in the context of the outer query. These types of subqueries are supported by relational databases but not by column family databases. Instead, a column family with salesperson information could be included with sales transaction data that would likely be maintained in another column family (see Figure 9.8).

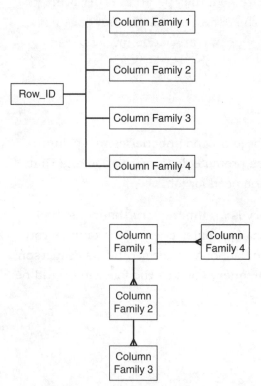

**Figure 9.8**   *Instead of using joins and subqueries, as in a relational databases, column family databases use denormalization to maintain related information using a common row identifier.*

This concludes the introduction to the logical model of column family databases. It is now time to consider architectural approaches to implementing column family databases.

# Architectures Used in Column Family Databases

Broadly speaking, there are two commonly used types of architectures used with distributed databases: multiple node type and peer-to-peer type. Multiple node type architectures have at least two types of nodes, although there may be more.

HBase is built on Hadoop and makes use of various Hadoop nodes, including name nodes, data nodes, and a centralized server for maintaining configuration data about the cluster. Peer-to-peer type architectures have only one type of node. Cassandra, for example, has a single type of node. Any node can assume responsibility for any service or task that must be run in the cluster.

## HBase Architecture: Variety of Nodes

Apache HBase uses the Hadoop infrastructure. A full description of Hadoop architecture is beyond the scope of this chapter, but the most important parts for HBase are outlined here.

The Hadoop File System, HDFS, uses a master-slave architecture that consists of name nodes and data nodes. The name nodes manage the file system and provide for centralized metadata management. Data nodes actually store data and replicate data as required by configuration parameters.

Zookeeper is a type of node that enables coordination between nodes within a Hadoop cluster. Zookeeper maintains a shared hierarchical namespace. Because clients need to communicate with Zookeeper, it is a potential single point of failure for HBase. Zookeeper designers mitigate risks of failure by replicating Zookeeper data to multiple nodes.

In addition to the Hadoop services used by HBase, the database also has server processes for managing metadata about the distribution of table data. RegionServers are instances that manage Regions, which are storage units for HBase table data. When a table is first created in HBase, all data is stored in a single Region. As the volume of data grows, additional Regions are created and data is partitioned between the multiple Regions. RegionServers, which host Regions, are designed to run with 20–200 Regions per server; each Region should store between 5GB and 20GB of table data.[3] A Master Server oversees the operation of RegionServers (see Figure 9.9).

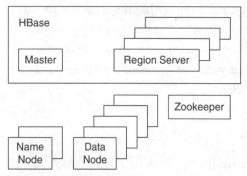

**Figure 9.9**   *Apache HBase depends on multiple types of nodes that make up the Hadoop environment.*

When a client device needs to read or write data from HBase, it can contact the Zookeeper server to find the name of the server that stores information about the corresponding Region's storage location within the cluster. The client device can then cache that information so it does not need to query Zookeeper again for those device details. The client then queries the server with the Region information to find out which server has data for a given row key (in the case of a read) or which server should receive data associated with a row key (in the case of the write).

An advantage of this type of architecture is that servers can be deployed and tuned for specific tasks, for example, managing the

---

3. The Apache HBase Reference Guide: http://hbase.apache.org/book/regions.arch.html.

Zookeeper. It does, however, require system administrators to manage multiple configurations and to tune each configuration separately. An alternative approach is to use a single type of node that can assume any role required in the cluster. Cassandra uses this approach.

## Cassandra Architecture: Peer-to-Peer

Apache Cassandra, like Apache HBase, is designed for high availability, scalability, and consistency. Cassandra takes a different architectural approach than HBase. Rather than use a hierarchical structure with fixed functions per server, Cassandra uses a peer-to-peer model (see Figure 9.10). All Cassandra nodes run the same software. They may, however, serve different functions for the cluster.

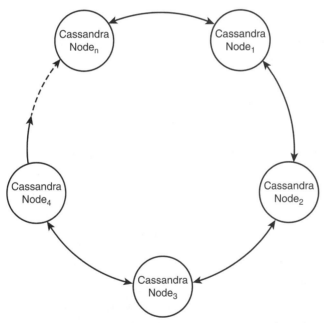

**Figure 9.10**  *Cassandra uses a peer-to-peer architecture in which all nodes are the same.*

There are several advantages to the peer-to-peer approach. The first is simplicity. No node can be a single point of failure. Scaling up and down is fairly straightforward: Servers are added or removed from the cluster. Servers in a peer-to-peer network communicate with each other and, eventually, new nodes are assigned a set of data to manage. When a node is removed, servers hosting replicas of data from the removed node respond to read and write requests.

Because peer-to-peer networks do not have a single master coordinating server, the servers in the cluster are responsible for managing a number of operations that a master server would handle, including the following:

- Sharing information about the state of servers in the cluster

- Ensuring nodes have the latest version of data

- Ensuring write data is stored when the server that should receive the write is unavailable

Cassandra has protocols to implement all of these functions.

## Getting the Word Around: Gossip Protocol

Sharing information about the state of servers in a cluster can sound like a trivial problem. Each server can simply ping or request update information from each of the other servers. The problem is that this type of all-servers-to-all-other-servers protocol can quickly increase the volume of traffic on the network and the amount of time each server has to dedicate to communicating with other servers.

Consider a variety of scenarios. When there are only two servers in a cluster, they each request information from and receive information from each other; 2 messages are exchanged. If you add a third server to the cluster, the servers generate 6 messages between the three of them. Increase the number to four servers, and they generate 12 messages. By the time you reach a 100-node cluster, 9,900 messages are sent through the cluster to communicate status information. The number of messages sent is a function of the number of servers in the cluster. If *N* is the number of servers, then N×(N–1) is the number of messages needed to update all servers with information about all other servers (see Figure 9.11).

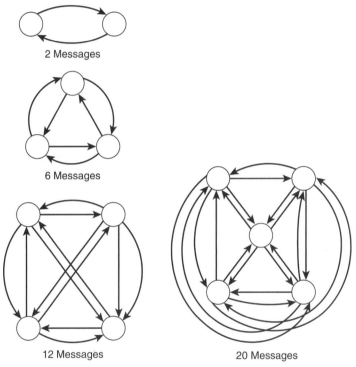

2 Messages

6 Messages

12 Messages          20 Messages

**Figure 9.11**   *The number of messages sent in a complete server-to-server communication protocol grows more rapidly each time a server is added to the cluster.*

A more-efficient method of sharing information is to have each server update another server about itself as well as all the servers it knows about. Those servers can then share what they know with a second set of other servers. The second set, which might receive information from a few different servers, can pass on all the status information it has been sent instead of just passing on its own information.

To get an idea of how efficient an information-sharing scheme can be, consider a seven-node cluster. Servers 1 and 2 send status information to Server 3. Servers 4 and 5 send status information to Server 6. Servers 3 and 6 send their own status information plus status information about two other servers to Server 7. Server 7 now has information about every server in the cluster. Server 7 sends the complete set of information to Servers 3 and 6. Server 3 then passes the information on to Servers 1 and 2 while Server 6 passes the information on to Servers 4 and 5. All nodes in the cluster now have complete status information about the cluster.

> ❖ **Note** Cassandra's protocol and gossip protocols in general do not operate exactly like this example. Gossip protocols implement random selection, and there may be some redundancy in information delivery. Rather than try to depict the complexities of a random process, a deterministic protocol example is used instead. In both random and deterministic protocols, aggregating information into fewer messages can convey the same amount of information more efficiently than nonaggregating protocols.

Cassandra's gossip protocol works as follows:[4]

- A node in the cluster initiates a gossip session with a randomly selected node.

- The initiating node sends a starter message (known as a GossipDigestSyn message) to a target node.

- The target node replies with an acknowledgment (known as a GossipDigestAck message).

- After receiving the acknowledgment from the target node, the initiating node sends a final acknowledgment (a GossipDigestAck2 message) to the target node.

---

4. Eben Hewitt. *Cassandra: The Definitive Guide.* Sebastopol, CA: O'Reilly Media, Inc., 2010.

In the course of this message exchange, each server is updated about the state of servers as known by the other server. In addition, version information about each server's state is exchanged. With this additional piece of data, each party in the exchange can determine which of the two has the most up-to-date data about each of the servers discussed.

## Thermodynamics and Distributed Database: Why We Need Anti-Entropy

If you have studied physics, you might have come across the laws of thermodynamics. The second law of thermodynamics describes a feature of entropy, which is the state of randomness and lack of order in a system or object. A broken glass, for example, has higher entropy than an unbroken glass. The second law of thermodynamics states that the amount of entropy (or disorder) in a closed system does not decrease. A broken glass does not repair itself and restore itself to the state of less entropy found in an unbroken glass.

Databases, especially distributed databases, are subject to a kind of entropy, too. The mechanical parts of a database server are certainly subject to entropy—just ask anyone who has suffered a disk failure—but that is not the kind of entropy discussed here. Distributed database designers have to address information entropy. Information entropy increases when data is inconsistent in the database. If one replica of data indicates that Lucinda Jones last made a purchase on January 15, 2014, and another replica has data that indicates she last made a purchase on November 23, 2014, the system is in an inconsistent state.

Cassandra uses an anti-entropy algorithm, that is, one that increases order, to correct inconsistencies between replicas. When a server initiates an anti-entropy session with another server, it sends a hash data structure, known as a Merkle or hash tree, derived from the data in a column family. The receiving server calculates a hash data structure from its copy of the column family. If they do not match, the servers determine which of the two has the latest information and updates the server with the outdated data (see Figure 9.12).

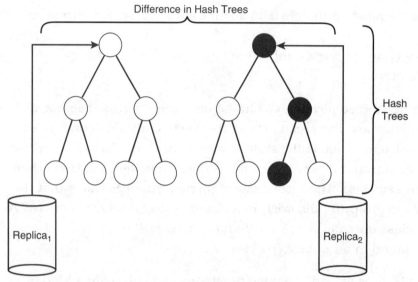

**Figure 9.12**    *Cassandra regularly compares replicas of data to ensure they are up to date. Hashes are used to make this a relatively fast operation.*

## Hold This for Me: Hinted Handoff

Cassandra is known for being well suited for write-intensive applications. This is probably due in part to its ability to keep accepting write requests even when the server that is responsible for handling the write request is unavailable. To understand how this high-availability write service works, let's take a step back and consider how read operations work.

Figure 9.13 shows the basic flow of information when a client device makes a request to the Cassandra database.

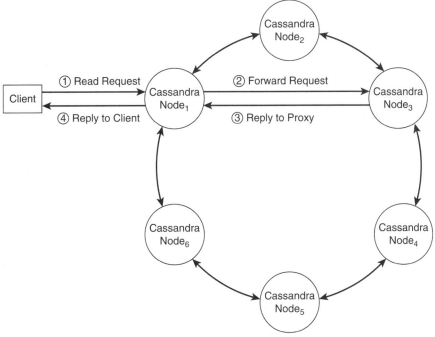

**Figure 9.13**  *Any node in a Cassandra cluster can handle a client request. All nodes have information about the state of the cluster and can act as a proxy for a client, forwarding the request to the appropriate node in the cluster.*

A client device needs to request data from the database. It issues a read operation and Node 1 receives the request. Node 1 uses the row key in the read request and looks up information about which node should process the request. It determines that Node 2 is responsible for data associated with that row key and passes the information on to it. Node 2 performs the read operation and sends the data back to Node 1. Node 1, in turn, passes the read results back to the client.

Now consider a similar situation but with a write request. The client sends a request to Node 1 to write data associated with a row key. Node 1 queries its local copy of metadata about the cluster and determines that Node 3 should process this request. Node 1, however, knows that Node 3 is unavailable because the gossip protocol informed

Node 1 about the status of Node 3 a few seconds ago. Rather than lose the write information or change the permanent location of data associated with that row key, Node 1 initiates a hinted handoff.

A hinted handoff entails storing information about the write operation on a proxy node and periodically checking the status of the unavailable node. When that node becomes available again, the node with the write information sends, or "hands off," the write request to the recently recovered node (see Figure 9.14).

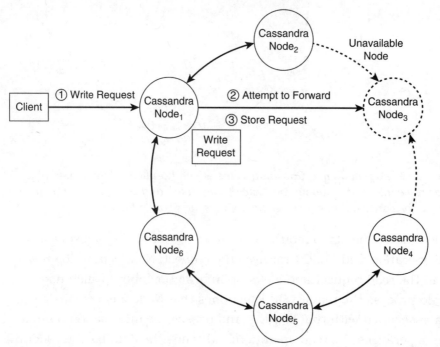

**Figure 9.14**   *If a node is unavailable, then other nodes can receive write requests on its behalf and forward them to the intended node when it becomes available.*

The architectures of column family databases allow for significant scalability. They can also be challenging to deploy and manage. It is important to choose a type of database that fits your needs but also minimizes the administrative overhead, development effort, and compute resources required.

# When to Use Column Family Databases

Column family databases are appropriate choices for large-scale database deployments that require high levels of write performance, a large number of servers or multi–data center availability.

Cassandra's peer-to-peer architecture with support for hinted handoff means the database will always be able to accept write operations as long as at least one node is functioning and reachable. Write-intensive operations, such as those found in social networking applications, are good candidates for using column family databases.

> ❖ **Tip** If your write-intensive application also requires transactions, then a column family database may not be the best choice. You might want to consider a hybrid approach that uses a database that supports ACID transactions (for example, a relational database or a key-value database such as FoundationDB[5]).

Column family databases are also appropriate when a large number of servers are required to meet expected workloads. Although column family databases can run on a single node, this configuration is more appropriate for development, testing, and getting to know a database management system. Column family databases typically run with more than several servers. If you find one or a few servers satisfy your performance requirements, you might find that key-value, document, or even relational databases are a better option.

Cassandra supports multi–data center deployment, including multi–data center replication. If you require continuous availability even in the event of a data center outage, then consider Cassandra for your deployment.

---

5. FoundationDB. "ACID Claims." https://foundationdb.com/acid-claims.

If you are considering column family databases for the flexibility of the data model, be sure to evaluate key-value and document databases. You may find they meet your requirements and run well in an environment with a single server or a small number of servers.

## Summary

Column family databases are some of the most scalable databases available. They provide developers with the flexibility to change the columns of a column family. They also support high availability, in some cases even cross–data center availability.

The next two chapters delve deeper into column family databases. Chapter 10, "Column Family Database Terminology," describes key terminology you will need to understand data modeling for column family databases as well as additional terms related to implementation. Chapter 11, "Designing for Column Family Databases," focuses on data modeling techniques and implementation issues developers should understand when deploying applications built on column family databases.

## Review Questions

1. Name at least three core features of Google BigTable.

2. Why are time stamps used in Google BigTable?

3. Identify one similarity between column family databases and key-value databases.

4. Identify one similarity between column family databases and document databases.

5. Identify one similarity between column family databases and relational databases.

6. What types of Hadoop nodes are used by HBase?

7. Describe the essential characteristics of a peer-to-peer architecture.

8. Why does Cassandra use a gossip protocol to exchange server status information?

9. What is the purpose of the anti-entropy protocol used by Cassandra?

10. When would you use a column family database instead of another type of NoSQL database?

# References

Apache HBase Reference Guide: http://hbase.apache.org/book/regions.arch.html

Biow, Chris, and Miles Ward. "PetaMongo: A Petabyte Database for as Little as $200." AWS re:Invent Conference, 2013: http://www.slideshare.net/mongodb/petamongo-a-petabyte-database-for-as-little-as-200

Chang, Fay, et al. "BigTable: A Distributed Storage System for Structured Data." OSDI'06: Seventh Symposium on Operating System Design and Implementation, Seattle, WA, November, 2006: http://research.google.com/archive/bigtable.html

FoundationDB. "ACID Claims": https://foundationdb.com/acid-claims

Hewitt, Eben. *Cassandra: The Definitive Guide.* Sebastopol, CA: O'Reilly Media, Inc., 2010.

■ ■ ■ ■ ■ ■ ■ ■ ■ ■ **10**

# Column Family Database Terminology

*"Uttering a word is like striking a note on the keyboard of the imagination."*
—LUDWIG WITTGENSTEIN
PHILOSOPHER

## Topics Covered In This Chapter

Basic Components of Column Family Databases

Structures and Processes: Implementing Column Family Databases

Processes and Protocols

When you read documentation and books about column family databases, you will see many familiar terms. Columns, partitions, and keyspaces are just a few of the commonly used terms you will see. When you are trying to understand a new technology, it often helps when the new technology uses the same terms used in existing technology—that is, unless they mean something else.

This chapter consists of descriptions of words and terms used in column family databases. The definitions are specific to column family databases. There are no minimalist definitions designed to satisfy a logician's desire for parsimony. The descriptions are designed to meet the needs of database designers, software developers, and others interested in understanding what makes column family databases different from other databases.

The next section of this chapter focuses on the elements of column family databases that you should understand to get started working with databases like Cassandra and HBase. Developers of column family databases will regularly deal with these components.

Next, the focus moves onto terms associated with implementing column family databases. Many of these terms refer to data structures or processes that are not obvious to application developers, but are essential for efficient implementation of the database.

> ❖ **Note** To use a column family database, you do not need to know the details of how partitioning works, but it helps—quite a bit. If some of the terminology in the implementation section seems obscure and too low level to matter to you (for example, Bloom filters and gossip protocols), then you can skim the material now.

# Basic Components of Column Family Databases

The basic components of a column family database are the data structures developers deal with the most. These are the data structures that developers define explicitly, such as a column. The terms described in this section include

- Keyspace
- Row key
- Column
- Column families

With these basic components, you can start constructing a column family database.

## Keyspace

A *keyspace* is the top-level data structure in a column family database (see Figure 10.1). It is top level in the sense that all other data structures you would create as a database designer are contained within a keyspace. A keyspace is analogous to a schema in a relational database. Typically, you will have one keyspace for each of your applications.

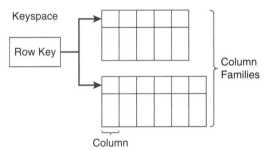

**Figure 10.1** *A keyspace is a top-level container that logically holds column families, row keys, and related data structures. Typically, there is one keyspace per application.*

## Row Key

A *row key* uniquely identifies a row in a column family. It serves some of the same purposes as a primary key in a relational database (see Figure 10.2).

Row keys are one of the components used to uniquely identify values stored in a database. The others are column family names, column names, and a version ordering mechanism, such as a time stamp.

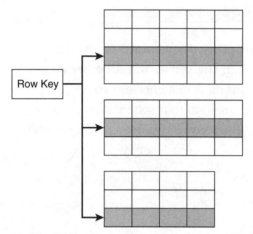

**Figure 10.2**   *A row key uniquely identifies a row and has a role in determining the order in which data is stored.*

In addition to uniquely identifying rows, row keys are also used to partition and order data. In HBase, rows are stored in lexicographic order of row keys. You can think of this as alphabetic ordering with additional orderings for nonalphabetic characters.

In Cassandra, rows are stored in an order determined by an object known as a partitioner. Cassandra uses a random partitioner by default. As the name implies, the partitioner randomly distributes rows across nodes. Cassandra also provides an order-preserving partitioner, which can provide lexicographic ordering.

## Column

A *column* is the data structure for storing a single value in a database (see Figure 10.3). Depending on the type of column family database you are using, you might find values are represented simply as a string of bytes. This minimizes the overhead on the database because it does not validate data types. HBase takes this approach.

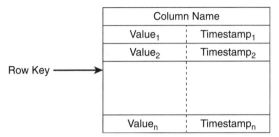

**Figure 10.3**  *A column, along with a row key and version stamp, uniquely identifies values.*

In other cases, you might be able to specify data types ranging from integers and strings to lists and maps. Cassandra's Query Language (CQL) offers almost 20 different data types.

Values can vary in length. For example, a value could be as simple as a single integer, such as 12, or as complex as a highly structured XML document.

Columns are members of column family databases. Database designers define column families when they create a database. However, developers can add columns any time after that. Just as you can insert data into a relational table, you can create new columns in column family databases.

Columns have three parts:

- A column name

- A time stamp or other version stamp

- A value

The column name serves the same function as a key in a key-value pair: It refers to a value.

The time stamp or other version stamp is a way to order values of a column. As the value of a column is updated, the new value is inserted into the database and a time stamp or other version stamp is recorded along with the column name and value. The version mechanism allows the database to store multiple values associated with a column while maintaining the ability to readily identify the latest value. Column family databases vary in the types of version control mechanisms used.

## Column Families

Column families are collections of related columns. Columns that are frequently used together should be grouped into the same column family. For example, a customer's address information, such as street, city, state, and zip code, should be grouped together in a single column family.

Column families are stored in a keyspace. Each row in a column family is uniquely identified by a row key. This makes a column family analogous to a table in a relational database (see Figure 10.4). There are important differences, however. Data in relational database tables is not necessarily maintained in a predefined order. Rows in relational tables are not versioned the way they are in column family databases.

| Street | City | State | Province | Zip | Postal Code | Country |
|---|---|---|---|---|---|---|
| 178 Main St. | Boise | ID | | 83701 | | U.S. |
| 89 Woodridge | Baltimore | MD | | 21218 | | U.S. |
| 293 Archer St. | Ottawa | | ON | | K1A 2C5 | Canada |
| 8713 Alberta DR | Vancouver | | BC | | VSK 0AI | Canada |

**Figure 10.4**   *Column families are analogous to relational database tables: They store multiple rows and multiple columns. There are, however, significant differences between the two, including varying columns by row.*

Perhaps most importantly, columns in a relational database table are not as dynamic as in column family databases. Adding a column in a relational database requires changing its schema definition. Adding a column in a column family database just requires making a reference to it from a client application, for example, inserting a value to a column name.

In many ways, the data structures that database application designers work with are just the tip of the column family database iceberg. There are many more components of column family databases that support the more apparent structures.

The next section focuses on these underlying structures and processes that implement essential functions of column family databases.

## Structures and Processes: Implementing Column Family Databases

Column family databases are complicated. There are many processes that continually run in order to ensure the database functions as expected. There are also sophisticated data structures that significantly improve performance over more naive implementations.

### Internal Structures and Configuration Parameters of Column Family Databases

Internal structures and configuration parameters of column family databases span the full range of the database—from the lowest level of storing a single value up to the high-level components of the database. Several are particularly important for database application designers and developers to understand:

- Cluster
- Partition

- Commit log

- Bloom filter

- Replication count

- Consistency level

Clusters and partitions are commonly used in distributed databases and are probably familiar topics by now. Vector clocks are used in version management. The commit log and Bloom filter are supporting data structures that improve integrity and availability of data as well as the performance of read operations.

Replication count and consistency level are configuration parameters that allow database administrators to customize functionality of the column family database according to the needs of applications using it.

## Old Friends: Clusters and Partitions

Clusters and partitions enable distributed databases to coordinate processing and data storage across a set of servers.

### Cluster

A *cluster* is a set of servers configured to function together. Servers sometimes have differentiated functions and sometimes they do not (see Figure 10.5).

HBase is a part of the Hadoop infrastructure. It uses the various types of servers to implement the functional requirements of Hadoop. Hadoop implementation details are outside the scope of this book.[1]

---

1. The interested reader should see *Professional Hadoop Solutions* by Boris Lublinsky, Kevin T. Smith, and Alexy Yakubovich (Worx, 2013).

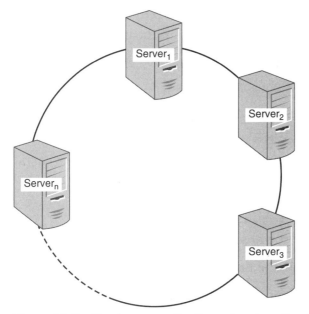

**Figure 10.5** *Clusters are collections of servers functioning together to implement a distributed service, such as a column family database.*

Cassandra, on the other hand, uses a single type of node. There are no master or slave nodes. Each node shares similar responsibilities, including

- Accepting read and write requests

- Forwarding read and write requests to servers able to fulfill the requests

- Gathering and sharing information about the state of servers in the clusters

- Helping compensate for failed nodes by storing write requests for the failed node until it is restored

These operations are all required to maintain a functional distributed database. At the same time, these operations are too low level to concern database application developers. If they had to write code to ensure they sent read and write requests to the proper server or had to maintain state information about each server in the cluster, it would add significantly more code to the application.

## Partition

A *partition* is a logical subset of a database. Partitions are usually used to store a set of data based on some attribute of the data (see Figure 10.6). For example, a database might assign data to a particular partition based on one of the following:

- A range of values, such as the value of a row ID

- A hash value, such as the hash value of a column name

- A list of values, such as the names of states or provinces

- A composite of two or more of the above options

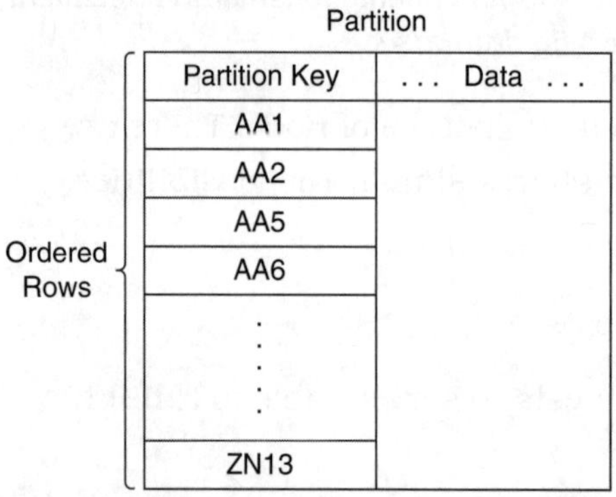

**Figure 10.6**  *Partitions store data ordered by partition key.*

Each node or server within a column family cluster maintains one or more partitions.

When a client application requests data, the request is routed to a server with the partition containing the requested data. A request could go to a central server in a master-slave architecture or to any server in a peer-to-peer architecture. In either case, the request is for-warded to the appropriate server.

In practice, multiple servers may store copies of the same partition. This improves the chances of successfully reading and writing data even in the event of server failures. It can also help improve perfor-mance because all servers with copies of a partition can respond to requests for data from that partition. This model effectively implements load balancing.

## Taking a Look Under the Hood: More Column Family Database Components

In addition to the structures and procedures you will routinely work with, there are a few less visible components of column family data-bases worth understanding. These include

- Commit logs
- Bloom filter
- Consistency level

These components are not obvious to most developers, but they play crucial roles in achieving availability and performance.

### Commit Log

If your application writes data to a database and receives a successful status response, you reasonably expect the data to be stored on per-sistent storage. Even if a server fails immediately after sending a write success response, you should be able to retrieve your data once the server restarts (see Figure 10.7).

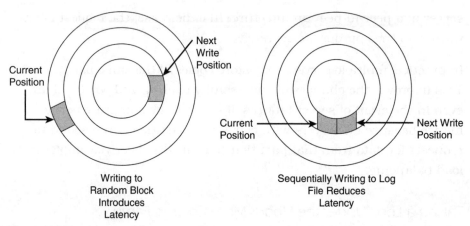

**Figure 10.7**  *A commit log saves data written to the database prior to writing it to partitions. This reduces the latency introduced by random writes on disks.*

One way to ensure this is to have the database write data to disk (or other persistent storage) before sending the success response. The database could do this, but it would have to wait for the read/write heads to be in the correct position on the disk before writing the data. If the database did this for every write, it could significantly cut down on write performance.

Instead of writing data immediately to its partition and disk block, column family databases can employ commit logs. These are append only files that always write data to the end of the file.

> ❖ **Tip**  When database administrators dedicate a disk to a commit log, there are no other write processes competing to write data to the disk. This reduces the need for random seeks and reduces latency.

In the event of a failure, the database management system reads the commit log on recovery. Any entries in the commit log that have not been saved to partitions are then written to appropriate partitions (see Figure 10.8).

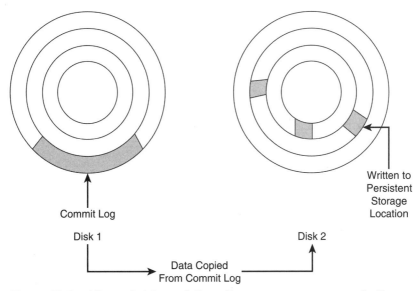

**Figure 10.8** *After a database failure, the recovery process reads the commit log and writes entries to partitions. The database remains unavailable to users until all commit log entries are written to partitions.*

### Bloom Filter

Anything that reduces the number of blocks read from disk or solid state device can help improve performance. Applying Bloom filters is one such technique.

A *Bloom filter* tests whether or not an element is a member of a set (see Figure 10.9). Unlike a typical member function, the Bloom filter sometimes returns an incorrect answer. It could return a positive response in cases where the tested element is not a member of the set. This is known as a false-positive. Bloom filters never return a negative response unless the element is not in the set.

Bloom filters help reduce the number of read operations by avoiding reading partitions or other data structures that definitely do not contain a sought-after piece of data.

| Member Function | | |
|---|---|---|
| Input Set | Test Element | In Set |
| {a,b,c} | a | Yes |
| {a,b,c} | c | Yes |
| {a,b,c} | e | No |

| Bloom Filter | | |
|---|---|---|
| Input Set | Test Element | In Set |
| {a,b,c} | a | Yes |
| {a,b,c} | c | Yes |
| {a,b,c} | e | Yes |
| {a,b,c} | f | No |
| {a,b,c} | g | No |

Low
Probability
but
Possible

**Figure 10.9**  *Member functions always return accurate results. Bloom filters usually return accurate results but sometimes make false-positive errors.*

Another way to achieve the same benefit is to use a hash function. For example, assume you partition customer data using a hash function on a person's last name and city. The hash function would return a single value for each last name–city combination. The application would only need to read that one partition. Why should database developers use Bloom filters that sometimes return incorrect?

Bloom filters use less memory than typical hash functions, and the savings can be significant for the large-scale databases typically deployed in column family databases. Because a Bloom filter is a probabilistic data structure, you can tune your implementation according to the error rate you would like to achieve. The more memory you allocate for the Bloom filter, the smaller your error rate. If you can tolerate a 1% false-positive rate, you can implement a Bloom filter using about 10 bits per element. If you can afford another 5 bits per element, your error rate can reduce to 0.1%.

Both HBase and Cassandra make use of Bloom filters to avoid unnecessary disk seeks.

**Consistency Level**

*Consistency level* refers to the consistency between copies of data on different replicas. In the strictest sense, data is consistent only if all replicas have the same data. At the other end of the spectrum, you could consider the data "consistent" as long as it is persistently written to at least one replica. There are several intermediate levels as well.

Consistency level is set according to several, sometimes competing, requirements:

- How fast should write operations return a success status after saving data to persistent storage?

- Is it acceptable for two users to look up a set of columns by the same row ID and receive different data?

- If your application runs across multiple data centers and one of the data centers fails, must the remaining functioning data centers have the latest data?

- Can you tolerate some inconsistency in reads but need updates saved to two or more replicas?

In many cases, a low consistency level can satisfy requirements. Consider an application that collects sensor data every minute from hundreds of industrial sensors. If data is occasionally lost, the data sets will have missing values.

❖ **Note** A small number of missing values may not even be noticeable because this kind of data is often aggregated into sums, averages, standard deviations, and other descriptive statistics. In addition, missing data is a common problem in scientific and social science research; statisticians have developed a number of methods of compensating for missing data.

Other situations call for a moderate consistency level. Players using an online game reasonably expect to have the state of their game saved when they pause or stop playing on one device to switch to another. Even losing a small amount of data could frustrate users who have to repeat play and possibly lose gains made in the game.

To avoid disrupting players' games in the event of a server failure, an underlying column family database could be configured with a consistency level requiring writes to two or three replicas. Using a higher level of consistency would increase availability but at the cost of slowing write operations and possibly adversely affecting gameplay.

The highest levels of consistency, such as writing replicas to multiple replicas in multiple data centers, should be saved for the most demanding fault-tolerant applications.

# Processes and Protocols

In addition to the data structures described above, a number of important background processes are responsible for maintaining a functional column family database.

## Replication

Replication is a process closely related to consistency level. Whereas the consistency level determines how many replicas to keep, the replication process determines where to place replicas and how to keep them up to date.

In the simplest case, the server for the first replica is determined by hash function, and additional replicas are placed according to the relative position of other servers. For example, all nodes in Cassandra are in a logical ring. Once the first replica is placed, additional replicas are stored on successive nodes in the ring in the clockwise direction.

Column family databases can also use network topology to determine where to place replicas. For example, replicas may be created on different racks within a data center to ensure availability in the event of a rack failure.

## Anti-Entropy

*Anti-entropy* is the process of detecting differences in replicas. From a performance perspective, it is important to detect and resolve inconsistencies with a minimum amount of data exchange.

The naive way to compare replicas is to send a copy of one replica to the node storing another replica and compare the two. This is obviously inefficient. Even with high-write applications, much of the data sent from the source is the same as the data on the target node. Column family databases can exploit the fact that much of replica data may not change between anti-entropy checks. They do this by sending hashes of data instead of the data itself.

One method employs a tree of hashes, also known as a Merkle tree (see Figure 10.10). The leaf nodes contain hashes of a data set. The nodes above the leaf nodes contain a hash of the hashes in the leaf nodes. Each successive layer contains the hash of hashes in the level below. The root node contains the hash of the entire collection of data sets.

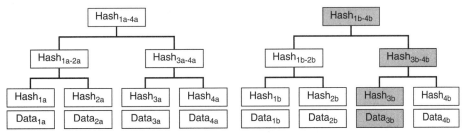

**Figure 10.10** *Hash trees, or Merkle trees, allow for rapid checks on consistency between two data sets. In this example, data3a and data3b are different, resulting in different hash values in each level from the data block to the root.*

Anti-entropy processes can calculate hash trees on all replicas. One replica sends its hash tree to another node. That node compares the hash values in the two root nodes. If both are the same, then there is no difference in the replicas. If there is a difference, then the anti-entropy process can compare the hash values at the next level down.

At least one pair of these hash values will differ between replicas. The process of traversing the tree continues until the process reaches one or more leaf nodes that have changed. Only the data associated with those leaf nodes needs to be exchanged.

## Gossip Protocol

A fundamental challenge in any distributed system is keeping member nodes up to date on information about other members of the system. This is not too much of a problem when the number of nodes in a cluster is small, say fewer than 10 servers. If every node in a server has to communicate with every other node, then the number of messages can quickly grow.

Table 10.1 shows how the number of messages that must be sent in complete communications protocol increases at the rate of $n \times (n-1)/2$, where $n$ is the number of nodes in the cluster.

**Table 10.1**    *Number of Messages Sent Per Node*

| Number of Nodes | Number of Messages for Complete Communication |
| --- | --- |
| 2 | 2 |
| 3 | 6 |
| 4 | 12 |
| 5 | 20 |
| 10 | 90 |
| 15 | 210 |
| 20 | 380 |
| 25 | 600 |
| 50 | 2,450 |
| 100 | 9,900 |

Instead of having every node communicate with every other node, it is more efficient to have nodes share information about themselves as well as other nodes from which they have received updates. Consider a cluster with 10 nodes. If each node communicated with every other node, the system will send a total of 90 messages to ensure all nodes have up-to-date information.

Figure 10.11 shows that when using a gossip protocol—in which each node sends information about itself and all information it has received from other nodes—all nodes can be updated with a fraction of the number of messages required for complete communication.

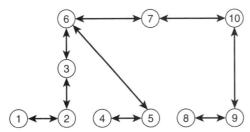

**Figure 10.11**   *Gossip protocols spread information with fewer messages than a protocol that requires all nodes to communicate with all other nodes.*

## Hinted Handoff

Replicas enable read availability even if some nodes have failed. They do not address how to handle a write operation that is directed to a node that is down. The hinted handoff mechanism is designed to solve this problem.

If a write operation is directed to a node that is unavailable, the operation can be redirected to another node, such as another replica node or a node designated to receive write operations when the target node is down.

The node receiving the redirected write message creates a data structure to store information about the write operation and where it should ultimately be sent. The hinted handoff periodically checks the status of the target server and sends the write operation when the target is available.

Storing a hinted handoff data structure is not the same as writing to a replica. Hinted handoffs are stored in their own data structures and are managed by the hinted handoff process. Once the write data is successfully written to the target node, it can be considered a successful write for the purposes of consistency and replication.

## Summary

Column family databases share some terminology with relational databases, but there are important differences in how those terms are used. Columns, for example, can have similar characteristics in both relational and column family databases, but they are implemented differently. Columns can be programmatically added to column family databases but require schema changes in relational databases. It is important to keep these differences in mind when working with column family databases.

The basic, logical components of a column family database are namespaces, column families, columns, and row keys. You should be familiar with these components when working with any column family database.

To understand the physical implementation of a column family database, you should understand at least partitions and clusters. To ensure you have adequately addressed availability and performance requirements, you should understand how commit logs are used and the trade-offs in setting replication parameters and consistency levels. For those who like to dig into details, it helps to understand Bloom filters, anti-entropy, gossip protocols, and hinted handoffs.

## Review Questions

1. What is a keyspace? What is an analogous data structure in a relational database?

2. How do columns in column family databases differ from columns in relational databases?

3. When should columns be grouped together in a column family? When should they be in separate column families?

4. Describe how partitions are used in column family databases.

5. What are the performance advantages of using a commit log?

6. What are the advantages of using a Bloom filter?

7. What factors should you consider when setting a consistency level?

8. What factors should you consider when setting a replication strategy?

9. Why are hash trees used in anti-entropy processes?

10. What are the advantages of using a gossip protocol?

11. Describe how hinted handoff can help improve the availability of write operations.

## References

Apache Cassandra Glossary: http://io.typepad.com/glossary.html

Apache HBase Reference Guide: http://hbase.apache.org/book.html

Bloom Filter: http://en.wikipedia.org/wiki/Bloom_filter

Hewitt, Eben. *Cassandra: The Definitive Guide.* Sebastopol, CA: O'Reilly Media, Inc., 2010.

Merkle Filter: http://en.wikipedia.org/wiki/Merkle_tree

# 11

# Designing for Column Family Databases

*"A good designer must rely on experience, on precise, logic thinking;*
*and on pedantic exactness. No magic will do."*
—Niklaus Wirth
Computer Scientist

## Topics Covered In This Chapter

Guidelines for Designing Tables

Guidelines for Indexing

Tools for Working with Big Data

Case Study: Customer Data Analysis

Users drive the design of a column family database. This might seem illogical at first. After all, shouldn't experienced designers with knowledge of the database management system take the lead on design? Actually, designers follow the lead of users. It is users who determine the questions that will be asked of the database application. They might have questions such as these:

- How many new orders were placed in the Northwest region yesterday?

- When did a particular customer last place an order?

- What orders are en route to customers in London, England?

- What products in the Ohio warehouse have fewer than the stock keeping minimum number of items?

Only when you have questions like these can you design for a column family database. Like other NoSQL databases, design starts with queries.

Queries provide information needed to effectively design column family databases. The information includes

- Entities
- Attributes of entities
- Query criteria
- Derived values

Entities represent things that can range from concrete things, such as customers and products, to abstractions such as a service level agreement or a credit score history. Entities are modeled as rows in column family databases. A single row should correspond to a single entity. Rows are uniquely identified by row keys.

Attributes of entities are modeled using columns. Queries include references to columns to specify criteria for selecting entities and to specify a set of attributes to return.

Designers use the selection criteria to determine optimal ways to organize data with tables and partitions. For example, queries that require range scans, such as selecting all orders placed between two dates, are best served by tables that order the data in the same order it will be scanned.

Designers use the set of attributes to return to help determine how to group attributes in column families. It is most efficient to store columns together that are frequently used together.

❖ **Tip** When designers see queries that include derived values, such as a count of orders placed yesterday or the average dollar value of an order, it is an indication that additional attributes may be needed to store derived data.

Information about entities, attributes, query criteria, and derived values is a starting point for column family design. Designers start with this information and then use the features of column family databases to select the most appropriate implementation.

❖ **Note** When you first learn about column family databases, it is useful to draw parallels between relational databases and column family databases. When you have learned enough of the basics to start to design column family database applications, it is time to forget the relational analogies.

Column family databases are implemented differently than relational databases. Thinking they are essentially the same could lead to poor design decisions. It is important to understand:

- Column family databases are implemented as sparse, multidimensional maps.
- Columns can vary between rows.
- Columns can be added dynamically.
- Joins are not used; data is denormalized instead.

These characteristics of column family databases will influence design guidelines detailed in the following sections. Guidelines are presented for the major logical components of the column family database. In the case of keyspaces, there are few guidelines other than to use a separate keyspace for each application. This is based on the fact that applications will have different query patterns and, as noted previously, column family database design is largely driven by those queries.

> ❖ **Note**  HBase and Cassandra are two popular column family databases. They have many features in common. They differ in others. For example, HBase uses a time stamp to keep multiple versions of column values. Cassandra uses time stamp-like data too, but for conflict resolution, not for storing multiple values. Implementation details can also vary between versions of column family database systems. What was true of an earlier version of Cassandra might not be true of the latest version.

## Guidelines for Designing Tables

One of your first design decisions is to determine the tables in your schema. The following are several guidelines to keep in mind when designing tables:

- Denormalize instead of join.

- Make use of valueless columns.

- Use both column names and column values to store data.

- Model an entity with a single row.

- Avoid hotspotting in row keys.

- Keep an appropriate number of column value versions.

- Avoid complex data structures in column values.

It should be noted that some of these recommendations, such as using an appropriate number of column value versions, are not applicable to all column family database systems.

## Denormalize Instead of Join

Tables model entities, so it is reasonable to expect to have one table per entity. Column family databases often need fewer tables than their relational counterparts. This is because column family databases denormalize data to avoid the need for joins. For example, in a relational database, you typically use three tables to represent a many-to-many relationship: two tables for the related entities and one table for the many-to-many relation.

Figure 11.1 shows how to model customers who bought multiple products and products that were purchased by multiple customers.

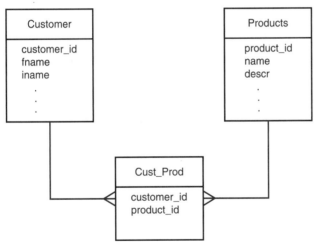

**Figure 11.1**  *In relational databases, many-to-many relations are modeled with a table for storing primary keys of the two entities in a many-to-many relationship.*

Figure 11.2 shows how to accomplish the same modeling goal with denormalized data. Each customer includes a set of column names that correspond to purchased products. Similarly, products include a list of customer IDs that indicate the set of customers that purchased those products.

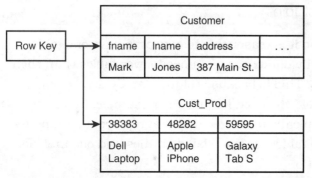

**Figure 11.2**   *In a column family database, many-to-many relationships are captured by denormalizing data.*

## Make Use of Valueless Columns

You might have noticed something strange about the previous example of using column names to hold actual data about customers and products. Instead of having a column with a name like `'ProductPurchased1'` with value `'PR_B1839'`, the table simply stores the product ID as the column name.

> ❖ **Tip** Using column names to store data can have advantages. For example, in Cassandra, data stored in column names is stored in sort order, but data stored in column values is not.

Of course, you could store a value associated with a column name. If a column name indicates the presence or absence of something, you could assign a *T* or *F* to indicate true or false. This, however, would take additional storage without increasing the amount of information stored in the column.

## Use Both Column Names and Column Values to Store Data

A variation on the use of valueless columns uses the column value for denormalization. For example, in a database about customers and products, the features of the product, such as description, size, color, and weight, are stored in the products table. If your application users want to produce a report listing products bought by a customer, they probably want the product name in addition to its identifier. Because you are dealing with large volumes of data (otherwise you would not be using a column family database), you do not want to join or query both the customer and the product table to produce the report.

As you saw in Figure 11.2, the customer table includes a list of column names indicating the product ID of items purchased by the customer. Because the column value is not used for anything else, you can store the product name there, as shown in Figure 11.3.

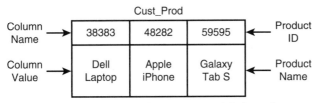

**Figure 11.3**  *Both the column name and the column value can store data.*

Keeping a copy of the product name in the customer table will increase the amount of storage used. That is one of the downsides of denormalized data. The benefit, however, is that the report of customers and the products they bought is produced by referencing only one table instead of two. In effect, you are trading the need for additional storage for improved read performance.

## Model an Entity with a Single Row

A single entity, such as a particular customer or a specific product, should have all its attributes in a single row. This can lead to cases in which some rows store more column values than others, but that is not uncommon in column family databases.

Let's consider the product table in more detail. The retailer designing the application sells several different types of products, including appliances, books, and clothing. They all share some common attributes, such as price, stock keeping unit (SKU), and inventory level. They each have unique features as well. Appliances have form factors, voltage, and energy certifications. Books have authors, publishers, and copyright dates. Clothing items have fabrics, size, and cleaning instructions. One way to model this is with several tables, as shown in Figure 11.4.

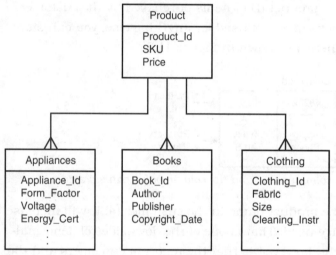

**Figure 11.4** *Entities can have attributes stored in multiple tables, but this is not recommended for column family databases.*

Column family databases do not provide the same level of transaction control as relational databases. Typically, writes to a row are atomic. If you update several columns in a table, they will all be updated, or none of them will be.

❖ **Caution** If you need to update two separate tables, such as a product table and a books table, it is conceivable the updates to the product table succeed, but the updates to the book table do not. In such a case, you would be left with inconsistent data.

## Avoid Hotspotting in Row Keys

Distributed systems enable you to take advantage of large numbers of servers to solve problems. It is inefficient to direct an excessive amount of work at one or a few machines while others are underutilized.

Hotspotting occurs when many operations are performed on a small number of servers (see Figure 11. 5). Consider an example of how this can occur in HBase.

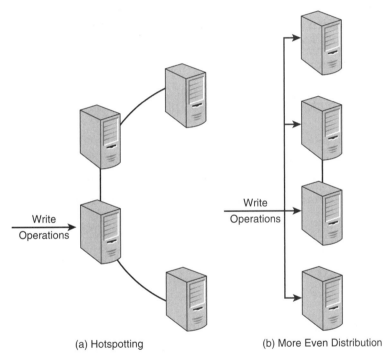

(a) Hotspotting                    (b) More Even Distribution

**Figure 11.5**   *(a) Hotspotting leads to underutilization of cluster resources while (b) more even distribution of operations leads to more efficient use of resources.*

HBase uses lexigraphic ordering of rows. Let's assume you are loading data into a table and the key value for the table is a sequential number assigned by a source system. The data is stored in a file in sequential order. As HBase loads each record, it will likely write it to the same server that received the prior record and to a data block near the data block of the prior record. This helps avoid disk latency, but it means a single server is working consistently while others are underutilized.

> ❖ **Tip** In a real-world scenario, you would probably load multiple files in parallel to utilize other servers while maintaining the benefits of reduced disk latency.

You can prevent hotspotting by hashing sequential values generated by other systems. Alternatively, you could add a random string as a prefix to the sequential value. This would eliminate the effects of the lexicographic order of the source file on the data load process.

## Keep an Appropriate Number of Column Value Versions

HBase enables you to store multiple versions of a column value. Column values are time-stamped so you can determine the latest and earliest values. Like other forms of version control, this feature is useful if you need to roll back changes you have made to column values.

> ❖ **Tip** You should keep as many versions as your application requirements dictate, but no more. Additional versions will obviously require more storage.

HBase enables you to set a minimum and maximum number of versions (see Figure 11.6). It will not remove versions if it would leave a column value with less than the minimum number of versions. When the number of versions exceeds the maximum number of versions, the oldest versions are removed during data compaction operations.

| Column Family | | |
|---|---|---|
| Column Name$_1$ | Column Name$_2$ | Column Name$_3$ |
| value$_{1a}$ : timestamp$_{1a}$ | value$_{2a}$ : timestamp$_{2a}$ | value$_{3a}$ : timestamp$_{3a}$ |
| value$_{1b}$ : timestamp$_{1b}$ | value$_{2b}$ : timestamp$_{2b}$ | value$_{3b}$ : timestamp$_{3b}$ |
| value$_{1c}$ : timestamp$_{1c}$ | value$_{2c}$ : timestamp$_{2c}$ | value$_{3c}$ : timestamp$_{3c}$ |

**Figure 11.6** *HBase provides for column value versions. The number of versions maintained is controlled by database parameters, which can be changed according to application requirements.*

## Avoid Complex Data Structures in Column Values

You might recall from the discussion of document databases that embedded objects are commonly used with documents. A JSON document about a customer, for example, might contain an embedded document storing address information, such as the following:

```
{
    "customer_id":187693,
    "name": "Kiera Brown",
    "address" : {
            "street" : "1232 Sandy Blvd.",
            "city" :  "Vancouver",
            "state" :  "Washington",
            "zip" :  "99121"
                },
    "first_order" : "01/15/2013",
    "last_order" : " 06/27/2014"
}
```

❖ **Tip** This type of data structure may be stored in a column value, but it is not recommended unless there is a specific reason to maintain this structure. If you are simply treating this object as a string and will only store and fetch it, then it is reasonable to store the string as is. If you expect to use the database to query or operate on the values within the structure, then it is better to decompose the structure.

Using separate columns for each attribute makes it easier to apply database features to the attributes. For example, creating separate columns for street, city, state, and zip means you can create secondary indexes on those values.

Also, separating attributes into individual columns allows you to use different column families if needed. Both the ability to use secondary indexes and the option of separating columns according to how they are used can lead to improved database performance.

As you can see from this discussion of guidelines for table design, there are a number of factors to consider when working with column family databases.  One of the most important considerations with regard to performance is indexing.

## Guidelines for Indexing

Indexes allow for rapid lookup of data in a table. For example, if you want to look up customers in a particular state, you could use a statement such as the following (in Cassandra query language, CQL):

```
SELECT
    fname, lname
FROM
    customers
WHERE
    state = 'OR';
```

A database index functions much like the index in a book. You can look up an entry in a book index to find the pages that reference that word or term. Similarly, in column family databases, you can look up a column value, such as state abbreviation, to find rows that reference that column value. In many cases, using an index allows the database engine to retrieve data faster than it otherwise would.

It is helpful to distinguish two kinds of indexes: primary and secondary. Primary indexes are indexes on the row keys of a table. They are automatically maintained by the column family database system. Secondary indexes are indexes created on one or more column values. Either the database system or your application can create and manage secondary indexes. Not all column family databases provide automatically managed secondary indexes, but you can create and manage tables as secondary indexes in all column family database systems.

## When to Use Secondary Indexes Managed by the Column Family Database System

As a general rule, if you need secondary indexes on column values and the column family database system provides automatically managed secondary indexes, then you should use them. The alternative, maintaining tables as indexes, is described in the next section.

The primary advantage of using automatically managed secondary indexes is they require less code to maintain than the alternative. In Cassandra, for example, you could create an index in CQL using the following statement:

```
CREATE INDEX state ON customers(state);
```

Cassandra will then create and manage all data structures needed to maintain the index. It will also determine the optimal use of indexes. For example, if you have an index on state and last name column values and you queried the following, Cassandra would choose which index to use first:

```
SELECT
    fname, lname
FROM
    customers
WHERE
    state = 'OR'
AND
    lname = 'Smith'
```

Typically, the database system will use the most selective index first. For example, if there are 10,000 customers in Oregon and 1,500 customers with the last name Smith, then it would use the lname secondary index first. It might then use the state index to determine, which, if any, of the 1,500 customers with the last name Smith are in Oregon.

The automatic use of secondary indexes has another major advantage because you do not have to change your code to use the indexes. Imagine you built an application according to the query requirements of your users and over time those requirements change. Now, your application has to generate a report based on state and last name instead of just state.

You could create a secondary index on the last name column and the database system would automatically use it when appropriate. As you will see in the next section, the tables as indexes method requires changes to your code.

There are times when you should not use automatically managed indexes. Avoid, or at least carefully test, the use of indexes in the following cases:

- There is a small number of distinct values in a column.

- There are many unique values in a column.

- The column values are sparse.

When the number of distinct values in a column (known as the cardinality of the column) is small, indexes will not help performance much—it might even hurt (see Figure 11.7). For example, if you have a column with values Yes and No, an index will probably not help much, especially if there are roughly equal numbers of each value.

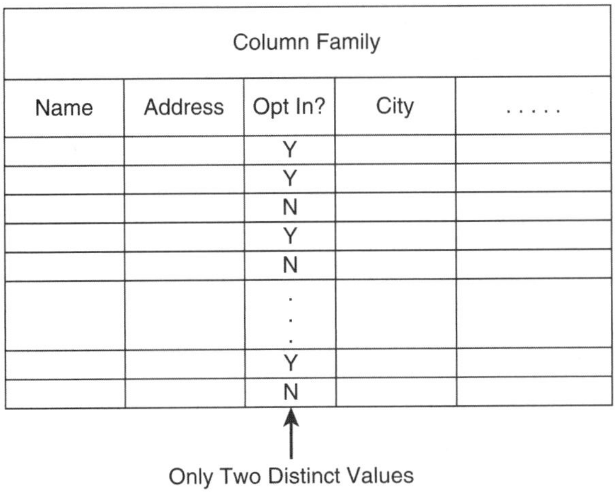

Only Two Distinct Values

**Figure 11.7** *Columns with few distinct values are not good candidates for secondary indexes.*

At the other end of the cardinality spectrum are columns with many distinct values, such as street addresses and email addresses (see Figure 11.8). Again, automatically managed indexes may not help much here because the index will have to maintain so much data it could take more time to search the index and retrieve the data than to scan the tables for the particular value.

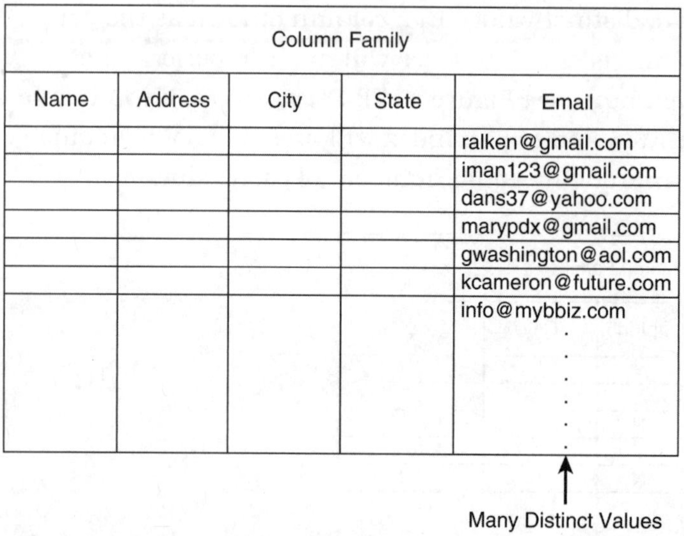

| Column Family | | | | |
|---|---|---|---|---|
| Name | Address | City | State | Email |
| | | | | ralken@gmail.com |
| | | | | iman123@gmail.com |
| | | | | dans37@yahoo.com |
| | | | | marypdx@gmail.com |
| | | | | gwashington@aol.com |
| | | | | kcameron@future.com |
| | | | | info@mybbiz.com |
| | | | | . |
| | | | | . |
| | | | | . |
| | | | | . |

Many Distinct Values

**Figure 11.8**   *Rows with too many distinct values are also not good candidates for indexes.*

In cases where many of the rows do not use a column, a secondary index may not help. For example, if most of your customers are in the United States, then their addresses will include a value in the state column. For those customers who live in Canada, they will have values in the province column instead of in the state column. Because most of your customers are in the United States, the province column will have sparse data. An index will not likely help with that column (see Figure 11.9).

> ❖ **Note** If you are not sure whether indexes will help, test their use if possible. Be sure to use realistically sized test data. If you create test data yourself, try to ensure it has the same range of values and distribution of values that you would see in real data. If your test data varies significantly in size or distribution, your results might not be informative for your actual use case.

A second approach to indexing is to build and manage indexes yourself using tables as indexes.

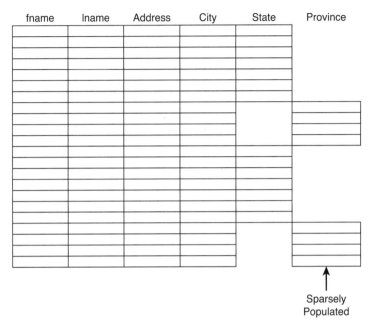

**Figure 11.9**  *Sparsely populated columns should not be indexed.*

## When to Create and Manage Secondary Indexes Using Tables

If your column family database system does not support automatically managed secondary indexes or the column you would like to index has many distinct values, you might benefit from creating and managing your own indexes.

Indexes created and managed by your application use the same table, column family, and column data structures used to store your data. Instead of using a statement such as CREATE INDEX to make data structures managed by the database system, you explicitly create tables to store data you would like to access via the index.

Let's return to the customer and product database. Your end users would like to generate reports that list all customers who bought a particular product. They would also like a report on particular products and which customers bought them.

In the first situation, you would want to quickly find information about a product, such as its name and description. The existing product table meets this requirement. Next, you would want to quickly find all customers who bought that product. A time-efficient way to do this is to keep a table that uses the product identifier as the row key and uses customer identifiers as column names. The column values can be used to store additional information about the customers, such as their names. In the example shown in Figure 11.10, the necessary data is stored in the Cust _ by _ Prod table.

**Customer**

| Row key | fname | lname | street | city | state |
|---|---|---|---|---|---|
| 123 | Jane | Smith | 387 Main St | Boise | ID |
| 287 | Mark | Jones | 192 Wellfleet Dr | Austin | TX |
| 1987 | Harsha | Badal | 298 Commercial St | Provincetown | MA |
| 2405 | Senica | Washington | 98 Morton Ave | Windsor | CT |
| 3902 | Marg | O'Malley | 981 Circle Dr | Santa Fe | NM |

**Product**

| Row key | name | descr | qty_avail | category | |
|---|---|---|---|---|---|
| 38383 | Dell Latitude E6410 | Laptop with ... | 124 | Computer | |
| 48282 | Apple iPhone | iPhone 6 with ... | 345 | Phone | |
| 59595 | Galaxy Tab S | Samsung tablet ... | 743 | Tablet | |

**Cust_by_Prod**

| Row key | 123 | 287 | 1987 | 2405 | 3902 |
|---|---|---|---|---|---|
| 38383 | Smith | | Badal | | |
| 48282 | Smith | Jones | | | O'Malley |
| 59595 | | | | Washington | |

**Prod_by_Cust**

| Row key | 38383 | 48282 | 59595 | | |
|---|---|---|---|---|---|
| 123 | Dell Latitude E6410 | Apple iPhone | | | |
| 287 | | Apple iPhone | | | |
| 1987 | Dell Latitude E6410 | | | | |
| 2405 | | | Galaxy Tab S | | |
| 3902 | | Apple iPhone | | | |

**Figure 11.10**  *Example of tables as indexes method.*

A similar approach works for the second report as well. To list all products purchased by a customer, you start with the customer table to find the customer identifier and any information about the customer needed for the report, for example, address, credit score, last purchase date, and so forth. Information about the products purchased is found in the Prod _ by _ Cust table shown in Figure 11.10.

> ❖ **Tip** Using tables as secondary indexes will, of course, require more storage than if no additional tables were used. The same is the case when using column family database systems to manage indexes. In both cases, you are trading additional storage space for better performance.

When using tables as indexes, you will be responsible for maintaining the indexes. You have two broad options with regard to the timing of updates. You could update the index whenever there is a change to the base tables, for example, when a customer makes a purchase. Alternatively, you could run a batch job at regular intervals to update the index tables.

Updating index tables at the same time you update the base tables keeps the indexes up to date at all times. This is a significant advantage if the reports that use the index table could be run at any time. A drawback of this approach is that your application will have to perform two write operations, one to the base table and one to the index table. This could lead to longer latencies during write operations.

Updating index tables with batch jobs has the advantage of not adding additional work to write operations. The obvious disadvantage is that there is a period of time when the data in the base tables and the indexes is out of synchronization. This might be acceptable in some cases. For example, if the reports that use the index tables only run at night as part of a larger batch job, then the index tables could be updated just prior to running the report. Your reporting requirements should guide your choice of update strategy (see Figure 11.11).

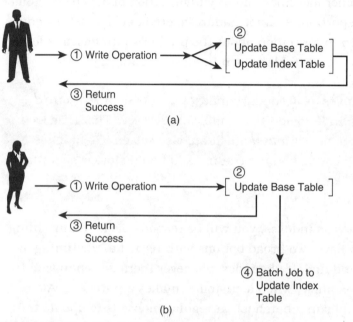

(a)

(b)

**Figure 11.11**    *(a) Updating an index table during write operations keeps data synchronized but increases the time needed to complete a write operation. (b) Batch updates introduce periods of time when the data is not synchronized, but this may be acceptable in some cases.*

## Tools for Working with Big Data

NoSQL database options, such as key-value, document, and graph databases, are used with a wide range of applications with varying data sizes. Column family databases certainly could be used with small data sets, but other database types are probably better options.

❖ **Note** If you find yourself working with Apache HBase or Cassandra, two popular column family databases, you are probably dealing with Big Data.

The term *Big Data* does not have a precise definition. Informally, data sets that are too large to efficiently store and analyze in relational databases are considered Big Data. Internet search companies, such as Yahoo!, found early that relational databases would not meet the needs of a web search service. They went on to create the Hadoop platform, which is now an Apache project with broad community support.

A more formal and commonly used definition is due to the Gartner research group.[1] Gartner defines Big Data as high velocity, high volume, and/or high variety. Velocity refers to the speed at which data is generated or changed. Volume refers to the size of the data. Variety refers to the range of data types and the scope of information included in the data.

A database with information about weather, traffic, population, and cell phone use must contend with large volumes of rapidly generated data about different entities and in different forms. A column family database would be a good option for such a database.

Databases are designed to store and retrieve data, and they perform these operations well. There are, however, a number of supporting and related tasks that are usually required to get the most out of your database. These tasks include

- Extracting, transforming, and loading data (ETL)

- Analyzing data

- Monitoring database performance

Innovative designers and developers created NoSQL databases to address an emerging need. Similarly, a wide community of designers and developers has created tools to perform additional operations required to support Big Data services.

---

1. Laney Douglas. "The Importance of 'Big Data': A Definition." http://www.gartner.com/resId=2057415.

## Extracting, Transforming, and Loading Big Data

Moving large amounts of data is challenging for several reasons, including

- Insufficient network throughput for the volume of data
- The time required to copy large volumes of data
- The potential for corrupting data during transmission
- Storing large amounts of data at the source and target

Data warehousing developers have faced these same problems for decades, and the challenges have gotten only more difficult with Big Data. There are many ETL tools available for data warehouse developers. Scaling ETL to Big Data volumes and variety requires attention to factors that are not common to smaller data warehouse implementations.

Examples of ETL tools for Big Data include

- Apache Flume
- Apache Sqoop
- Apache Pig

Each of these addresses particular needs in Big Data ETL and, like HBase, is part of the Hadoop ecosystem of tools.

Apache Flume is designed to move large amounts of log data, but it can be used for other types of data as well. It is a distributed system, so it has many of the benefits you have probably come to expect from such systems: reliability, scalability, and fault tolerance. It uses a streaming event model to capture and deliver data. When an event occurs, such as data is written to a log file, data is sent to Flume. Flume sends the data through a channel, which is an abstraction for delivering the data to one or more destinations.

Apache Sqoop works with relational databases to move data to and from Big Data sources, such as the Hadoop file system and to the HBase column family database. Sqoop also allows developers to run massively parallel computations in the form of MapReduce jobs.

> ▶ *MapReduce is described in more detail in the "Tools for Analyzing Big Data" section, later in this chapter.*

Apache Pig is a data flow language that provides a succinct way to transform data. The programming language, known as Pig Latin, has high-level statements for loading, filtering, aggregating, and joining data. Pig programs are translated into MapReduce jobs.

## Analyzing Big Data

One of the reasons companies and other organizations collect Big Data is that such data holds potentially valuable insights. That is, someone can glean those insights from all the data. There are many ways to analyze data, look for patterns, and otherwise extract useful information. Two broad disciplines are useful here: statistics and machine learning.

### Describing and Predicting with Statistics

Statistics is the branch of mathematics that studies how to describe large data sets, also known as populations in statistics parlance, and how to make inference from data. Descriptive statistics are particularly useful for understanding the characteristics of your data.

> ❖ **Note** Something as simple as an average and a standard deviation, which is a measure of the spread in your data, can give you a useful picture of your data, especially when comparing it with other, related data.

Figure 11.12 shows an example of the dollar value of average orders in the months of November and December. Notice that in November, the average was lower than in December and there was more variation in the size of orders. December orders have a higher average and less variation. Perhaps last-minute holiday shoppers had to purchase as much as possible from one retailer in order to finish their shopping.

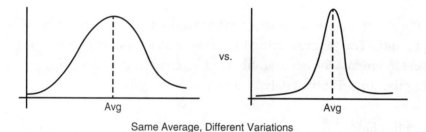

Same Average, Different Variations

**Figure 11.12**   *Descriptive statistics help us understand the composition of our data and how it compares with other, related data sets.*

Predictive, or inferential, statistics is the study of methods for making predictions based on data (see Figure 11.13). For example, if the average December order has been increasing by 1% each year for the past 10 years, you might predict that this year's December average will increase by 1% as well. This is a trivial example, but predictive statistics can be used for much more complex problems that include confounding factors, such as seasonal variations and differences in data set sizes.

❖ **Note** There is much more to statistics and machine learning than presented here. See the "References" section at the end of the chapter for additional resources in these areas.

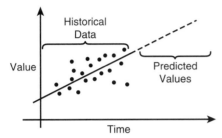

**Figure 11.13**  *Predictive statistics help us make inferences about new situations using existing data.*

### Finding Patterns with Machine Learning

Machine learning is another discipline proving useful for Big Data analysis. Machine learning incorporates methods from several disciplines, including computer science, artificial intelligence, statistics, linear algebra, and others. Many services might be taken for granted, such as getting personal recommendations based on past purchases, analyzing the sentiment in social media posts, fraud detection, and machine translation, but all depend on machine-learning techniques.

One area of machine learning, called unsupervised learning, is useful for exploring large data sets. A common unsupervised learning method is clustering. Clustering algorithms are helpful when you want to find nonapparent structures or common patterns in data. For example, your company may have a cluster of customers who tend to shop late at night and early in the week. Marketing professionals can devise incentives targeted at this particular group to increase the average dollar value of their purchases.

Supervised learning techniques provide the means to learn from examples. A credit card company, for example, has large volumes of data on legitimate credit card transactions as well as data on fraudulent transactions. There are many ways to use this data to create classifiers, which are programs that can analyze transactions and classify them as either legitimate or fraudulent.

### Tools for Analyzing Big Data

NoSQL database users have the option of using freely available distributed platforms for building their own tools or using available statistics and machine-learning tools. Four widely used tools are

- MapReduce

- Spark

- R

- Mahout

MapReduce and Spark are distributed platforms. R is a widely used statistics package, and Mahout is a machine-learning system designed for Big Data.

MapReduce is a programming model used for distributed, parallel processing. MapReduce programs consist of two primary components: a mapping function and a reducing function. The MapReduce engine applies the mapping function to a set of input data to generate a stream of output values. Those values are then transformed by a reducing function, which often performs aggregating operations, like counting, summing, or averaging the input data. The MapReduce model is a core part of the Apache Hadoop project and is widely used for Big Data analysis.

Spark is another distributed computational platform. Spark was designed by researchers at the University of California, Berkley, as an alternative to MapReduce. Both are designed to solve similar types of problems, but they take different approaches. MapReduce writes much data to disk, whereas Spark makes more use of memory. MapReduce employs a fairly rigid computational model (map operation followed by reduce operation), whereas Spark allows for more general computational models.

R is an open source statistics platform. The core platform contains modules for many common statistical functions. Libraries with additional capabilities are added to the R environment as needed by users. Libraries are available to support machine learning and data mining, specialized disciplines (for example, aquatic sciences), visualization, and specialized statistical methods. R did not start out as a tool for Big Data, but at least two libraries are available that support Big Data analysis.

Mahout is an Apache project developing machine-learning tools for Big Data. Mahout machine-learning packages were originally written as MapReduce programs, but newer implementations are using Spark. Mahout is especially useful for recommendations, classification, and clustering.

## Tools for Monitoring Big Data

One of the primary responsibilities of system administrators is ensuring applications and servers are running as expected. When an application runs on a cluster of servers instead of a single server, the system administrator's job is even more difficult. General cluster-monitoring tools and database-specific tools can help with distributed systems management. Examples of these tools are

- Ganglia
- Hannibal for HBase
- OpsCenter for Cassandra

Ganglia is monitoring tool designed for high-performance clusters. It is not specific to any one type of database. It uses a hierarchical model to represent nodes in a cluster and manage communication between nodes. Ganglia is a freely available open source tool.

Hannibal is an open source monitoring tool for HBase. It is especially useful for monitoring and managing regions, which are high-level data structures used in distributing data. Hannibal includes visualization tools that allow administrators to quickly assess the current and historical state of data distribution in the cluster.

OpsCenter is another open source tool, but it is designed for the Cassandra database. OpsCenter gives system administrators a single point of access to information about the state of the cluster and jobs running on the cluster.

# Summary

Column family databases are designed for large volumes of data. They are flexible in regard to the type of data stored and the structure of schemas. Although you will find a good amount of overlap in terminology between relational database and column family databases, the similarity is only superficial. Column family databases optimize storage by using efficient data structures for sparse, multidimensional data sets.

To get the most out of your column family database, it is important to work with, and not against, the data structures and processes that implement the column family database. Guidelines outlined in this chapter can help when designing tables, column families, and columns.

The discussion of indexes demonstrates a common choice developers and designers face: Which is more important, time or space? When time—as in query response time—is important, use indexes. Column family databases automatically index on row keys. When you need secondary indexes on column values and your database system does not support them, you can implement your own indexes using tables. There are some disadvantages to this approach compared with database-supported secondary indexes, but the benefits often outweigh the disadvantages.

If you find yourself using a column family database, you are probably working with Big Data. It helps to use tools designed specifically for moving, processing, and managing Big Data and Big Data systems.

## Case Study: Customer Data Analysis

Chapter 1, "Different Databases for Different Requirements," introduced TransGlobal Transport and Shipping (TGTS), a fictitious transportation company that coordinates the movement of goods around the globe for businesses of all sizes. Chapter 8, "Designing for Document Databases," discussed how the shipping company could use document databases to help manage shipping manifests.

The following case study applies concepts you learned in this chapter to show how TGTS can use column family databases to store and analyze large volumes of data about its customers and their shipping practices.

### Understanding User Needs

Analysts at TGTS would like to understand how customer shipping patterns are changing. The analysts have several hypotheses about why some customers are shipping more and others are shipping less. They would like to have a large data store with a wide range of data, including

- All shipping orders for all customers since the start of the company

- All details kept in customer records

- News articles, industry newsletters, and other text on their customers' industries and markets

- Historical data about the shipping industry, especially financial databases

The variety and volume of data put this project into the Big Data category, so the development team decides to use a column family database. Next, they turn their attention to specific query requirements.

In the first phase of the project, analysts want to apply statistical and machine-learning techniques to get a better sense of the data. Questions include: Are there clusters of similar customers or shipping orders? How does the average value of order vary by customer and by time of year the shipment is made? They also want to run reports on specific customers and shipping routes. The queries for these reports are

- For a particular customer, what orders have been placed?

- For a particular order, what items were shipped?

- For a particular route, how many ships used that route in a given time period?

- For customers in a particular industry, how many shipments were made during a particular period of time?

The database designers have a good sense of the entities that need to be modeled in the first phase of the project. The column store database will need tables for

- Customers

- Orders

- Ships

- Routes

Customers will have a single column family with data about company name, addresses, contacts, industry, and market categories. Orders will have details about items shipped, such as names, descriptions, and weights. Ships will have details about the capacity, age, maintenance history, and other features of the vessels. Routes will store descriptive information about routes as well as geographic details of the route.

In addition to the tables for the four primary entities, the designers will implement tables as indexes for the following:

- Orders by customer

- Shipped items by order

- Ships by route

The tables as indexes allow for rapid retrieval of data as needed by the queries. Because these reports are run after data is loaded in batch, it is not a problem if the base tables and tables as indexes are not synchronized for some time during the load.

In addition, because some of the queries make a reference to a period of time, the designers will implement database-managed indexes on data columns. This will allow developers and users to issue queries and filter by date without having to use specialized index tables.

## Review Questions

1. What is the role of end-user queries in column family database design?

2. How can you avoid performing joins in column family databases?

3. Why should entities be modeled in a single row?

4. What is hotspotting, and why should it be avoided?

5. What are some disadvantages of using complex data structures as a column value?

6. Describe three scenarios in which you should not use secondary indexes.

7. What are the disadvantages of managing your own tables as indexes?

8.  What are two types of statistics? What are they each used for?

9.  What are two types of machine learning? What are they used for?

10. How is Spark different from MapReduce?

# References

Apache Cassandra Glossary: http://io.typepad.com/glossary.html

Apache HBase Reference Guide: http://hbase.apache.org/book.html

Bishop, Christopher M. *Pattern Recognition and Machine Learning.* vol. 4. no. 4. New York: Springer, 2006.

Chang, Fay, et al. "BigTable: A Distributed Storage System for Structured Data." OSDI'06: Seventh Symposium on Operating System Design and Implementation, Seattle, WA, November, 2006. http://research.google.com/archive/bigtable.html

FoundationDB. "ACID Claims." https://foundationdb.com/acid-claims

Hewitt, Eben. *Cassandra: The Definitive Guide.* Sebastopol, CA: O'Reilly Media, Inc., 2010.

Pedregosa, Fabian, et al. "Scikit-learn: Machine Learning in Python." *The Journal of Machine Learning Research* 12 (2011): 2825–2830.

Ratner, Bruce. *Statistical and Machine-Learning Data Mining: Techniques for Better Predictive Modeling and Analysis of Big Data.* Boca Raton: CRC Press, 2011.

Rice University, University of Houston Clear Lake, and Tufts University. "Online Statistics Education: An Interactive Multimedia Course of Study": http://onlinestatbook.com/

Wikibooks. "Statistics." http://en.wikibooks.org/wiki/Statistics

# ■ ■ ■ ■ ■ ■ ■ ■ ■ ■ ■ Part V

# Graph
# Databases

# 12

# Introduction to Graph Databases

*"They told me computers could only do arithmetic."*
—GRACE HOPPER
COMPUTER SCIENTIST AND U.S. NAVY REAR ADMIRAL

## Topics Covered In This Chapter

Design Criteria of Graph Databases

Graphs and Network Modeling

Advantages of Graph Databases

In this chapter, you learn about a specialized type of database known as a graph database. A graph database is based on a branch of mathematics known as graph theory. The techniques in this area of mathematics are useful for analyzing connections and links between entities. As you shall see, these techniques are quite useful in many data management areas.

## What Is a Graph?

Graphs are mathematical objects that consist of two parts: vertices and edges. Vertices are sometimes called nodes; however, this chapter avoids this term to prevent confusion because the term *node* can also refer to a server in a cluster.

Vertices represent things. They could be just about anything, including

- Cities

- Employees in a company

**363**

- Proteins

- Electrical circuits

- Junctions in a water line

- Organisms in an ecosystem

- Train stations

One thing that is common with all of these things is that they have relationships to other things—often in the same category. Cities are connected to other cities by roads. Employees work with other employees. Proteins interact with other proteins. Electrical circuits are linked to other electrical circuits. Junctions in water lines connect to other junctions. Organisms in ecosystems are predators and prey of other organisms. Train stations are connected to other train stations by railway lines.

The links or connections between entities are represented by edges. This might seem like an obvious representation for some relations, such as roads and railway lines between cities. However, it might be less obvious in other cases, such as interacting proteins and organisms in an ecosystem. The flexible nature of vertices and edges makes them well suited to model both concrete and abstract relations between things.

Figure 12.1 shows a simple graph with two vertices and one edge.

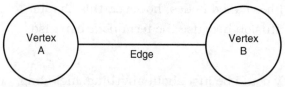

**Figure 12.1**   *A simple graph with two vertices and one edge.*

Some relations are long term (for example, roads between cities), whereas others are short term (for example, a person passing on a bacterial infection to another person). Additionally, some are physically obvious, whereas others have no physical instantiation. For instance, you can see a water line, but the manager-employee relationship in a business has no physical representation.

# Graphs and Network Modeling

At first glance, it is obvious that graphs are good for modeling networks. However, it might also appear that networks are specialized systems and not generalized to a wide range of problems; this assumption is incorrect. If you think of networks as things and relations between those things, you can start to see networks everywhere. Here are several examples to show the breadth of problems you can tackle by modeling systems as graphs.

## Modeling Geographic Locations

Highways and railways have two distinct properties of interest here: They are designed to link geographic locations and they last a long time.

Geographic locations are modeled as vertices. These could be cities, towns, or intersections of highways. Vertices have properties, like names, latitudes, and longitudes. In the case of towns and cities, they have populations and size measured in square miles or kilometers.

Highways and railways are modeled as edges between two vertices. They also have properties, such as length, year built, and maximum speed.

Highways could be modeled in two ways. A highway could be a single edge between two cities, in which case it models the road traffic in both directions. Alternatively, a graphical representation could use two edges, one to represent travel in each direction (for example, east to west and west to east). Which is the "right way" to model highways? It depends.

If your goal is to model distance and approximate travel times between cities, then a single edge might be sufficient. If you are interested in more detailed descriptions of highways, such as direction, number of lanes, current construction areas, and locations of accidents, then using two edges is a better option. When you use two edges between cities, it helps to indicate which direction traffic is flowing. This is done with a type of edge known as a directed edge (see Figure 12.2).

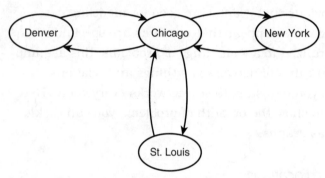

**Figure 12.2**    *Highways between cities are modeled as vertices and edges.*

## Modeling Infectious Diseases

Infectious diseases can spread from person to person. For example, a person coughs into his hand and bacteria and viruses are left on his hand. When that person shakes the hand of someone else, there is a chance that a pathogen is transmitted to the other person, who may eventually become infected. The spread of infectious disease is readily modeled using graphs.

Vertices represent people, whereas edges represent interactions between people, such as shaking hands or standing in close proximity. Both the vertices and the edges have properties that help represent the way diseases spread (see Figure 12.3).

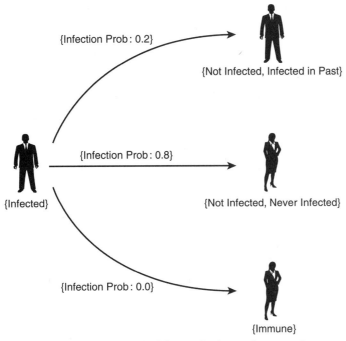

{Infection Prob: 0.2}

{Not Infected, Infected in Past}

{Infection Prob: 0.8}

{Infected}

{Not Infected, Never Infected}

{Infection Prob: 0.0}

{Immune}

**Figure 12.3** *The spread of flu and other infectious diseases is modeled as graphs.*

People have properties, such as age and weight. In the case of the infectious disease model, the most important property is infection status, which could be

- Not infected now, never infected before

- Not infected now, infected in the past

- Infected now

- Immune

You want to keep track of these properties because they influence the probability of becoming infected:

- If you are not infected now and never have been, you have a moderately high probability of becoming infected upon contact with an infected person.

- If you are not infected now but were infected in the past, you have probably acquired some immunity to the infectious disease. This means you have a low probability of getting infected upon contact with an infected person.

- If you are infected now and come in contact with another infected person, you will both continue to be infected. There is no change.

- If you are immune, either because of some natural immunity or medical immunization, then you will not become infected upon contact with another infected person.

The state of an infectious disease graph would change frequently as people interact; some people become infected while others recover from the disease. As you can see, this is much different from the railways and highways example, which is fairly static in terms of nodes and edges. Properties of cities and roads may change as populations change and car accidents occur. The infectious disease graph changes as people interact, something that happens frequently and rapidly.

Edges—or in this case, interactions between people—have properties. For example, there is a probability that someone will transmit a disease to another person by shaking hands. This interaction has a higher rate of transmission than two people standing in close proximity but not touching. Some pathogens require physical contact to spread disease, whereas other airborne diseases can transmit without direct contact. These are the kinds of properties that would be associated with edges.

Graphs are useful for more than modeling railways and disease transmission. Sometimes there is no flow or transmission of objects between vertices. Instead, some graphs model relations between things that persist over time.

## Modeling Abstract and Concrete Entities

Graphs are well suited to model abstract relations, like a part-of relation. For example, the state of Oregon is a part of the United States, and the province of Quebec is a part of Canada. The city of Portland is located in Oregon, and the city of Montreal is located in Quebec. This kind of hierarchical relationship is modeled in a special type of graph known as a tree.

A tree has a special vertex call the root. The root is the top of the hierarchy. Figure 12.4 shows two trees, one for the United States and one for Canada. Both show the relationship between national, regional, and local government entities.

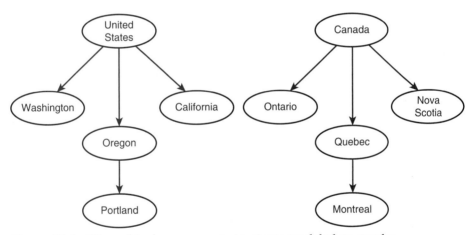

**Figure 12.4**  *Hierarchical government structures modeled as graphs.*

Notice that all nodes connect up to only one other vertex. The upper vertex is often called the parent vertex, and the lower vertices are called children vertices. Parent vertices can have multiple children vertices.

Trees are useful for modeling hierarchical relationships, such as organization charts, as well as part-of relations, such as parts of a car, as shown in Figure 12.5.

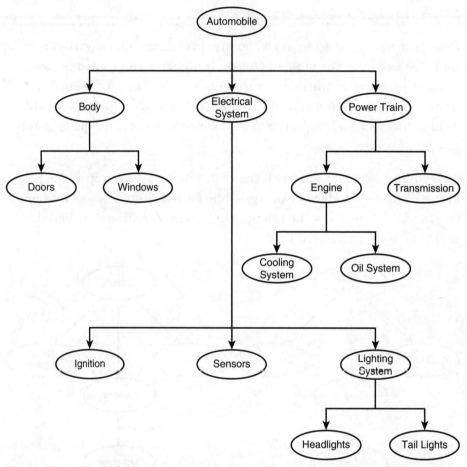

**Figure 12.5**   *Part-of relations, such as parts of a car, are modeled using a graph.*

The examples so far have focused on flows or relations between entities of the same type, such as cities and governments; graphs can also model relations between different types of entities.

## Modeling Social Media

Social networking sites like Facebook and LinkedIn allow users to interact and communicate with each other online. They have extended the way people communicate by introducing new ways of interacting, such as the "Like" button. This makes it quick and easy to indicate you like or appreciate someone else's post.

A social media "like" can be modeled as a link between a person and a post. Many people can like the same post, and people can have multiple posts each with a different number of likes. The vertices in this case would be people and posts. It is worth pointing out, not all vertices and edges have to be of the same type; there can be a mix of different types in a single graph.

Figure 12.6 shows an example of a people-like-posts graph. You will notice, unlike many other graphs, this has a special property. The edges only go from people to posts; there are no edges between people or between posts. This is a special type of graph known as a bipartite graph, and it is useful for modeling relations between different types of entities.

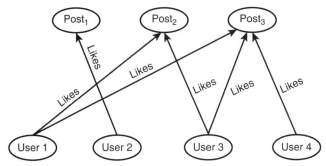

**Figure 12.6** *Social media posts and likes are modeled by graphs.*

As these examples show, graphs are capable of modeling a wide range of entities and relations. An obvious question probably comes to mind: What are good use cases for graph databases?

# Advantages of Graph Databases

Graph databases show explicit relations between entities. Vertices represent entities, and they are linked or connected by edges. In relational databases, connections are not represented as links. Instead, two entities share a common attribute value, which is known as a key.

## Query Faster by Avoiding Joins

To find connections or links in a relational database, you must perform an operation called a join. A join entails looking up a value from one table in another table. For example, in Figure 12.7, the table Students has a list of student names and IDs. The student ID is also used in the table Enrollment to indicate a student is enrolled in a course. To list all of the courses a student is enrolled in, you need to perform a join between two tables. This can be time consuming when using join operations frequently on large tables.

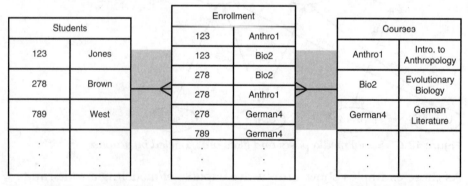

**Figure 12.7**   *Representing a student-course relation in a relational database.*

Alternatively, you can represent relations between a student and a course using a graph, as shown in Figure 12.8. The edges between students and courses allow users to quickly query all the courses a particular student is enrolled in.

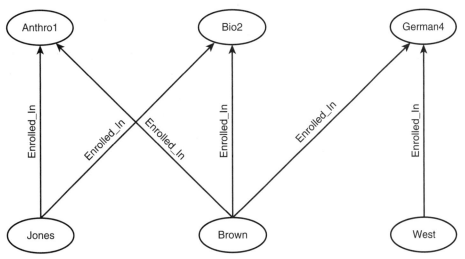

**Figure 12.8**    *Representing a student-course relation in a graph database.*

The infectious disease example shows even more dramatically how graphs can help avoid joins. Figure 12.9 shows a relational table with information about people and their state of infection. It also shows a table indicating interactions between people.

| Course_of_Infection | |
|---|---|
| Patient | Infected By |
| Patient A | Patient B |
| Patient B | Patient C |
| Patient C | Patient D |
| Patient D | Patient E |
| Patient E | Patient F |
| Patient F | Patient G |
| Patient G | <Null>  ⟵ Patient Zero |

**Figure 12.9**    *Finding Patient Zero in an infectious disease investigation.*

During an outbreak, it helps to understand either the source of an outbreak or the first person infected with a disease. Suppose you know Patient A was infected by Patient B, and Patient B was infected by Patient C, and so on. If you were to start with Patient A, you would need to perform a join to find she was infected by Patient B. Next, you would need to query the interaction table to find out Patient C had infected Patient B. The process would continue until you found the person who was not infected by someone else (that is, *Patient Zero*, or the *index case* in epidemiological parlance).

❖ **Tip** In a graph database, instead of performing joins, you follow edges from vertex to vertex. This is a much simpler and faster operation.

## Fun with Graphs

Graphs have even made their way into popular entertainment. Take the board game *Pandemic* from Z-Man Games, for instance. In *Pandemic*, players work together to suppress and eradicate four different infectious diseases, represented by colored plastic blocks. The game board displays numerous major cities across the world, and each city possesses between two and six lines connecting it to another city. Each line represents a pathway for transmission of a given disease. Throughout the game, players utilize unique powers assigned to them at the beginning of the game to remove the colored blocks from the board.

As you can see, *Pandemic*'s gameplay takes place within a graphical model. Cities act as the vertices, whereas the lines serve as edges. You may also attribute certain properties to the vertices and edges. For instance, each city has a certain number of lines connecting it to other cities, as well as a level of infection, represented by the number of colored blocks on a city. In this case, properties of the edges are more abstract. They include whether or not the lines connect two infected cites, two healthy cities, or one infected city and one healthy city.

## Simplified Modeling

Working with graph databases can simplify the modeling process. When you work with relational databases, you typically start by modeling the main entities in your domain. In the case of social media, this could be people and posts. In the case of infectious diseases, the main entity is just people. When you start to model information about interactions, it can start to get more complicated.

For example, in the social media area, many people may like a post and a post may be liked by many people. This is known as a many-to-many relation, which is modeled as another table, as shown in Figure 12.10.

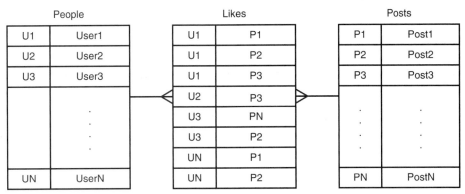

| People | | Likes | | Posts | |
|---|---|---|---|---|---|
| U1 | User1 | U1 | P1 | P1 | Post1 |
| U2 | User2 | U1 | P2 | P2 | Post2 |
| U3 | User3 | U1 | P3 | P3 | Post3 |
| | | U2 | P3 | | |
| | . | U3 | PN | . | . |
| | . | U3 | P2 | . | . |
| | . | UN | P1 | . | . |
| UN | UserN | UN | P2 | PN | PostN |

**Figure 12.10** *Modeling many-to-many relations in a relational database.*

In a graph database, there is no need to create tables to model many-to-many relations; instead, they are explicitly modeled using edges.

## Multiple Relations Between Entities

Using multiple types of edges allows database designers to readily model multiple relations between entities. This is particularly useful when modeling transportation options between entities. For example, a transportation company might want to consider road, rail, and air transportation between cities (see Figure 12.11). Each has different properties, such as time to deliver, cost, and government regulations.

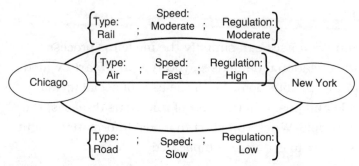

**Figure 12.11**   *Modeling multiple types of relations in a graph database.*

Multiple relations can be modeled in relational databases, but they are explicit and easy to understand when using a graph database.

## Summary

Interactions and relations between entities are commonplace. Graph theory provides a solid foundation for building graph databases and analyzing relations between entities. As the examples in this chapter show, the power of graph theory can be applied to a wide range of problems. The next chapter introduces additional terms and concepts that will be useful for analyzing graph data.

## Review Questions

1. What are the two components of a graph?

2. List at least three sample entities that can be modeled as vertices.

3. List at least three sample relations that can be modeled as edges.

4. What properties could you associate with a vertex representing a city?

5. What properties could you associate with an edge representing a highway between two cities?

6. Epidemiologists use graphs to model the spread of infection. What do vertices represent? What do edges represent?

7. Give an example of a part-of hierarchy.

8. How do graph databases avoid joins?

9. How is a person-likes-post graph different from other graphs used as examples in this chapter?

10. Give an example of a business application that would use multiple types of edges (relations) between vertices.

## References

Easley, David, and Jon Kleinberg. *Networks, Crowds, and Markets: Reasoning About a Highly Connected World.* Cambridge, England: Cambridge University Press, 2010.

Robinson, Ian, Jim Webber, and Emil Eifrem. *Graph Databases.* Sebastopol, CA: O'Reilly Media, Inc., 2013.

Trudeau, Richard J. *Introduction to Graph Theory.* Mineola, NY: Courier Dover Publications, 2013.

# 13

# Graph Database Terminology

*"If the industrial age was about building things,*
*the social era is about connecting things, people and ideas."*
—Nilofer Merchant
Founder and CEO, Rubicon Consulting

## Topics Covered In This Chapter

Elements of Graphs

Operations on Graphs

Properties of Graphs and Nodes

Types of Graphs

A graph is a fairly abstract concept. It includes two basic components: vertices and edges. Even with such a simple model, graphs are suitable for modeling a number of domain areas. This forms the foundation for their usefulness as a major type of NoSQL database.

When you consider other properties of graphs, such as weights on edges, and operations you can perform on graphs, such as taking an intersection of two graphs, you have even more capabilities from a modeling perspective.

The goal of this chapter is to define terminology about graphs, their components, operations on graphs, and properties of graphs. Graphs are different from tables and documents and have distinct properties. In this chapter, you learn how these differences enable you to create higher-level abstractions that can fit well with some problem domains, such as modeling social networks, transportation systems, and flow networks.

# Elements of Graphs

There are two basic building blocks of graphs: vertices and edges. This section introduces these two components. Using these two components, you can construct higher-level structures such as paths, which are sets of connected edges and vertices. You also learn about loops, a special type of path that sometimes requires specialized processing.

## Vertex

A *vertex* represents an entity marked with a unique identifier—analogous to a row key in a column family database or a primary key in a relational database.

> ❖ **Note**  Note that the term *node* is an acceptable replacement for *vertex*. However, this book only uses the latter to avoid confusion with the use of *node* to describe a service running in a cluster.

A vertex can represent virtually any entity that has a relation with another entity (see Figure 13.1). Vertices can represent

- People in a social network

- Cities connected by highways

- Proteins that interact with other proteins in the body

- Warehouses in a company's distribution network

- Compute servers in a cluster

**Figure 13.1**    *Vertices are used to represent objects.*

Vertices can have properties. For example, a vertex in a social network represents a person; it has properties like a name, an address, and a birth date. Similarly, a graph of a highway system uses vertices to represent cities. Cities have populations, a longitude and latitude, and a name, and are located in a geographic region.

## Edge

An *edge*, also known as a *link* or *arc*, defines relationships between vertices or objects connecting vertices (see Figure 13.2). For example, in a family tree database, vertices can represent people, whereas the edges represent the relationships between them, such as "daughter of" and "father of." In the case of a highway database, cities are represented with vertices, whereas edges represent highways linking the cities.

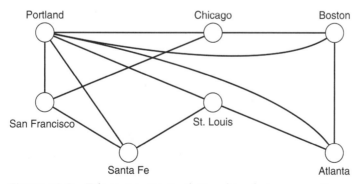

**Figure 13.2**    *Edges represent relationships between vertices.*

Much like vertices, edges have properties. For example, in the highway database, all edges will have properties, such as distance, speed limit, and number of lanes. In the family tree example, edges may have properties such as indicating whether two people are related by marriage, adoption, or biology.

A commonly used property is called the *weight* of an edge (see Figure 13.3). Weights represent some value about the relationship. For example, in the case of highways, weight could be the distance between cities. In a social network, weight could be an indication of how frequently the two individuals post on each other's walls or comment on each other's posts. In general, weights can represent cost, distance, or another measure of the relationship between objects represented by vertices.

❖ **Note** Not all graphs have weights. For instance, edge weight would not be a factor in a family tree graph.

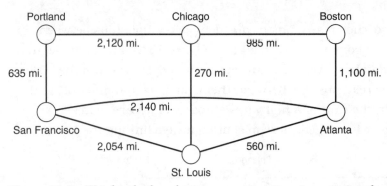

**Figure 13.3**  *Weighted edges have a numeric property associated with them.*

There are two types of edges: directed and undirected (see Figure 13.4). Directed edges have a direction. This is used to indicate how the relationship, as modeled by the edge, should be interpreted. For example, in a family relations graph, there is a direction associated with a "parent of" relation. However, direction is not always needed. The highway graph, for instance, could be undirected, assuming traffic flows both ways.

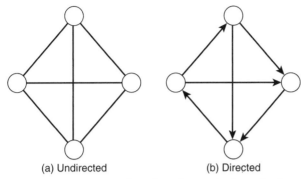

(a) Undirected                    (b) Directed

**Figure 13.4**   *Directed and undirected edges further refine properties of relationships between vertices by capturing directionality.*

## Path

A *path* through a graph is a set of vertices along with the edges between those vertices (see Figure 13.5). The vertices in a graph are all different from each other. If edges are directed, the path is a directed path. If the graph is undirected, the paths in it are undirected paths.

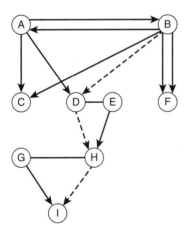

I ⟶ H ⟶ D ⟶ B    Ancestor Path

**Figure 13.5**   *A path is a set of vertices and edges through a graph. The vertices and edges from B to D to H to I are a path from vertex B to vertex I.*

Paths are important because they capture information about how vertices in a graph are related. For example, in a family graph, a person is an ancestor of someone else only if there is a directed path from the person to her ancestor. In the case of a family tree, there is only one path from a person to an ancestor. In the case of a highway graph, there may be multiple paths between cities.

A common problem encountered when working with graphs is to find the least weighted path between two vertices. The weight can represent cost of using the edge, time required to traverse the edge, or some other metric that you are trying to minimize.

## Loop

A *loop* is an edge that connects a vertex to itself (see Figure 13.6). For example, in biology, proteins can interact with other proteins. Some proteins interact with other protein molecules of the same type. A loop could be used to represent this. However, like direction, it might not make sense to allow loops in some graphs. For instance, a loop would not make much sense in a family tree graph; people cannot be their own parents or children.

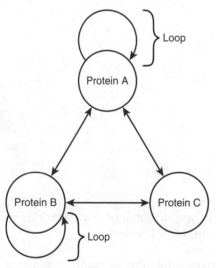

**Figure 13.6**   *A loop is an edge that links a vertex to itself.*

# Operations on Graphs

Common operations performed on databases include inserting, reading, updating, and deleting data. You do this in graph databases as well. In the case of relational, document, and column family databases, you often perform aggregations, such as counting or summing values from multiple rows in the database.

Graph databases are also well suited for an additional set of operations. Specifically, operations can be used to follow paths or detect repeating patterns in relationships between vertices.

The following sections cover three important operations unique to graphs:

- Union of graphs
- Intersection of graphs
- Graph traversal

## Union of Graphs

The *union of graphs* is the combined set of vertices and edges in a graph.

Consider two graphs. The first graph, A, has vertices 1, 2, 3, and 4, and the edges are {1, 2}, {1, 3}, and {1, 4}. The second graph, B, has vertices 1, 4, 5, and 6, and edges {1, 4}, {4, 5}, {4, 6}, and {5, 6}. Figure 13.7 shows the two graphs.

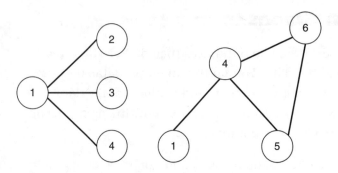

Graph A                              Graph B

**Figure 13.7**    *Two distinct graphs, A and B.*

The union of A and B is the set of vertices and edges from both graphs. The set of vertices is 1, 2, 3, 4, 5, and 6. The set of edges is {1, 2}, {1, 3}, {1, 4}, {4, 5}, {4, 6}, and {5, 6}. Because the two graphs share common vertices, the union produces a single graph (see Figure 13.8).

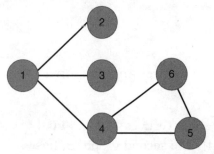

**Figure 13.8**    *Union of graphs A and B.*

## Intersection of Graphs

The *intersection of a graph* is the set of vertices and edges that are common to both graphs (see Figure 13.9). In the case of graphs A and B, the intersection of graphs includes vertices 1 and 4, as well as the edge {1, 4}.

**Figure 13.9**   *Intersection of graphs A and B.*

## Graph Traversal

*Graph traversal* is the process of visiting all vertices in a graph in a particular way (see Figure 13.10). The purpose of this is usually to either set or read some property value in a graph.

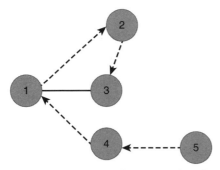

**Figure 13.10**   *Graph traversal is the process of visiting all nodes in a graph.*

For example, you might create a graph of all cities in the country that you would like to visit; cities are represented by vertices and highways by edges. You start at your home city and follow the highway with the shortest distance out of all edges between your starting city and another city on the graph.

After you visit the next city, you drive on to a third city. The third city is the city that is the shortest distance from the current city, unless you have already been to that city. For instance, you have already been to your home city, so even if your home city is closest to the second city, you would choose the next shortest route to an adjacent city. In this way, you could keep moving from city to city until you have visited all cities.

# Properties of Graphs and Nodes

Several properties of graphs and nodes are useful when comparing and analyzing graphs. These include

- Isomorphisms

- Order and Size

- Degree

- Closeness

- Betweenness

As you will see, these properties are useful when comparing graphs and when trying to identify particularly interesting vertices within a graph.

## Isomorphism

Two graphs are considered *isomorphic* if for each vertex in the first graph, there is a corresponding vertex in the other graph (see Figure 13.11). In addition, for each edge between a pair of vertices in the first graph, there is a corresponding edge between the corresponding vertices of the other graph.

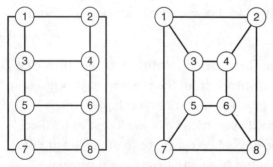

**Figure 13.11**   *Example of two isomorphic graphs.*

Graph isomorphism is important if you are trying to detect patterns in a set of graphs. In a large social network graph, there may be repeating patterns with interesting properties. For example, it may be possible to detect business collaborators by examining their links on a business social network.

Another branch of study that makes use of graphs is *epidemiology*, or the study of infectious diseases. For example, an epidemiologist who studies flu transmission in a city might build a graph of individuals and their connections to other individuals. Let's assume that they can collect data about who has the flu at any point in time and they want to determine how fast it spreads.

First, the flu may spread faster in some groups than others. This may be because of the characteristics of the individuals involved, or it could be because of patterns of interconnection that affect the rate of disease spread. If epidemiologists can identify patterns associated with infection, they could then identify other individuals by finding similar patterns and target them for intervention, education, and so on.

## Order and Size

Order and size are measures of how large a graph is. The order of a graph is the number of vertices, whereas the size of a graph is the number of edges in a graph.

The order and size of a graph are important to understand because they can affect the time and space required to perform operations. It is obvious that performing a union or intersection on a small graph would take less time than performing the same operation on a larger graph. It is also easy to assume that traversing a small graph will take less time than traversing a large graph.

Some problems sound simple but can quickly become too hard to solve in any reasonable amount of time. Consider a *clique*, which is a set of vertices in a graph that are all connected to each other. Finding cliques is impractical for large graphs.

Think of trying to find the largest subset of people in a social network that know each other; this is obviously a large undertaking. As you work with graphs and perform operations on graphs, consider how the order and size impact the time it takes to perform operations.

## Degree

*Degree* is the number of edges linked to a vertex and is one way to measure the importance of any given vertex in a graph. Vertices with high degrees are more directly connected to other vertices than vertices with low degrees. Degree is important when addressing problems of spreading information or properties through a network.

Consider a person with many family members and friends that he sees regularly; that person would have high degree. What if that person contracts the flu? It is easy to imagine it spreading to friends and family, and from there to people outside of the initial social circle. One person can infect many people if he has many connections.

As another example, think about the last time you were delayed in an airport because of bad weather. Delays in airports with high degrees, like Chicago and Atlanta, can generate ripple effects that lead to delays at other airports.

## Closeness

*Closeness* is a property of a vertex that indicates how far the vertex is from all others in the graph.

Closeness is an important measure if you want to understand the spread of information in a social network, an infectious disease in a community, or movement of materials in a distribution network.

Vertices with high closeness values can reach other vertices in the network faster than vertices with smaller closeness values. Marketers, for example, might want to target people in a social network with high closeness values to get the word out about a new product. Information will spread faster in the network if the marketer starts with someone with a high closeness value than with someone on the periphery of the network.

## Betweenness

In addition to understanding closeness, it is sometimes important to understand betweenness. *Betweenness* is a measure of how much of a bottleneck a given vertex is. Imagine a city on a river that has many roads but only one bridge (see Figure 13.12).

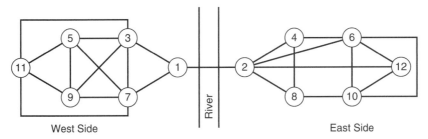

**Figure 13.12** *Betweenness helps identify bottlenecks in a graph.*

As you can see from the network, there are many ways, or paths, to move from one vertex to another on the west side of the network. Similarly, there are multiple paths to get from one vertex to another on the east side. There is only one edge that connects the west and east sides of the city, linking vertices 1 and 2.

Both vertices 1 and 2 will have high betweenness scores as they form a bottleneck in the graph. If vertex 1 or 2 were removed, it would leave the graph disconnected. However, if you removed nodes 4 or 9, for example, you could still move between any of the remaining nodes.

Betweenness helps identify potentially vulnerable parts of a network. For instance, you would not want a distribution network that depended on one bridge. If that bridge were damaged or the flow of traffic were disrupted, you would not be able to move materials to all vertices in the network.

# Types of Graphs

Graphs are useful for modeling structures and processes in many different domains. Sometimes, the graphs represent relations between entities such as people or cities. In other cases, graphs represent the flow of material or objects through a system, such as water flowing through a municipal water system or trucks on a highway. This section describes several distinct types of graphs that can be useful for your modeling need. These include

- Undirected and directed graphs

- Flow networks

- Bipartite graphs

- Multigraphs

- Weighted graphs

Graphs you create might share features from one or more of these types. For example, you might have directed and weighted graphs. It is important to remember that these types are not mutually exclusive.

## Undirected and Directed Graphs

An *undirected graph*, shown in Figure 13.13(a), is one in which the edges are not directed. This type of graph is used for modeling relations or flows where direction does not make sense. For example, you can model couples in a domestic relationship using undirected edges.

*Directed graphs*, shown in Figure 13.13 (b), are graphs with directed edges. You can model a parent-child relationship with directed edges.

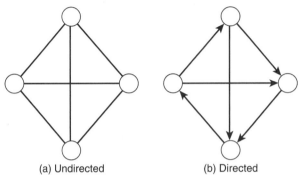

(a) Undirected            (b) Directed

**Figure 13.13**  *Undirected (a) and directed (b) graphs.*

There might be cases in which some edges in a graph are directed and some are not. For example, if you modeled employees in a business, some edges could represent a "reports to" relation between an employee and a manager. This would use a directed edge. On the other hand, a "works with" relation among peers would be without direction. It could also be modeled as two directional edges.

> ▶ *Refer to Chapter 14, "Designing for Graph Databases," to learn more about graph database design.*

## Flow Network

A *flow network* is a directed graph in which each edge has a capacity and each vertex has a set of incoming and outgoing edges. The sum of the capacity of incoming edges cannot be greater than the sum of the capacity of outgoing edges. The two exceptions to this rule are *source* and *sink* vertices. Sources have no inputs but do have outputs, whereas sinks have inputs but no outputs.

Flow networks are also called transportation networks (see Figure 13.14). Graph databases can be used to model flow networks, like road systems or transportation networks. They can also be used to model processes with continuous flows, such as a network of storm drains that take in rainwater (source) and allow it to flow into a river (sink).

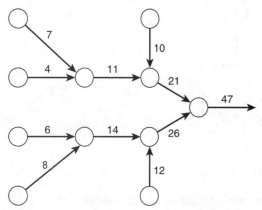

**Figure 13.14**   *Flow networks capture information about capacities of edges and how they can be combined using vertices.*

## Bipartite Graph

A *bipartite graph*, or *bigraph*, is a graph with two distinct sets of vertices where each vertex in one set is only connected to vertices in the other set (see Figure 13.15).

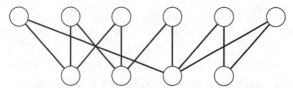

**Figure 13.15**   *A bipartite graph consists of two subgroups of nodes.*

Bipartite graphs are useful when modeling relationships between different types of objects. For example, one set of vertices might represent businesses and another might represent people. An edge between a given person and a business appears if the person works for that business. Other examples include teachers and students, members and groups, and train cars and trains.

## Multigraph

A *multigraph* is a graph with multiple edges between vertices (see Figure 13.16). Let's take a shipping company as an example.

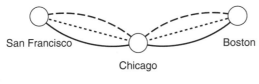

Multigraph

**Figure 13.16**   *A multigraph is used to represent multiple types of relations between vertices.*

The company could use a graph database for determining the least costly way to ship items between cities. Multiple edges between cities could represent various shipping options, such as shipping by truck, train, or plane. Each edge would have its own properties, such as the time taken to transport an item between two cities, cost per kilogram to ship, and so forth.

## Weighted Graph

A *weighted graph* is a graph in which each edge has a number assigned to it. The number can reflect a cost, a capacity, or some other measure of an edge. This is commonly used in optimization problems, such as finding the shortest path between vertices.

One way to find the shortest path is known as Dijkstra's algorithm, created by Edsger Dijkstra. Famous for his contributions to software design, the Dutch scientist actually shunned the use of computers in his own work for many years, instead opting for handwritten manuscripts.

Dijkstra's algorithm is used to find the shortest path in a network. This is ideal for routing packets on the Internet or finding the most efficient route for delivery trucks.

The algorithm states that the growth rate is equal to the number of vertices squared; this is one of those algorithms where it pays to understand size. Let's take a look at Table 13.1 for an illustration.

**Table 13.1**    *Growth Rate Calculation of Dijkstra's Algorithm*

| Number of Vertices | Time Units to Complete |
|:---:|:---:|
| 1 | 1 |
| 5 | 25 |
| 10 | 100 |
| 20 | 400 |
| 50 | 2,500 |
| 100 | 10,000 |
| 1000 | 1,000,000 |

As you can see, Dijkstra's algorithm takes time proportional to the number of vertices in the network. The time required to complete Dijkstra's algorithm increases exponentially as the number of vertices increases.

# Summary

Graphs are composed of two simple components: vertices and edges. This simplicity quickly gives way to a broad range of graph properties and features that are useful for modeling a number of phenomena.

Mathematicians and computer scientists have developed a wide array of algorithms for working with graphs. This combination of the ability to model many domains and apply general algorithms to those domains makes graphs a powerful way to represent data in a NoSQL database.

## Review Questions

1. Define a vertex.
2. Define an edge.
3. List at least three examples in which you can use graphs to model the domains.
4. Give an example of when you would use a weighted graph.
5. Give an example of when you would use a directed graph.
6. What is the difference between order and size?
7. Why is betweenness sometimes called a bottleneck measure?
8. How would an epidemiologist use closeness to understand the spread of a disease?
9. When would you use a multigraph?
10. What is Dijkstra's algorithm used for?

## References

Trudeau, Richard J. *Introduction to Graph Theory*. Mineola, NY: Dover, 1994.

Wikipedia. "Clique Problem": http://en.wikipedia.org/wiki/Clique_problem

Wikipedia. "Dijkstra's Algorithm": http://en.wikipedia.org/wiki/Dijkstra%27s_algorithm

Wikipedia. "Flow Network": http://en.wikipedia.org/wiki/Flow_network

# 14

# Designing for Graph Databases

*"We start with an idea which is then translated into a form, a structure."*
—Linda von Deursen
Graphic Designer, Faculty Yale University of Art

## Topics Covered In This Chapter

Getting Started with Graph Design

Querying a Graph

Tips and Traps of Graph Database Design

Case Study: Optimizing Transportation Routes

Graph database design has some things in common with other types of database design, but it has distinct characteristics as well. This chapter delves into details and examples of designing entity and relations between entities along with a description of two different ways of querying graph databases.

Graph databases have some unusual characteristics. Algorithms that run in reasonable time on small graphs can take a surprisingly long time with moderate or large graphs.

Design tips are included in this chapter to help you avoid, or at least recognize the potential for, such problems. This chapter concludes with a case study on the optimization of transportation routes.

# Getting Started with Graph Design

A common characteristic of NoSQL databases is the way you approach design, which is by asking what kinds of queries or analysis you will perform on the data. Graph databases are well suited to problem domains that are easily described in terms of entities and relations between those entities.

Entities can be virtually anything, from proteins to planets. Of course, other NoSQL databases and relational databases are well suited to modeling entities, too.

What makes a particular problem well suited for a graph database? A number of characteristics.

Graph database applications frequently include queries and analysis that involve

- Identifying relations between two entities
- Identifying common properties of edges from a node
- Calculating aggregate properties of edges from a node
- Calculating aggregate values of properties of nodes

Here are some examples of each of these types of queries:

- How many hops (that is, edges) does it take to get from vertex A to vertex B?
- How many edges between vertex A and vertex B have a cost that is less than 100?
- How many edges are linked to vertex A?
- What is the centrality measure of vertex B?
- Is vertex C a bottleneck; that is, if vertex C is removed, which parts of the graph become disconnected?

❖ **Note** You might have noticed these queries are different from queries associated with document and column family databases. There is less emphasis on selecting by particular properties, for example, how many vertices have at least 10 edges? Similarly, there is less emphasis on aggregating values across a group of entities. For example, in a column family database, you might have a query that selects all customer orders from the Northeast placed in the last month and sum the total value of those orders. These types of queries can be done in graph databases, but they do not reflect the flexibility and new ways of querying offered by graph databases.

The queries listed above are fairly abstract. They are stated in the terminology used by computer scientists and mathematicians when working with graphs. When it comes to designing graph databases, it is probably better to start with queries that reflect the problem domain.

## Designing a Social Network Graph Database

Imagine you are starting a new social networking site designed for NoSQL database developers. The goal is to support the NoSQL development community by providing a platform for sharing tips, asking questions, and keeping in touch with others working on similar problems. Let's assume this site will allow for developers to

- Join and leave the site

- Follow the postings of other developers

- Post questions for others with expertise in a particular area

- Suggest new connections with other developers based on shared interests

- Rank members according to their number of connections, posts, and answers

The model will start simple with just two entities: developers and posts. You can always add more later, but it helps to flesh out the relations and properties of a small number of entities at a time.

Properties of developers include

- Name

- Location

- NoSQL databases used

- Years of experience with NoSQL databases

- Areas of interest, such as data modeling, performance tuning, and security

Developers will be asked for this information when they register at the site. Posts have several properties as well, such as

- Date created

- Topic keywords

- Post type (for example, question, tip, news)

- Title

- Body of post

The application will automatically assign date created as well as topic keywords. The person posting the message will fill in the other properties (see Figure 14.1).

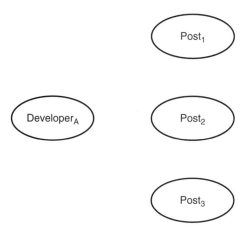

**Figure 14.1**    *Developers and posts are two types of entities in the NoSQL social network.*

Next, consider the relations between entities. Entities may have one or more relations to other entities. Because there are two types of entities, there can be four possible combinations of entity-relation-entity:

- Developer-relation-developer
- Developer-relation-post
- Post-relation-developer
- Post-relation-post

The term *relation* is a placeholder in the preceding list. As a graph database designer, one of your first tasks is to identify each of these relations.

❖ **Tip** It helps to consider all possible combinations of entities having relations when the number of entity types is small. Some of the combinations may not be relevant to the types of queries you will pose. You can eliminate them from consideration. This process helps reduce the chance that you miss a relevant relation early in the design phase.

As the number of entities grows, you might want to focus on combinations that are reasonably likely to support your queries.

The "follows" relation is the only relation between developers in the simple model (see Figure 14.2). If Robert Smith follows Andrea Wilson, then Robert will see all of Andrea's posts when he logs on to the NoSQL social network. The site designers believe the followers of a developer might be interested in who that developer follows as well. For example, if Andrea follows Charles Vita, then Robert should see Charles's posts as well. You can imagine adding posts from the developers Charles follows, but that could start to overwhelm Robert's feed.

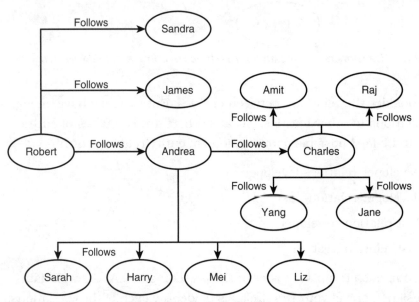

**Figure 14.2**   *Sample set of "follows" relations in a NoSQL developer social network.*

The designers do not have to decide now how deep of a path to pursue looking for posts to show to Robert. The way graph databases are designed makes it easy to alter application features with minor changes to queries. No change in the underlying model is required.

The relation between developers and posts is "created"; that is, developers create posts. This implies a reverse relationship; that is, that posts are "created by" developers. There are two ways to model this:

- A designer could create a directed edge of type "created" from the developer vertex to the post vertex and another directed edge from the post to the developer of type "created by," as shown in Figure 14.3(a).

- Because one of these relations always implies the other, you can avoid using two directed edges by using a single, possibly undirected, edge, as shown in Figure 14.3(b).

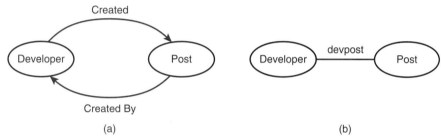

**Figure 14.3**   *Developer and post with two directed edges (a); one edge not directed (b).*

## Queries Drive Design (Again)

There is no one correct way to model a graph database for all possible problems. If you have queries that frequently involved gathering posts and then looking up the creators of those posts, it makes sense to have a created by relation.

By creating such an edge, you implement a direct link between the post and the developer. It is this feature that allows graph database designers to avoid working with joins to retrieve data from related entities. Following edges between vertices is a simple and fast operation, so it is possible to follow long paths or a large number of paths between vertices without adversely impacting performance.

At first glance, the post-relation-post may not appear useful. After all, posts do not create other posts. However, there is no rule that says all relations between entities need to be the same type. In fact, one of the powerful features of graph database modeling is the ability to use different types of relations. For example, a post may be created in response to another post. This is particularly useful for questions.

Imagine that Robert posted the question: Is there a faster way than Dijkstra's algorithm to find the shortest path (see Figure 14.4)? Andrea and Charles might each reply with their own answers. Robert then posts another question to clarify his understanding of Andrea's response. Andrea responds with additional details. Meanwhile, Edith Woolfe adds additional details to Charles's post. The resulting graph of posts is a tree with Robert's initial post as the root and branches that follow the two parts of the conversation thread.

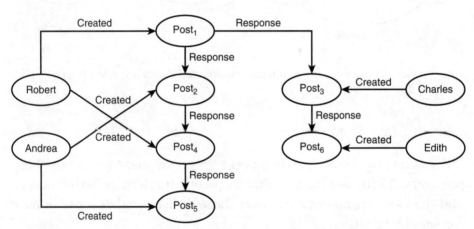

**Figure 14.4**    *A conversation thread started with Robert posting a question.*

Let's return the queries that reference vertices and edges and rewrite them in terms of the NoSQL social network example.

As Table 14.1 shows, abstract queries map to useful queries about graph databases. Some queries are based on paths, such as the distance between two nodes; for example, "How many follows relations are between Developer A and Developer B?" Other queries take into account the global structure of the graph, such as "If a developer left the social network, would there be disconnected groups of developers?"

**Table 14.1**   *Mapping from Graph-Specific Queries That Apply to Any Graph to Queries That Apply to a Social Network Graph*

| Graph-Centric Query | Domain-Specific Query |
|---|---|
| How many hops (that is, edges) does it take to get from vertex A to vertex B? | How many follows relations are between Developer A and Developer B? |
| How many incoming edges are incident to vertex A? | How many developers follow Andrea Wilson? |
| What is the centrality measure of vertex B? | How well connected is Edith Woolfe in the social network? |
| Is vertex C a bottleneck; that is, if vertex C is removed, which parts of the graph become disconnected? | If a developer left the social network, would there be disconnected groups of developers? |

When you design graph databases, you start with domain-specific queries. Ultimately, you will want to map these domain-specific queries to graph-specific queries that reference vertices, edges, and graph measures, like centrality and betweenness.

When you have your domain-specific queries mapped to graph-specific queries, you have the full range of graph query tools and graph algorithms available to you to analyze and explore your data.

The following are the basic steps to getting started with graph database design:

- Identify the queries you would like to perform.

- Identify entities in the graph.

- Identify relations between entities

- Map domain-specific queries to more abstract queries so you can implement graph queries and use graph algorithms to compute additional properties of nodes.

Queries drive the design of graph databases. The next sections delve into details about how to perform those queries.

# Querying a Graph

The motto of the Perl programing language is "There is more than one way to do it." The same statement applies to querying graphs.

The Cypher query language provides a declarative, SQL-like language for building queries. Cypher is used with the Neo4j graph database (neo4j.com). Alternatively, developers can use Gremlin, a graph traversal language that works with a number of different graph databases.

The goal in this section is not to teach you the details of these query languages, but to give you a flavor for how each works and show examples of how each language is used.

## Cypher: Declarative Querying

Before you can query a graph, you must create one. Cypher statements to create vertices for the preceding NoSQL social network include

```
CREATE (robert:Developer { name: 'Robert Smith' })
CREATE (andrea:Developer { name: 'Andrea Wilson' })
CREATE (charles:Developer { name: 'Charles Vita' })
```

These three statements create three vertices. The text `robert:`
`Developer` creates a developer vertex with a label of `robert`. The text
`{ name: 'Robert Smith' }` adds a property to the node to store the
name of the developer.

Edges are added with `create` statements as well. For example:

```
CREATE (robert)-[FOLLOWS]->(andrea)
CREATE (andrea)-[FOLLOWS]->(charles)
```

To query nodes in Cypher, use the `MATCH` command, which returns all developers in the social network:

```
MATCH (developer:DEVELOPER)
RETURN (developer)
```

A comparable query in SQL is

```
SELECT *
FROM developer
```

SQL is a declarative language designed to work with tables that consist of rows and columns. Cypher is a declarative language designed to work with graphs that consist of vertices and edges, so it is not surprising that there are ways to query based on both. For example, the following returns all developer nodes linked to Robert Smith:

```
MATCH (robert:Developer {name:'Robert
  Smith'})--(developer:DEVELOPER)
RETURN developers
```

The `MATCH` operation starts with the node `robert` and searches all edges that lead to vertices of type `DEVELOPER` and returns those that it finds.

Cypher is a rich language with support for many graph operations. It also has clauses found in SQL, such as the following:

- `WHERE`
- `ORDER BY`
- `LIMIT`
- `UNION`
- `COUNT`
- `DISTINCT`
- `SUM`
- `AVG`

Because Cypher is a declarative query language, you specify the criteria for selecting vertices and edges, but you do not specify how to retrieve them. If you want control over the way your query retrieves vertices and edges, you should consider using a graph traversal language such as Gremlin.

## Gremlin: Query by Graph Traversal

*Traverse* means to travel across or through. Graph traversal is the process of logically moving from one vertex to another over an edge. Instead of querying by specifying criteria for selecting vertices, as in Cypher, you specify vertices and rules for traversing them.

### Basic Graph Traversal

Consider the graph in Figure 14.5. The graph has seven vertices and nine directed edges. Some vertices have edges coming in, some have only edges going out, and others have both.

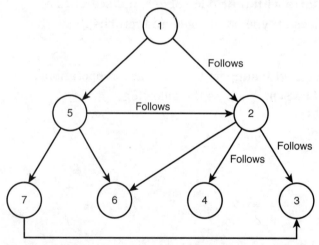

**Figure 14.5**   *Sample directed graph with vertices with only in, out, and both in and out edges.*

Let's assume a graph G is defined with the vertices and edges shown in Figure 14.5. You can create a variable in Gremlin to refer to a particular vertex, such as

```
v = G.v(1)
```

Gremlin also has special terms defined to refer to adjacent edges and vertices. These are

- outE—Outgoing directed edges from a vertex

- inE—Incoming directed edges from a vertex

- bothE—Both inward and outward directed edges from a vertex

- outV—Outgoing vertex of an edge

- inV—Incoming vertex of an edge

- bothV—Both incoming and outgoing vertex of an edge

These are useful for querying edges and graphs based on a starting vertex or edge. For example, if you queried v.outE, you would get the following resultset:

```
[1-follows-2]
[1-follows-5]
```

Because the variable v is defined as the vertex v(1) and there are two outgoing edges, Gremlin returns a descriptive string representing those two edges.

Consider the following example:

```
v2 = G.v(2)

v2.outE
 Results:
    [2-follows-3]
    [2-follows-4]
    [2-follows-6]
```

The vertex 2 has five incident edges, but only three edges are listed above. This is because the other two edges are inbound edges, not outbound edges.

If you want to return the vertices at the end of the outbound edge, you can refer to the inbound vertices of the edges listed in the last example with the following code:

```
v2.outE.inV
  Results:
     [3]
     [4]
     [6]
```

This model of querying allows you to string together additional combinations of edge and vertex specifications, such as v2.outE.inV. outE.inV.

Gremlin supports more complex query patterns as well.

### Traversing a Graph with Depth-First and Breadth-First Searches

There will be times when you do not have a specific starting point. Instead, you want to find all nodes that have a particular property. Cypher uses the MATCH statement for retrieving vertices.

In Gremlin, you can traverse the entire graph and as you visit each vertex, you can test it to determine if it meets your search criteria. For example, you could traverse the graph, starting at vertex 1 by visiting vertex 2, then vertex 3, then vertex 4, then vertex 5, then vertex 6, and finally vertex 7. This is an example of a depth-first search of a graph (see Figure 14.6).

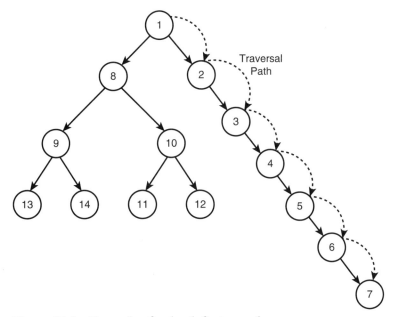

**Figure 14.6** *Example of a depth-first search.*

In a depth-first search, you start traversal at one vertex and select adjacent vertices. You then select the first vertex in that resultset and select adjacent vertices to it. You continue to select the first vertex in the resultset until there are no more edges to traverse.

At that point, you visit the next vertex in the latest resultset. If there are incident edges leading to other vertices, you visit those; otherwise, you continue to the next item in the latest resultset. When you exhaust all vertices in the latest resultset, you return to the resultset selected prior to that and begin the process again.

In a breadth-first search, you visit each of the vertices incident to the current vertex before visiting other vertices. Figure 14.7 shows an example of a breadth-first search traversal.

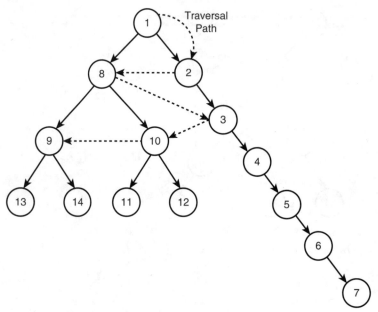

**Figure 14.7** *Example of a breadth-first search.*

Gremlin supports other specialized types of graph traversal, such as the flow rank pattern that allows for queries such as "rank developers by the number of posts we have both commented on."

❖ **Note** For details on the Gremlin language, see the Gremlin Wiki at https://github.com/tinkerpop/gremlin/wiki.

❖ **Note** Gremlin is part of the larger TinkerPop project that builds a common framework for graph databases and graph analysis applications. TinkerPop includes Blueprints, a database API analogous to JDBC and ODBC for relational databases; Pipes, a data flow framework for transforming streams of data; Furnace, a graph algorithm package; and Rexster, a graph server.

Graph databases support both declarative and traversal-based query methods. Choosing the more appropriate model will, as always, depend on your requirements.

Declarative languages,  such as Cypher, are well suited to problems that require selecting vertices based on their properties. It is also useful when you need to apply aggregate operations, such as grouping or summing values from vertex properties.

Traversal languages, such as Gremlin, provide more control over how the query is executed. Developers, for example, can choose between searching by depth-first or breadth-first methods.

# Tips and Traps of Graph Database Design

Applications using graph databases can take advantage of the vertex-edge data model to implement efficient query and analysis capabilities. At the same time, graph operations that run in reasonable time with modest-size graphs may take too long to complete when the graph grows larger.

This section discusses several techniques that can be used to optimize performance when working with graphs.

### Use Indexes to Improve Retrieval Time

Some graph databases provide for indexes on nodes. Neo4j, for example, provides a `CREATE INDEX` command that allows developers to specify properties to index. The Cypher query processor automatically uses indexes, when they are available, to improve the query performance of `WHERE` and `IN` operations.

## Use Appropriate Types of Edges

Edges may be directed or undirected. Directed edges are used when the relation between two vertices is not symmetrical. For example, in the NoSQL social network, Robert follows Andrea, but Andrea does not follow Robert. If Andrea were to follow Robert, there would be an additional edge, directed inward toward Robert from Andrea.

Undirected edges are used for symmetrical relations, such as the distance between two cities (see Figure 14.8).

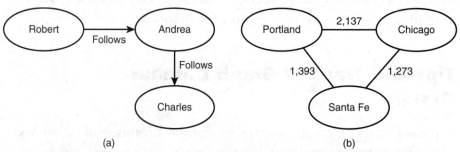

(a)                                                              (b)

**Figure 14.8**   *Undirected edges are used for symmetrical relations; directed edges are used for nonsymmetrical relations.*

❖ **Tip** Graph processing is memory intensive. Keep this in mind as you design your graph.

Simple edges with no properties require little storage, so there is not necessarily a storage penalty for using them. If, however, edges have a large number of properties or large values (for example, BLOBs), then the amount of storage required can be significant.

Consider whether your relations between two vertices require one undirected or two directed nodes. Also, consider how you code property values. Reducing the size of values that are used in a large number of edges can help reduce memory requirements.

## Watch for Cycles When Traversing Graphs

Cycles are paths that lead back to themselves. The graph in Figure 14.9 has a cycle A-B-C-D-E-F-A.

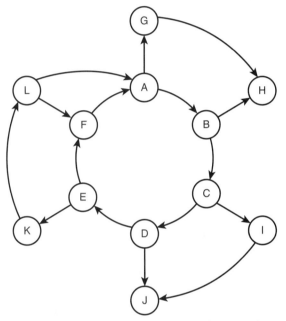

**Figure 14.9** *Cycles can cause problems with traversal if they are not accounted for in the traversal algorithm.*

If you were to start a traversal at vertex A and then followed a path through vertices B, C, D, E, and F, you would end up back at A. If there is no indication that you have already visited A, you could find yourself in an endless cycle of revisiting the same six nodes over and over again.

❖ **Tip** When writing your own graph-processing algorithms, consider the possibility of cycles. Not all graphs have them—trees, for example, do not.

If you might encounter cycles, keep track of which vertices have already been visited. This can be as simple as maintaining a set named `visitedNodes`.

Each time you visit a node, you first check to see if that node is in the set `visitedNodes`. If it is, you return with processing the node; otherwise, you process the node and add it to the set.

## Consider the Scalability of Your Graph Database

The graph database systems available today can work with millions of vertices and edges using a single server. You should consider how your applications and analysis tools will scale as the following occurs:

- The number of nodes and edges grow

- The number of users grow

- The number and size of properties on vertices and edges grow

Increases in each of these three areas can put additional demands on a database server. Many graph databases are designed to run on a single server. If your server can no longer meet performance requirements, you have to scale vertically, that is, get a bigger server.

> ❖ **Note** This is an unusual situation for NoSQL databases, which are generally designed for scalability. Titan (http://thinkaurelius. github.io/titan/), a graph database designed to scale horizontally— that is, by adding more servers—uses other NoSQL databases such as Cassandra for basic storage and retrieval functions. Because Titan supports Gremlin and the TinkerPop graph platform, you could start with another graph database that supports Gremlin and migrate to Titan when you need to horizontally scale.

Also consider the algorithms you use to analyze data in the graph. The time required to perform some types of analysis grows rapidly as you add more vertices. For example, Dijkstra's algorithm for finding the shortest paths in a network takes a time related to the square of the number of vertices in a graph.

To find the largest group of people who all follow each other (known as a maximal clique) in the NoSQL social network requires time that grows exponentially with the number of people.

Table 14.2 shows examples of time required to run Dijkstra's algorithm and solve the maximal clique problem. Be careful when using graph algorithms. Some that run in reasonable amounts of time with small graphs will not finish in reasonable amounts of time if the graphs grow too large. This table assumes a time of two units to complete the operations on a single vertex.

**Table 14.2** *Solving a Maximal Clique Problem*

| Number of Vertices | Time to Find Shortest Path | Time to Find Maximal Clique |
|---|---|---|
| 1 | 2 | 2 |
| 10 | 200 | 1,024 |
| 20 | 800 | 1,048,576 |
| 30 | 1,800 | 1,073,741,824 |
| 40 | 3,200 | 1,099,511,627,776 |
| 50 | 5,000 | 1,125,899,906,842,620 |

## Summary

Graph databases are well suited to a wide range of applications. Graph database designers should start with the queries they will run on the database to identify the entities and relations between entities that should be modeled. Depending on the types of relations, edges may be directed or undirected.

Graph databases support both declarative and traversal query options. Designers should use optimization features, such as indexes, when available to improve the overall performance of graph database operations.

## Case Study: Optimizing Transportation Routes

A client of TransGlobal Transport and Shipping (TGTS), a fictitious transportation company, has hired the analytics company to help optimize its shipping routes. The client ships parcels from manufacturing sites to distribution centers and then to customer sites. It has used a simple method for shipping parcels but suspects its approach is less than optimal.

### Understanding User Needs

Analysts at TGTS have several meetings with executives, shipping managers, and other employees responsible for parcel shipping. They learn that the client uses two methods for shipping:

- If there is no need for rush shipping, an employee from the manufacturing site will drive a shipment of parcels to the nearest hub airport. From there, it is flown to a distribution center closest to the ultimate customer destination. An employee from the distribution center then drives the package from the distribution center to the customer's location.

- If there is a rush order, an employee from the manufacturing site drives the shipment to the closest regional airport and the parcel is flown to the closet regional airport to the customer.

The client has data indicating that the first method is less expensive than the second, which is only used in order to meet time constraints on delivery.

The analysts collect information about the client's shipping costs between all of its facilities and its customer sites.

## Designing a Graph Analysis Solution

The TGTS analysts quickly realize that the client is using only a small subset of all possible routes. They determine that Dijkstra's algorithm can be used with data from a graph database to find the least-cost path between all locations.

The set of least-cost paths will provide the optimal route for deliveries without time constraints. It does not, however, address the need to consider time constraints as well as costs.

The analysts decide to use edge properties to store both the cost of moving a parcel between the two locations and the time required to move it.

> ❖ **Tip** Because the cost of shipping a parcel will vary by weight, the TGTS analysts use a unit cost, such as cost per kilogram, to represent the cost of the edge.

The time property is the average time it takes to ship a parcel between locations. The client has historical data for many of the edges, but not all. For those edges without shipment time data, the analysts estimate based on the shipping time of packages between similar types of facilities.

The TGTS analysts create a database of shortest paths between all facilities and store the total cost and total time required to ship a parcel. They realize that sometimes the least-cost path will not meet time constraints on delivery, so the analysts develop their own algorithm to find the least-cost path that does meet the time constraints.

The algorithm takes as input a start facility, an end facility, and the time available for delivery. As the algorithm traverses each facility (vertex), it records the cumulative cost and time required to ship a parcel between the two facilities. If at any time, the cumulative time exceeds the time available for delivery, the path is discarded.

All remaining paths are stored in a list sorted by cost. The first path in the list is the least-cost path created so far. The algorithm continues with the least-cost path and finds all facilities linked to the latest facility in the least-cost path.

If any of those facilities is the final destination, the algorithm terminates and outputs the least-cost path with a delivery time within constraints. Otherwise, it continues to find facilities linked to the last facility in the current least-cost path.

As this example shows, well-established algorithms can provide the foundation for graph analysis problems. There are times, however, that slight variations on the algorithm are required to accommodate the particular requirements of the problem under study.

# Review Questions

1. What is the benefit of mapping domain-specific queries into graph-specific queries?

2. Which is more like SQL, Cypher or Gremlin?

3. How is the `MATCH` statement like a SQL `SELECT` statement?

4. What are the `inE` and `outE` terms used for in Gremlin?

5. Which type of edge should be used for a nonsymmetrical relation, a directed or undirected edge?

6. What is the difference between a declarative and a traversal query language for graph databases?

7. What is a depth-first search?

8. What is a breadth-first search?

9. Why are cycles a potential problem when performing graph operations?

10. Why is scalability such an important consideration when working with graphs?

# References

Gremlin: https://github.com/tinkerpop/gremlin/wiki

Neo4j Manual: http://neo4j.com/docs/

Titan Distributed Graph Database: http://thinkaurelius.github.io/titan/

Wikipedia. "Dijkstra's Algorithm": http://en.wikipedia.org/wiki/Dijkstra%27s_algorithm

# ■ Part VI

# Choosing a Database for Your Application

# 15

# Guidelines for Selecting a Database

*"One's philosophy is not best expressed in words;
it is expressed in the choices one makes."*
—Eleanor Roosevelt
Politician, activist, and diplomat

## Topics Covered In This Chapter

Choosing a NoSQL Database

Using NoSQL and Relational Databases Together

Developers have never had as many good database options as they have today. Relational databases have a long and proven track record of successful use in a wide range of applications. These databases have been so successful they virtually eliminated the widespread use of earlier database models, such as file-based, hierarchical, and network databases. It was not until the advent of commercial web systems, such as search engines, that relational databases strained to meet developers' demands.

The growing demands for web-scale data management systems drove a renaissance in nonrelational database design. Yahoo! developed Hadoop. Google created BigTable. Amazon designed and deployed DynamoDB. Instead of keeping their intellectual property locked up in a corporate vault somewhere, these companies published papers and, in some cases, released code for others to build on. This in turn allowed other developers to build on those designs and expand the ecosystem of NoSQL databases and supporting tools.

If you are a developer starting a data management project today, you will have to decide which type of database management system to use. Your major options are

- Relational databases, such as PostgreSQL, MySQL, and Microsoft SQL Server

- Key-value databases, such as Redis, Riak, and Oracle BerkeleyDB

- Document databases, such as MongoDB, CouchDB, and CouchBase

- Column family databases, such as Cassandra and HBase

- Graph databases, such as Neo4j and Titan

❖ **Note** Discussing relational database design in any detail is outside the scope of this book, but if you think a relational database might be an option for you, see Michael Hernandez's, *Database Design for Mere Mortals: A Hands-On Guide to Relational Database Design* for guidance.

For those best served by a NoSQL option, this chapter includes some points to consider as you evaluate your options.

## Choosing a NoSQL Database

In relational database design, the structure and relations of entities drives design—not so in NoSQL database design. Of course, you will model entities and relations, but performance is more important than preserving the relational model.

The relational model emerged for pragmatic reasons, that is, data anomalies and difficulty reusing existing databases for new applications. NoSQL databases also emerged for pragmatic reasons, specifically, the inability to scale to meet growing demands for high volumes of read and write operations.

In exchange for improved read and write performance, you may lose other features of relational databases, such as immediate consistency and ACID transactions (although this is not always the case).

Throughout this book, queries have driven the design of data models. This is the case because queries describe how data will be used. Queries are also a good starting point for understanding how well various NoSQL databases will meet your needs. You will also need to understand other factors, such as

- The volume of reads and writes
- Tolerance for inconsistent data in replicas
- The nature of relations between entities and how that affects query patterns
- Availability and disaster recovery requirements
- The need for flexibility in data models
- Latency requirements

The following sections provide some sample use cases and some criteria for matching different NoSQL database models to different requirements.

## Criteria for Selecting Key-Value Databases

Key-value databases are well suited to applications that have frequent small reads and writes along with simple data models. The values stored in key-value databases may be simple scalar values, such as integers or Booleans, but they may be structured data types, such as lists and JSON structures.

Key-value databases generally have simple query facilities that allow you to look up a value by its key. Some key-value databases support search features that provide for somewhat more flexibility. Developers can use tricks, such as enumerated keys, to implement range queries, but these databases usually lack the query capabilities of document, column family, and graph databases.

Key-value databases are used in a wide range of applications, such as the following:

- Caching data from relational databases to improve performance
- Tracking transient attributes in a web application, such as a shopping cart
- Storing configuration and user data information for mobile applications
- Storing large objects, such as images and audio files

❖ **Note** In addition to key-value databases you install and run on the premises, there are a number of cloud-based choices as well. Amazon Web Services offers SimpleDB and DynamoDB, whereas Microsoft Azure's Table service provides for key-value storage.

## Use Cases and Criteria for Selecting Document Databases

Document databases are designed for flexibility. If an application requires the ability to store varying attributes along with large amounts of data, then document databases are a good option. For example, to represent products in a relational database, a modeler may use a table for common attributes and additional tables for each sub-type of product to store attributes used only in the subtype of product. Document databases can handle this situation easily.

Document databases provide for embedded documents, which are useful for denormalizing. Instead of storing data in different tables, data that is frequently queried together is stored together in the same document.

Document databases improve on the query capabilities of key-value databases with indexing and the ability to filter documents based on attributes in the document.

Document databases are probably the most popular of the NoSQL databases because of their flexibility, performance, and ease of use.

These databases are well suited to a number of use cases, including

- Back-end support for websites with high volumes of reads and writes

- Managing data types with variable attributes, such as products

- Tracking variable types of metadata

- Applications that use JSON data structures

- Applications benefiting from denormalization by embedding structures within structures

Document databases are also available from cloud services such as Microsoft Azure Document and Cloudant's database.

## Use Cases and Criteria for Selecting Column Family Databases

Column family databases are designed for large volumes of data, read and write performance, and high availability. Google introduced Big-Table to address the needs of its services. Facebook developed Cassandra to back its Inbox Search service.

These database management systems run on clusters of multiple servers. If your data is small enough to run with a single server, then a column family database is probably more than you need—consider a document or key-value database instead.

Column family databases are well suited for use with

- Applications that require the ability to always write to the database

- Applications that are geographically distributed over multiple data centers

- Applications that can tolerate some short-term inconsistency in replicas

- Applications with dynamic fields

- Applications with the potential for truly large volumes of data, such as hundreds of terabytes

Google demonstrated the capabilities of Cassandra running the Google Compute Engine.[1] Google engineers deployed

- 330 Google Compute Engine virtual machines

- 300 1TB Persistent Disk volumes

- Debian Linux

- Datastax Cassandra 2.2

- Data was written to two nodes (Quorum commit of 2)

- 30 virtual machines to generate 3 billion records of 170 bytes each

With this configuration, the Cassandra cluster reached one million writes per second with 95% completing in under 23 milliseconds. When one-third of the nodes were lost, the one million writes were sustained but with higher latency.

---

1. Google. 2014, March 20. "Cassandra Hits One Million Writes Per Second on Google Compute Engine." http://googlecloudplatform.blogspot.com/2014/03/cassandra-hits-one-million-writes-per-second-on-google-compute-engine.html

Several areas can use this kind of Big Data processing capability, such as

- Security analytics using network traffic and log data mode
- Big Science, such as bioinformatics using genetic and proteomic data
- Stock market analysis using trade data
- Web-scale applications such as search
- Social network services

Key-value, document, and column family databases are well suited to a wide range of applications. Graph databases, however, are best suited to a particular type of problem.

## Use Cases and Criteria for Selecting Graph Databases

Problem domains that lend themselves to representations as networks of connected entities are well suited for graph databases. One way to assess the usefulness of a graph database is to determine if instances of entities have relations to other instances of entities.

For example, two orders in an e-commerce application probably have no connection to each other. They might be ordered by the same customer, but that is a shared attribute, not a connection.

Similarly, a game player's configuration and game state have little to do with other game players' configurations. Entities like these are readily modeled with key-value, document, or relational databases.

Now consider examples mentioned in the discussion of graph databases, such as highways connecting cities, proteins interacting with other proteins, and employees working with other employees. In all of these cases, there is some type of connection, link, or direct relationship between two instances of entities.

These are the types of problem domains that are well suited to graph databases. Other examples of these types of problem domains include

- Network and IT infrastructure management
- Identity and access management
- Business process management
- Recommending products and services
- Social networking

From these examples, it is clear that when there is a need to model explicit relations between entities and rapidly traverse paths between entities, then graph databases are a good database option.

Large-scale graph processing, such as with large social networks, may actually use column family databases for storage and retrieval. Graph operations are built on top of the database management system. The Titan graph database and analysis platform takes this approach.

Key-value, document, column family, and graph databases meet different types of needs. Unlike relational databases that essentially displaced their predecessors, these NoSQL databases will continue to coexist with each other and relational databases because there is a growing need for different types of applications with varying require-ments and competing demands.

# Using NoSQL and Relational Databases Together

NoSQL and relational databases are complementary. Relational data-bases offer many features that protect the integrity of data and reduce the risk of data anomalies. Relational databases incur operational overhead providing these features.

In some use cases, performance is more important than ensuring immediate consistency or supporting ACID transactions. In these cases, NoSQL databases may be the better solution. Choosing a database is a process of choosing the right tool for the job. The more varied your set of jobs, the more varied your toolkit.

Modern data management infrastructure is responsible for a wider range of applications and data types than ever before. When E. F. Codd developed the relational model in the 1970s, businesses and governments were the primary users of databases.

The personal computer, smartphones, and tablets did not exist. The Internet was used by government and academic researchers; the World Wide Web was almost 20 years into the future. The Global Positioning System (GPS) was not fully operational until 1995.

Today, IT professionals are working with more of the same types of business data that existed in the 1970s as well as new types, such as social media and detailed customer demographics and preference data.

Mobile devices generate large volumes of data about users' behaviors and location. The instrumentation of cars, appliances, and other devices, referred to as the Internet of Things (IoT), is another potential data source. With so many changes in the scope and size of data and applications, it is no surprise that additional database management techniques are needed.

Relational databases will continue to support transaction processing systems and business intelligence applications. Decades of work with transaction processing systems and data warehouses has led to best practices and design principles that continue to meet the needs of businesses, governments, and other organizations.

At the same time, these organizations are adapting to technologies that did not exist when the relational model was first formulated.

Customer-facing web applications, mobile services, and Big Data analytics might work well with relational databases, but in some cases they do not.

The current technology landscape requires a variety of database technologies. Just as there is no best programming language, there is no best database management system. There are database systems better suited to some problems than others, and the job of developers and designers is to find the best database for the requirements at hand.

## Summary

Application developers have choices about which programming language they use, which development environments they work in, and which web frameworks they deploy. They also have choices when it comes to database management systems. The different types of database management systems were all developed to solve real-world problems that could not be solved as well with other types of databases.

One of the jobs of developers and designers is to choose an appropriate database system for their applications. You do this by understanding your problem domain and your user requirements. Often you will have options. You could use a key-value store or a document database in some cases. Other times, a graph database might be the best fit. Do not be surprised if you find yourself working with key-value databases one day and graph databases the next. The choice of database should be driven by your needs.

## Review Questions

1. Name two use cases for key-value databases.
2. Describe two reasons for choosing a key-value database for your application.

3. Name two use cases for document databases.

4. Describe two reasons for choosing a document database for your application.

5. Name two use cases for column family databases.

6. Describe two reasons for choosing a column family database for your application.

7. Name two use cases for graph databases.

8. Describe two reasons for choosing a graph database for your application.

9. Name two types of applications well suited for relational databases.

10. Discuss the need for both NoSQL and relational databases in enterprise data management.

## References

Apache Foundation. Apache Cassandra Glossary:
http://io.typepad.com/glossary.html

Apache Foundation. Apache CouchDB 1.6 Documentation:
http://docs.couchdb.org/en/1.6.1/

Apache Foundation. Apache HBase Reference Guide:
http://hbase.apache.org/book/regions.arch.html

Basho Technologies, Inc. Riak Documentation:
http://docs.basho.com/riak/latest/

Bishop, Christopher M. *Pattern Recognition and Machine Learning.* New York: Springer, 2006.

Chang, Fay, et al. "BigTable: A Distributed Storage System for Structured Data." OSDI'06: Seventh Symposium on Operating System Design and Implementation, Seattle, WA, November, 2006.
http://research.google.com/archive/bigtable.html

Chodorow, Kristina. *50 Tips and Tricks for MongoDB Developers*. Sebastopol, CA: O'Reilly Media, Inc., 2011.

Chodorow, Kristina. *MongoDB: The Definitive Guide*. Sebastopol, CA: O'Reilly Media, Inc., 2013.

Copeland, Rick. *MongoDB Applied Design Patterns*. Sebastopol, CA: O'Reilly Media, Inc., 2013.

Couchbase. Couchbase Documentation: http://docs.couchbase.com/

FoundationDB. "ACID Claims": https://foundationdb.com/acid-claims

FoundationDB. Key-Value Store 2.0 Documentation: https://foundationdb.com/key-value-store/documentation/index.html

Gremlin: https://github.com/tinkerpop/gremlin/wiki

Han, Jing, et al. "Survey on NoSQL Database." Pervasive computing and applications (ICPCA), 2011 6th International Conference on IEEE, 2011.

Hewitt, Eben. *Cassandra: The Definitive Guide*. Sebastopol, CA: O'Reilly Media, Inc., 2010.

Katsov, Ilya. "NoSQL Data Modeling Techniques." *Highly Scalable Blog*. March 1, 2012. http://highlyscalable.wordpress.com/2012/03/01/nosql-data-modeling-techniques/

MongoDB. MongoDB 2.6 Manual: http://docs.mongodb.org/manual/

Neo Technologies, Inc. Neo4j Manual: http://neo4j.com/docs/

Oracle Corporation. Oracle NoSQL Database, 12c Release 1: http://docs.oracle.com/cd/NOSQL/html/index.html

OrientDB. OrientDB Manual, version 2.0: http://www.orientechnologies.com/docs/last/

Redis. Redis Documentation: http://redis.io/documentation

Titan Distributed Graph Database: http://thinkaurelius.github.io/titan/

# Part VII
# *Appendices*

# A

# Answers to Chapter Review Questions

This appendix provides answers to review questions throughout the book.

## Chapter 1

1.  If the layout of records in a flat file data management system changes, what else must change?

    **Answer:** Data access programs will have to change.

2.  What kind of relation is supported in a hierarchical data management system?

    a. Parent-child

    b. Many-to-many

    c. Many-to-many-to-many

    d. No relations are allowed.

    **Answer:** A. Parent-child relations are supported in hierarchical data management systems.

3.  What kind of relation is supported in network data management systems?

    a. Parent-child

    b. Many-to-many

    c. Both parent-child and many-to-many

    d. No relations are allowed

    **Answer:** C. Both parent-child and many-to-many relations are supported in network data management systems.

4.  Give an example of a SQL data manipulation language statement.

    **Answer:** Examples could include INSERT, DELETE, UPDATE, and SELECT. The following is an INSERT example:

    ```
    INSERT INTO employee (emp_id, first_name, last_name)
      VALUES (1234, 'Jane', 'Smith')
    ```

5.  Give an example of a SQL data definition language statement.

    **Answer:** The CREATE TABLE statement is a data definition statement. The following is an example of CREATE TABLE:

    ```
    CREATE TABLE employee (
        emp_id  int,
        emp_first_name varchar(25),
        emp_last_name varchar(25),
        emp_address varchar(50),
        emp_city varchar(50),
        emp_state varchar(2),
        emp_zip varchar(5),
        emp_position_title varchar(30)
        )
    ```

6.  What is scaling up?

    **Answer:** Scaling entails upgrading an existing database server to add additional processors, memory, network bandwidth, or other resources that would improve performance on a database management system. It could also entail replacing an existing server with one that has more CPUs, memory, and so forth.

7.  What is scaling out?

    **Answer:** Scaling out entails adding servers to a cluster.

8.  Are NoSQL databases likely to displace relational databases as relational databases displaced earlier types of data management systems?

    **Answer:** No, relational databases and NoSQL databases meet different types of needs.

9. Name four required components of a relational database management system (RDBMS).

   **Answer:**

   - Storage management programs

   - Memory management programs

   - Data dictionary

   - Query language

10. Name three common major components of a database application.

    **Answer:**

    - A user interface

    - Business logic

    - Database code

11. Name four motivating factors for database designers and other IT professionals to develop and use NoSQL databases.

    **Answer:**

    - Scalability

    - Cost

    - Flexibility

    - Availability

# Chapter 2

1. What is a distributed system?

   **Answer:** Systems that run on multiple servers are known as distributed systems.

2.  Describe a two-phase commit. Does it help ensure consistency or availability?

    **Answer:** A two-phase commit is a transaction that requires writing data to two separate locations. In the first phase of the operation, the database writes, or commits, the data to the disk of the primary server. In the second phase of the operation, the database writes data to the disk of the backup server.

    **Answer:** Two-phase commits help ensure consistency.

3.  What do the *C* and *A* in the CAP theorem stand for? Give an example of how designing for one of those properties can lead to difficulties in maintaining the other.

    **Answer:** *C* stands for consistency; *A* stands for availability.

    When using a two-phase commit, the database favors consistency but at the risk of the most recent data not being available for a brief period of time. While the two-phase commit is executing, other queries to the data are blocked. The updated data is unavailable until the two-phase commit finishes. This favors consistency over availability.

4.  The *E* in BASE stands for eventually consistent. What does that mean?

    **Answer:** *E* stands for eventually consistent, which means that some replicas might be inconsistent for some period of time but will become consistent at some point.

5.  Describe monotonic write consistency. Why is it so important?

    **Answer:** Monotonic write consistency ensures that if you were to issue several update commands, they would be executed in the order you issued them. This ensures that the results of a set of commands are predictable. Repeating the same commands with the same starting data will yield the same results.

6. How many values can be stored with a single key in a key-value database?

   **Answer:** One.

7. What is a namespace? Why is it important in key-value databases?

   **Answer:** A namespace is a collection of identifiers. Keys must be unique within a namespace.

8. How do document databases differ from key-value databases?

   **Answer:** Instead of storing each attribute of an entity with a separate key, document databases store multiple attributes in a single document. Users can query and retrieve documents by filtering on key-value pairs within a document.

9. Describe two differences between document databases and relational databases.

   **Answer:** Document databases do not require a fixed, predefined schema. Also, documents can have embedded documents and lists of multiple values within a document.

10. Name two data structures used in column family databases.

    **Answer:** Columns and column families.

11. What are the two fundamental data structures in a graph database?

    **Answer:** Nodes and relations, also known as vertices and edges.

12. You are assigned the task of building a database to model employees and who they work with in your company. The database must be able to answer queries such as how many employees does Employee A work with? And, does Employee A work with anyone who works with Employee B? Which type of NoSQL database would naturally fit with these requirements?

    **Answer:** A graph database because these queries require working with relations between employees. Employees can be modeled as vertices, and the "works with" relation can be modeled as an edge.

# Chapter 3

1.  How are associative arrays different from arrays?

    **Answer:** An associative array is a data structure, like an array, but is not restricted to using integers as indexes or limiting values to the same type. Associative arrays generalize the idea of an ordered list indexed by an identifier to include arbitrary values for identifiers and values.

2.  How can you use a cache to improve relational database performance?

    **Answer:** An in-memory cache is an associative array. The values retrieved from the relational database could be stored in the cache by creating a key for each value stored. Programs that access customer data will typically check the cache first for data and if it is not found in the cache, the program will then query the database. Retrieving data from memory is faster than retrieving it from disk.

3.  What is a namespace?

    **Answer:** A namespace is a logical data structure for organizing key-value pairs. Keys must be unique within a namespace. Namespaces are sometimes called buckets.

4.  Describe a way of constructing keys that captures some information about entities and attribute types.

    **Answer:** A developer could use a key-naming convention that uses a table name, primary key value, and an attribute name to create a key, such as customer: 1982737:firstName.

5.  Name three common features of key-value databases.

    **Answer:**

    *   Simplicity

    *   Speed

    *   Scalability

6. What is a hash function? Include important characteristics of hash functions in your definition.

   **Answer:** A hash function is a function that can take an arbitrary string of characters and produce a (usually) unique, fixed-length string of characters. Hash functions map to what appear to be random outputs.

7. How can hash functions help distribute writes over multiple servers?

   **Answer:** One way to take advantage of the hash value is to start by dividing the hash value by the number of servers. Sometimes the hash value will divide evenly by the number of servers and sometimes not. The remainder can be used to determine which of the servers should receive a write operation.

8. What is one type of practical limitation on values stored in key-value databases?

   **Answer:** Different implementations of key-value databases have different restrictions on values. For example, some key-value databases will typically have some limit on the size of values. Some might allow multiple megabytes in each value, but others might have smaller size limitations. Even in cases in which you can store extremely large values, you might run into performance problems that lead you to work with smaller data values.

9. How does the lack of a query language affect application developers using key-value databases?

   **Answer:** Key-value databases do not support query languages for searching over values. Application developers can implement search operations in their applications. Alternatively, some key-value databases incorporate search functionality directly into the database.

10. How can a search system help improve the performance of applications that use key-value databases?

    **Answer:** A built-in search system would index the string values stored in the database and create an index for rapid retrieval. Rather than search all values for a string, the search system keeps a list of words with the keys of each key-value pair in which that word appears.

# Chapter 4

1.  What are data models? How do they differ from data structures?

    **Answer:** Data models are abstractions that help organize the information conveyed by the data in databases. Data structures are well-defined data storage structures that are implemented using elements of underlying hardware, particularly random access memory and persistent data storage, such as hard drives and flash devices. Data models provide a level of organization and abstraction above data structures.

2.  What is a partition?

    **Answer:** A partition is a logical subdivision of a larger structure. Clusters, or groups of servers, can be organized into partitions. A partitioned cluster is a group of servers in which servers or instances of key-value database software running on servers are assigned to manage subsets of a database.

3.  Define two types of clusters. Which type is typically used with key-value data stores?

    **Answer:** Clusters may be loosely or tightly coupled. Loosely coupled clusters consist of fairly independent servers that complete many functions on their own with minimal coordination with other servers in the cluster. Tightly coupled clusters tend to have high levels of communication between servers. This is needed to support more coordinated operations, or calculations, on the cluster. Key-value clusters tend to be loosely coupled.

4. What are the advantages of having a large number of replicas? What are the disadvantages?

   **Answer:** The more replicas you have, the less likely you will lose data; however, you might have lower performance with a large number of replicas.

   It is possible for replicas to have different versions of data. All the versions will eventually be consistent, but sometimes they may be out of sync for short periods.

5. Why would you want to receive a response from more than one replica when reading a value from a key-value data store?

   **Answer:** To minimize the risk of reading old, out-of-date data, you can specify the number of nodes that must respond with the same answer to a read request before a response is returned to the calling application.

6. Under what circumstances would you want to have a large number of replicas?

   **Answer:** If you have little tolerance for losing data, a higher replica number is recommended.

7. Why are hash functions used with key-value databases?

   **Answer:** Hash functions are generally designed to distribute inputs evenly over the set of all possible outputs. The output space can be quite large. No matter how similar your keys are, they are evenly distributed across the range of possible output values. The ranges of output values can be assigned to partitions and you can be reasonably assured that each partition will receive approximately the same amount of data.

8. What is a collision?

   **Answer:** A collision occurs when two distinct inputs to a hash function produce the same output.

9. Describe one way to handle a collision so that no data is lost.

    **Answer:** Instead of storing just one value, a hash table can store lists of values.

10. Discuss the relation between speed of compression and the size of compressed data.

    **Answer:** There is a trade-off between the speed of compression/ decompression and the size of the compressed data. Faster compression algorithms can lead to larger compressed data than other, slower algorithms.

# Chapter 5

1. Describe four characteristics of a well-designed key-naming convention.

    **Answer:**

    • Use meaningful and unambiguous naming components, such as 'cust' for customer or 'inv' for inventory.

    • Use range-based components when you would like to retrieve ranges of values. Ranges include dates or integer counters.

    • Use a common delimiter when appending components to make a key. The ':' is a commonly used delimiter, but any character that will not otherwise appear in the key will work.

    • Keep keys as short as possible without sacrificing the other characteristics mentioned in this list.

2. Name two types of restrictions key-value databases can place on keys.

    **Answer:** Restrictions can be placed on key size and data types.

3. Describe the difference between range partitioning and hash partitioning.

   **Answer:** Range partitioning works by grouping contiguous values and sending them to the same node in a cluster. Hash partitioning distributes values evenly across the cluster.

4. How can structured data types help reduce read latency (that is, the time needed to retrieve a block of data from a disk)?

   **Answer:** By storing commonly used values together in a list or other structure, you reduce the number of disk seeks that must be performed to read all the needed data. Key-value databases will usually store the entire structure together in a data block so there is no need to hash multiple keys and retrieve multiple data blocks.

5. Describe the Time to Live (TTL) key pattern.

   **Answer:** A TTL parameter specifies a time that a key-value record is allowed to exist. The TTL pattern is sometimes useful with keys in a key-value database, especially when caching data in limited memory servers or keys are used to hold a resource for some specified period of time.

6. Which design pattern provides some of the features of relational transactions?

   **Answer:** Emulating tables.

7. When would you want to use the Aggregate pattern?

   **Answer:** Aggregation is used to support different attributes for different subtypes of an entity. For example, a concert venue could have two subtypes, seated and nonseated.

8. What are enumerable keys?

   **Answer:** Enumerable keys are keys that use counters or sequences to generate new keys. Enumerable keys are often created using an entity type prefix along with the generated number.

9. How can enumerable keys help with range queries?

   **Answer:** A range of keys can be retrieved by using a loop to generate the set of keys between the lower and upper bounds. For example, a `for` loop starting at 1 and ending with 3 could be used to generate the following keys: 'ticketLog:20140617:1', 'ticketLog:20140617:2', and 'ticketLog:20140617:3'.

10. How would you modify the design of TGTS Tracker to include a user's preferred language in the configuration?

    **Answer:** A language preference could be added to the customer value list. For example,

    ```
    TrackerNS[cust:4719364] = {name:' Prime Machine,
        Inc.', currency:'USD', language:'EN'}
    ```

# Chapter 6

1. Define a document with respect to document databases.

   **Answer:** Documents in document databases are composed of a set of attribute tags and values. Developers can make up their own set of attribute tags; they are not constrained to a predefined set of tags for specifying structure.

2. Name two types of formats for storing data in a document database.

   **Answer:** JSON and XML.

3. List at least three syntax rules for JSON objects.

   **Answer:**

   - Data is organized in key-value pairs, similar to key-value databases.

   - Documents consist of name-value pairs separated by commas.

   - Documents start with a { and end with a }.

   - Names are strings, such as `"customer _ id"` and `"address"`.

- Values can be numbers, strings, Booleans (true or false), arrays, objects, or the null value.

- The values of arrays are listed within square brackets, such as [ and ].

- The values of objects are listed as key-value pairs within curly brackets, such as { and }.

4. Create a sample document for a small appliance with the following attributes: appliance ID, name, description, height, width, length, and shipping weight. Use the JSON format.

   **Answer:**

   ```
   { "appliance ID":    132738,
     "name": "Toaster Model X",
     "description": "Large 4 bagel toaster",
     "height":   "9 in.",
      "width":   "7.5 in",
      "length": "12 in",
      "shipping weight": "3.2 lbs"
   }
   ```

5. Why are highly abstract entities often avoided when modeling document collections?

   **Answer:** Highly abstract entities can lead to document collections with many subtypes. These subtypes will need type indicators to support the frequent filtering required when different document types are in the same collection. Large collections can lead to inefficient retrieval operations.

6. When is it reasonable to use highly abstract entities?

   **Answer:** Abstract entities should be used when many of the queries used against a collection apply to all or many subtypes, for example, in a products document collection. Also, if there is a potential for the number of subtypes to grow into the tens or hundreds, it could become difficult to manage collections for all of those subtypes.

7. Using the db.books collection described in this chapter, write a command to insert a book to the collection. Use MongoDB syntax.

   **Answer:**
   ```
   db.books.insert( {"title":"Mother Night", "author":
     "Kurt Vonnegut, Jr."} )
   ```

8. Using the db.books collection described in this chapter, write a command to remove books by Isaac Asimov. Use MongoDB syntax.

   **Answer:**
   ```
   db.books.remove("author": "Isaac Asimov"})
   ```

9. Using the db.books collection described in this chapter, write a command to retrieve all books with quantity greater than or equal to 20. Use MongoDB syntax.

   **Answer:**
   ```
   db.books.find( {"quantity" : {"$gte" : 20 }})
   ```

10. Which query operator is used to search for values in a single key?

    **Answer:** The $in operator is used to search for a value in a single key.

# Chapter 7

1. Describe how documents are analogous to rows in relational databases.

   **Answer:** Documents are ordered sets of key-value pairs. Keys are used to reference particular values and are analogous to column names in relational tables. Values in a document database are analogous to values stored in a row of a relational database table.

2. Describe how collections are analogous to tables in relational databases.

   **Answer:** Collections are sets of documents; tables are sets of rows. Both documents and rows have unique identifiers and may have other attributes as well.

3.  Define a schema.

    **Answer:** A schema is a formal specification of a database structure.

4.  Why are document databases considered schemaless?

    **Answer:** Document databases do not require data modelers to formally specify the structure of documents.

5.  Why are document databases considered polymorphic?

    **Answer:** A document database is polymorphic because the documents that exist in collections can have many different forms.

6.  How does vertical partitioning differ from horizontal partitioning, or sharding?

    **Answer:** Vertical partitioning is a technique for improving database performance by separating columns of a relational table into multiple separate tables. This technique is particularly useful when you have some columns that are frequently accessed and others that are not.

    Horizontal partitioning is the process of dividing a database by documents in a document database or by rows in a relational database. These parts of the database, known as shards, are stored on separate servers.

7.  What is a shard key?

    **Answer:** A shard key is one or more keys or fields that exist in all documents in a collection that is used to separate documents into different partitions.

8.  What is the purpose of the partitioning algorithm in sharding?

    **Answer:** The partitioning algorithm determines how to distribute documents over shards. Common techniques include range, hash, and list partitioning.

9.  What is normalization?

    **Answer:** Database normalization is the process of organizing data into tables in such a way as to reduce the potential for data anomalies. An anomaly is an inconsistency in the data. Normalization reduces the amount of redundant data in the database.

10. Why would you want to denormalize collections in a document database?

    **Answer:** Denormalization is used to improve performance over normalized versions of databases.

# Chapter 8

1.  What are the advantages of normalization?

    **Answer:** Normalization reduces redundant data and mitigates the risk of data anomalies.

2.  What are the advantages of denormalization?

    **Answer:** Denormalization can improve query performance over more normalized models.

3.  Why are joins such costly operations?

    **Answer:** Joins retrieve data from multiple tables. Joins use loops, hashes, and merge operations. As the size of tables grows, these operations take longer as more data blocks need to be read. Indexes can improve performance, but they also require disk seeks to retrieve data blocks holding index data.

4.  How do document database modelers avoid costly joins?

    **Answer:** They use denormalized data models. The basic idea is that data models store data that is used together in a single data structure, such as a table in a relational database or in a document in a document database. This increases the likelihood that all the data in a document is in a single data block or at least adjacent data blocks.

5. How can adding data to a document cause more work for the I/O subsystem in addition to adding the data to a document?

   **Answer:** Too much denormalization will lead to large documents that will likely lead to unnecessary data read from persistent storage.

6. How can you, as a document database modeler, help avoid that extra work mentioned in Question 5?

   **Answer:** Let queries drive how you design documents. Try to include only fields that are frequently used together in documents. If you have two or more distinct sets of requirements for the same type of data, consider using two document collections each tailored to the different requirements.

7. Describe a situation where it would make sense to have many indexes on your document collections.

   **Answer:** Read-heavy applications, especially those with ad hoc query requirements, might need many indexes. Business intelligence and other analytic applications can fall into this category. Read-heavy applications with ad hoc query requirements should have indexes on virtually all fields used to help filter results. For example, if it was common for users to query documents from a particular sales region or with order items in a certain product category, then the sales region and product category fields should be indexed.

8. What would cause you to minimize the number of indexes on your document collection?

   **Answer:** Data modelers tend to try to minimize the number of indexes in write-heavy applications. Because indexes are data structures that must be created and updated, their use will consume CPU, persistent storage, and memory resources and increase the time needed to insert or update a document in the database.

9. Describe how to model a many-to-many relationship.

   **Answer:** Many-to-many relationships are modeled using two collec-tions—one for each type of entity. Each collection maintains a list of identifiers that reference related entities. For example, a docu-ment with course data would include an array of student IDs, and a student document would include a list of course IDs.

10. Describe three ways to model hierarchies in a document database.

   **Answer:** Parent references, child references, listing all ancestors.

# Chapter 9

1. Name at least three core features of Google BigTable.

   **Answer:**

   • Developers maintain dynamic control over columns.

   • Data values are indexed by row identifier, column name, and a time stamp.

   • Data modelers and developers have control over location of data.

   • Reads and writes of a row are atomic.

   • Rows are maintained in a sorted order.

2. Why are time stamps used in Google BigTable?

   **Answer:** The time stamp orders versions of the column value. When a new value is written to a BigTable database, the old value is not overwritten. Instead, a new value is added along with a time stamp. The time stamp allows applications to determine the latest version of a column value.

3. Identify one similarity between column family databases and key-value databases.

   **Answer:** Column families are analogous to keyspaces in key-value databases. In both key-value databases and Cassandra, a keyspace is the outermost logical structure used by data modelers and developers.

4. Identify one similarity between column family databases and document databases.

   **Answer:** Column family and document databases support similar types of querying that allow you to select subsets of data available in a row.

   Column family databases, like document databases, do not require all columns in all rows. In both column family and document databases, columns or fields can be added as needed by developers.

5. Identify one similarity between column family databases and relational databases.

   **Answer:** Both column family databases and relational databases use unique identifiers for rows of data. These are known as row keys in column family databases and as primary keys in relational databases. Both row keys and primary keys are indexed for rapid retrieval.

6. What types of Hadoop nodes are used by HBase?

   **Answer:** Name nodes and data nodes.

7. Describe the essential characteristics of a peer-to-peer architecture.

   **Answer:** Peer-to-peer architectures have only one type of node. Any node can assume responsibility for any service or task that must be run in the cluster.

8. Why does Cassandra use a gossip protocol to exchange server status information?

   **Answer:** An "all-servers-to-all-other-servers" protocol can quickly increase the volume of traffic on the network and the amount of time each server has to dedicate to communicating with other servers. The number of messages sent is a function of the number of servers in the cluster. If $N$ is the number of servers, then $N \times (N-1)$ is the number of messages needed to update all servers with information about all other servers. Gossip protocols are more efficient because one server can update another server about itself as well as all the servers it knows about.

9.  What is the purpose of the anti-entropy protocol used by Cassandra?

    **Answer:** Anti-entropy algorithms correct inconsistencies between replicas.

10. When would you use a column family database instead of another type of NoSQL database?

    **Answer:** Column family databases are appropriate choices for large-scale database deployments that require high levels of write performance, a large number of servers, or multi–data center availability.

    Column family databases are also appropriate when a large number of servers are required to meet expected workloads.

# Chapter 10

1.  What is a keyspace? What is an analogous data structure in a relational database?

    **Answer:** A keyspace is the top-level data structure in a column family database. It is top level in the sense that all other data structures you would create as a database designer are contained within a keyspace. A keyspace is analogous to a schema in a relational database.

2.  How do columns in column family databases differ from columns in relational databases?

    **Answer:** Columns in column families are dynamic. Columns in a relational database table are not as dynamic as in column family databases. Adding a column in a relational database requires changing its schema definition. Adding a column in a column family database just requires making a reference to it from a client application, for example, inserting a value to a column name.

3. When should columns be grouped together in a column family? When should they be in separate column families?

   **Answer:** Columns that are frequently used together should be grouped in the same column family.

4. Describe how partitions are used in column family databases.

   **Answer:** A partition is a logical subset of a database. Partitions are usually used to store a set of data based on some attribute of the data. Each node or server within a column family cluster maintains one or more partitions.

   When a client application requests data, the request is routed to a server with the partition containing the requested data. A request could go to a central server in a master-slave architecture or to any server in a peer-to-peer architecture. In either case, the request is forwarded to the appropriate server.

5. What are the performance advantages of using a commit log?

   **Answer:** Commit logs are append-only files that always write data to the end of the file. When database administrators dedicate a disk to a commit log, there are no other write processes competing to write data to the disk. This reduces the need for random seeks and reduces latency.

6. What are the advantages of using a Bloom filter?

   **Answer:** A Bloom filter tests whether or not an element is a member of a set, such as a partition. Bloom filters never return a negative response unless the element is not in the set; it may, however, return a true response in cases when the element is not in the set. Bloom filters are used to reduce the number of blocks read from disks or solid state devices.

7. What factors should you consider when setting a consistency level?

   **Answer:** A consistency level is set according to several, sometimes competing, requirements:

   - How fast should write operations return a success status after saving data to persistent storage?

   - Is it acceptable for two users to look up a set of columns by the same row ID and receive different data?

   - If your application runs across multiple data centers and one of the data centers fails, must the remaining functioning data centers have the latest data?

   - Can you tolerate some inconsistency in reads but need updates saved to two or more replicas?

8. What factors should you consider when setting a replication strategy?

   **Answer:** One method uses the ring structure of a cluster. When data is written to a node, it is replicated to the two adjacent nodes in the cluster. The other method uses network topology to determine where to replicate data. For example, replicas may be created on different racks within a data center to ensure availability in the event of a rack failure.

9. Why are hash trees used in anti-entropy processes?

   **Answer:** The naive way to compare replicas is to send a copy of one replica to the node storing another replica and compare the two. Even with high-write applications, much of the data sent from the source is the same as the data on the target node. Column family databases can exploit the fact that much of replica data may not change between anti-entropy checks. They do this by sending hashes of data instead of the data itself.

10. What are the advantages of using a gossip protocol?

    **Answer:** Instead of having every node communicate with every other node, it is more efficient to have nodes share information about themselves as well as other nodes from which they have received updates. This avoids the rapid increase in the number of messages that must be sent when compared with each node communicating with all other nodes.

11. Describe how hinted handoff can help improve the availability of write operations.

    **Answer:** If a write operation is directed to a node that is unavailable, the operation can be redirected to another node, such as another replica node or a node designated to receive write operations when the target node is down.

    The node receiving the redirected write message creates a data structure to store information about the write operation and where it should ultimately be sent. The hinted handoff periodically checks the status of the target server and sends the write operation when the target is available.

# Chapter 11

1.  What is the role of end-user queries in column family database design?

    **Answer:** Queries provide information needed to effectively design column family databases. The information includes entities, attributes of entities, query criteria, and derived values. It is users who determine the questions that will be asked of the database application and drive the data model design.

2.  How can you avoid performing joins in column family databases?

    **Answer:** Denormalization is used to avoid joins.

3.  Why should entities be modeled in a single row?

    **Answer:** Column family databases do not provide the same level of transaction control as relational databases. Typically, writes to a row are atomic. If you update several columns in a table, they will all be updated or none of them will be. If you need to update two separate tables, such as a product table and a books table, it is conceivable that the updates to the product table succeed but the updates to the book table do not. In such a case, you would be left with inconsistent data.

4.  What is hotspotting, and why should it be avoided?

    **Answer:** Hotspotting occurs when many operations are performed on a small number of servers. It is inefficient to direct an excessive amount of work at one or a few machines while there are others that are underutilized.

5.  What are some disadvantages of using complex data structures as a column value?

    **Answer:** Not all column family database features work well with complex data structures. Using separate columns for each attribute makes it easier to apply database features to the attributes. For example, creating separate columns for street, city, state, and zip means you can create secondary indexes on those values.

6.  Describe three scenarios in which you should not use secondary indexes.

    **Answer:**

    -   There are a small number of distinct values in a column.

    -   There are many unique values in a column.

    -   The column values are sparse.

7. What are the disadvantages of managing your own tables as indexes?

   **Answer:** When using tables as indexes, you will be responsible for maintaining the indexes. You could update the index whenever there is a change to the base tables; for example, a customer makes a purchase. Alternatively, you could run a batch job at regular intervals to update the index tables.

   Updating index tables at the same time you update the base tables keeps the indexes up to date at all times. A drawback of this approach is that your application will have to perform two write operations, one to the base table and one to the index table. This could lead to longer latencies during write operations.

   Updating index tables with batch jobs has the advantage of not adding additional work to write operations. The obvious disadvantage is that there is a period of time when the data in the base tables and the indexes is out of synchronization.

8. What are two types of statistics? What are they each used for?

   **Answer:** Descriptive statistics are used for understanding the characteristics of your data. Predictive, or inferential, statistics is the study of methods for making predictions based on data.

9. What are two types of machine learning? What are they used for?

   **Answer:** Unsupervised learning is useful for exploring large data sets with techniques such as clustering. Supervised learning techniques provide the means to learn from examples. These techniques can be used to create classifiers.

10. How is Spark different from MapReduce?

    **Answer:** MapReduce writes much data to disk, whereas Spark makes more use of memory. MapReduce employs a fairly rigid computational model (map operation followed by reduce operation), whereas Spark allows for more general computational models.

# Chapter 12

1.  What are the two components of a graph?

    **Answer:** Vertices and edges.

2.  List at least three sample entities that can be modeled as vertices.

    **Answer:**

    - Cities

    - Employees in a company

    - Proteins

    - Electrical circuits

    - Junctions in a water line

    - Organisms in an ecosystem

    - Train stations

    - A person infected with a contagious disease

3.  List at least three sample relations that can be modeled as edges.

    **Answer:**

    - Roads connecting cities

    - Employees working with other employees

    - Proteins interacting with other proteins

    - Electrical components linked to other electrical components

    - Water lines connecting junctions

    - Predators and prey in ecosystems

    - Rail lines connecting train stations

    - Disease transmission between an infected and uninfected person

4. What properties could you associate with a vertex representing a city?

   **Answer:**

   - City name

   - Population

   - Longitude and latitude

   - Points of interest

5. What properties could you associate with an edge representing a highway between two cities?

   **Answer:**

   - Length

   - Year built

   - Maximum speed

6. Epidemiologists use graphs to model the spread of infection. What do vertices represent? What do edges represent?

   **Answer:** Vertices represent people. Edges represent interactions between people, such as shaking hands or standing in close proximity.

7. Give an example of a part-of hierarchy.

   **Answer:**

   - Federal, state/provincial/local governments

   - Part of a car hierarchy

8. How do graph databases avoid joins?

   **Answer:** In a graph database, instead of performing joins, you follow edges from vertex to vertex.

9.  How is a person-likes-post graph different from other graphs used as examples in this chapter?

    **Answer:** This is an example of a bipartite graph.

10. Give an example of a business application that would use multiple types of edges (relations) between vertices.

    **Answer:** A transportation company might want to consider road, rail, and air transportation between cities. Each has different options, such as time to deliver, cost, and government regulations.

# Chapter 13

1.  Define a vertex.

    **Answer:** A vertex represents an entity marked with a unique identifier. A vertex can represent virtually any entity that has a relation with another entity.

2.  Define an edge.

    **Answer:** Edges define relationships between vertices.

3.  List at least three examples in which you can use graphs to model the domains.

    **Answer:**

    *   Transportation networks

    *   Social networks

    *   Spread of infectious diseases

    *   Electrical circuits

    *   Networks, such as the Internet

4.  Give an example of when you would use a weighted graph.

    **Answer:**

    *   In the case of highways, weight could be the distance between cities.

- In a social network, weight could be an indication of how frequently the two individuals post on each other's walls or comment on each other's posts.

5. Give an example of when you would use a directed graph.

   **Answer:** In a family relations graph, there is a direction associated with a "parent of" relation.

6. What is the difference between order and size?

   **Answer:** The order of a graph is the number of vertices in the graph. The size is the number of edges in a graph.

7. Why is betweenness sometimes called a bottleneck measure?

   **Answer:** Betweenness is a measure of how important a vertex is to connecting different parts of a graph. If all paths from one part of the network to another part must go through a single vertex, then it can become a bottleneck. Such vertices have high betweenness scores.

8. How would an epidemiologist use closeness to understand the spread of a disease?

   **Answer:** Closeness is a property of a vertex that indicates how far the vertex is from all others in the graph. People (vertices) with high closeness scores have short paths to others in the network. Diseases can spread faster from people with high closeness scores than from those with low closeness scores.

9. When would you use a multigraph?

   **Answer:** Multigraphs are graphs with multiple edges between vertices. Multiple edges between cities could represent various shipping options, such as shipping by truck, train, or plane.

10. What is Dijkstra's algorithm used for?

    **Answer:** Dijkstra's algorithm is used to find the shortest paths in a network.

# Chapter 14

1.  What is the benefit of mapping domain-specific queries into graph-specific queries?

    **Answer:** Once you have your domain-specific queries mapped to graph-specific queries, you have the full range of graph query tools and graph algorithms available to you to analyze and explore your data.

2.  Which is more like SQL, Cypher or Gremlin?

    **Answer:** Cypher.

3.  How is the MATCH statement like a SQL SELECT statement?

    **Answer:** MATCH is used to retrieve data from a graph database. MATCH supports filtering based on properties.

4.  What are the inE and outE terms used for in Gremlin?

    **Answer:** inE is a reference to incoming edges of a vertex; outE is a reference to outgoing edges of a vertex.

5.  Which type of edge should be used for a nonsymmetrical relation, a directed or undirected edge?

    **Answer:** A directed edge.

6.  What is the difference between a declarative and a traversal query language for graph databases?

    **Answer:** Declarative languages express what is to be retrieved; traversal languages specify how to retrieve data.

7.  What is a depth-first search?

    **Answer:** In a depth-first search, you start traversal at one vertex and select adjacent vertices. You then select the first vertex in that resultset and select adjacent vertices to it. You continue to select the first vertex in the resultset until there are no more edges to traverse. At that point, you visit the next vertex in the latest resultset. If there are incident edges leading to other vertices, you visit those; otherwise, you continue to the next item in the latest resultset.

When you exhaust all vertices in the latest resultset, you return to the resultset selected prior to that and begin the process again.

8.  What is a breadth-first search?

    **Answer:** In a breadth-first search, you visit each of the vertices incident to the current vertex before visiting other vertices.

9.  Why are cycles a potential problem when performing graph operations?

    **Answer:** Cycles can lead to traversing the same vertices repeatedly. Keeping track of visited vertices is one way to avoid problems with cycles.

10. Why is scalability such an important consideration when working with graphs?

    **Answer:** Scalability in graph databases must address growth in

    - Vertices and edges

    - Number of users

    - Number and size of properties on vertices and edges

# Chapter 15

1.  Name two use cases for key-value databases.

    **Answer:**

    - Caching data from relational databases to improve performance

    - Tracking transient attributes in a web application, such as a shopping cart

2.  Describe two reasons for choosing a key-value database for your application.

    **Answer:**

    - There is a need for variable attributes.

    - The problem domain requires a relatively simple data model.

3. Name two use cases for document databases.

   **Answer:**

   • Content management systems

   • Back-end support for mobile device applications

4. Describe two reasons for choosing a document database for your application.

   **Answer:**

   • There is a wide variety of query patterns.

   • There is a need for flexible data structures.

5. Name two use cases for column family databases.

   **Answer:**

   • Collecting and analyzing log data from a large number of devices

   • Analyzing customer characteristics to generate personalized offers

6. Describe two reasons for choosing a column family database for your application.

   **Answer:**

   • There is a need for multi–data center replication.

   • There is the need to work with Big Data–scale volumes of data.

7. Name two use cases for graph databases.

   **Answer:**

   • Modeling computer networks

   • Modeling social media networks

8. Describe two reasons for choosing a graph database for your application.

   **Answer:**

   - There is a need to model explicit relations between entities and rapidly traverse paths between entities.

   - There is an affinity between the problem domain, such as transportation networks, and graphs.

9. Name two types of applications well suited for relational databases.

   **Answer:**

   - Transaction processing

   - Data warehouses and data marts

10. Discuss the need for both NoSQL and relational databases in enterprise data management.

    **Answer:** NoSQL and relational databases are complementary. Relational databases offer many features that protect the integrity of data and reduce the risk of data anomalies. Relational databases incur operational overhead providing these features. In some use cases, performance is more important than ensuring immediate consistency or supporting ACID transactions. In these cases, NoSQL databases may be the better solution. Choosing a database is a process of choosing the right tool for the job. The more varied your set of jobs, the more varied your toolkit.

# B

# List of NoSQL Databases

### Aerospike

A key-value database available as open source software. Optimized for flash storage. For more details, see http://www.aerospike.com/.

### AllegroGraph

A commercial graph database with support for resource description format (RDF) data. For more details, see http://franz.com/agraph/allegrograph/.

### Amazon Web Services DynamoDB

A key-value and document database service provided by Amazon Web Services. This highly scalable service is designed for large key-value data stores; support for documents was recently added. Service cost is based on use. For more details, see aws.amazon.com/dynamodb.

### Amazon Web Services SimpleDB

A minimal key-value database provided by Amazon Web Services. Well suited for small databases that require query flexibility but do not require scalability. When scalability is required, AWS DynamoDB is a better option. Service cost is based on use. For more details, see aws.amazon.com/simpledb.

### Apache Accumulo

A column family database based on the Google BigTable design. Accumulo is open source software. Includes support for cell-based access controls. Built to work with the Hadoop ecosystem. For more details, see http://accumulo.apache.org/.

### Apache CouchDB

An open source document data store from the Apache Foundation. For more details, see http://couchdb.apache.org.

### Apache Giraph

An open source graph database designed for scalability. Based on Pregel, a graph database developed by Google. For more details, see giraph.apache.org.

### Apache HBase

A column family database based on the Google BigTable design. HBase is part of the Hadoop ecosystem. For more details, see http://hbase. apache.org.

### ArrangoDB

An open source, multimodal NoSQL database with support for key-value, document, and graph data models. For more details, see http://www.arrangodb.org.

### Cassandra

An open source wide column database based on Google BigTable and Amazon's DynamoDB designs. For more information, see http://cassandra.apache.org and http://www.datastax.com/docs.

### Cloudant

A commercial document database service based on CouchDB and owned by IBM. For more details, see https://cloudant.com.

### Couchbase

An open source document database derived from Apache CouchDB. For more information, see http://www.couchbase.com.

### FoundationDB

A commercial key-value database that supports ordered key values and ACID transactions. For more details, see https://foundationdb.com.

### Google Cloud Datastore

A commercial document database service from Google. See developers. google.com/datastore for more details.

### Hypertable

An open source implementation of Google BigTable. For more information, see http://hypertable.org/.

### Infinispan

An open source key-value data store that uses a distributed in-memory model to support a scalable key-value grid. For more details, see http://infinispan.org/.

### LevelDB

An open source key-value data store library from Google. This is a library for use with other applications. There is no client/server support; this must be provided by another application, if needed. For more details, see https://github.com/google/leveldb.

### MarkLogic

A commercial document database with support for native XML and resource description format (RDF) data. For more information, see http://www.marklogic.com.

### Microsoft Azure DocumentDB

A commercial service providing document database functionality in the Microsoft Azure cloud. See azure.microsoft.com/en-us/services/documentdb for more details.

### MongoDB

Probably the most popular document database. MongoDB is open source. For more details, see http://www.mongodb.org.

### Neo4j

A popular open source graph database that supports the Cypher query language. For more details, see http://neo4j.com.

### Oracle Berkeley DB

One of the oldest key-value data stores started as a project at the University of California at Berkeley. The open source code is now managed by Oracle. For more details, see www.oracle.com/technetwork/products/berkeleydb.

### OrientDB

An open source document database with some support for graph databases as well. For more information, see http://www.orientdb.org.

### RavenDB

An open source document database designed for use with the .NET Framework. For more details, see http://ravendb.net/.

### Redis

An open source key-value database that uses master-slave replication. For more details, see http://redis.io.

### Riak

Distributed key-value data store that, unlike Redis, does not use a master-slave architecture. For more details, see basho.com/products/riak-overview.

### Sparksee

A commercial graph database that includes a mobile version of the database for iOS and Android devices. For more details, see sparsity-technologies.com/#sparksee.

### Sqrrl

A commercial multimodal NoSQL database based on Apache Accumulo. Supports key-value, document, column family, and graph database models. For more details, see http://sqrrl.com.

### Titan

An open source distributed graph database that supports the Tinker-Pop platform. Uses Cassandra or other database for back-end, persistent storage. For more details, see http://thinkaurelius.github.io/titan/.

# Glossary

## A

### anti-entropy

Anti-entropy is the process of detecting differences in replicas. From a performance perspective, it is important to detect and resolve inconsistencies with a minimum amount of data exchange.

## B

### betweenness

Betweenness is a measure of how much of a bottleneck a given vertex is.

### bipartite graph

A bipartite graph, or bigraph, is a graph with two distinct sets of vertices where each vertex in one set is only connected to vertices in the other set.

### Bloom filter

A Bloom filter tests whether or not an element is a member of a set. Unlike a typical member function, the Bloom filter sometimes returns an incorrect answer. It could return a positive response in cases where the tested element is not a member of the set. This is known as a false positive. Bloom filters never return a negative response unless the element is not in the set.

## C

### CAP theorem

Also known as Brewer's theorem after the computer scientist who introduced it, the CAP theorem states that distributed databases cannot have consistency (C), availability (A), and partition protection (P) all at the same time. Consistency, in this case, means consistent copies of data on different servers. Availability refers to providing a response to any query. Partition protection means a network that connects two or more servers is unable to transmit network packets between the servers.

### closeness
Closeness is a property of a vertex that indicates how far the vertex is from all others in the graph.

### cluster
A cluster is a set of servers configured to function together. Servers sometimes have differentiated functions and sometimes they do not.

### collection
A collection is a group of documents. The documents within a collection are usually related to the same subject entity, such as employees, products, logged events, or customer profiles. It is possible to store unrelated documents in a collection, but this is not advised.

### collision
A collision occurs when two distinct inputs to a hash function produce the same output. When it is difficult to find two inputs that map to the same hash function output, the hash function is known as collision resistant. If a hash table is not collision resistant or if you encounter one of those rare cases in which two inputs map to the same output, you will need a collision resolution strategy.

### column
A column is the data structure for storing a single value in a column family database.

### column family
A column family is a collection of related columns. Columns that are frequently used together should be grouped into the same column family.

## commit log

Commit log files are used in databases to improve performance while ensuring recoverability. Instead of writing data immediately to their partition and disk block, column family databases can employ commit logs. These are append-only files that always write data to the end of the file. In the event of a failure, the database management system reads the commit log on recovery. Any entries in the commit log that have not been saved to partitions are written to appropriate partitions.

## compression

Compression is a data management technique that uses repeating patterns in data to reduce the storage needed to hold the data. A compression algorithm for databases should perform compression and decompression operations as fast as possible. This often entails a trade-off between the speed of compression/decompression and the size of the compressed data. Faster compression algorithms can lead to larger compressed data than other, slower algorithms.

## consistency level

Consistency level refers to the consistency between copies of data on different replicas. In the strictest sense, data is consistent only if all replicas have the same data. At the other end of the spectrum, you could consider the data "consistent" as long as it is persistently written to at least one replica. There are several intermediate levels as well.

# D

## degree

Degree is the number of edges linked to a vertex and is one way to measure the importance of any given vertex in a graph.

## directed graph

A directed graph is one in which the edges have a specified direction from one vertex to another.

## document

A document is a set of ordered key-value pairs. A key is a unique identifier used to look up a value. A value is an instance of any supported data type, such as a string, number, array, or list.

# E

## edge

An edge, also known as a link or arc, defines relationships between vertices or objects connecting vertices.

## embedded document

An embedded document enables document database users to store related data in a single document. This allows the document database to avoid a process called joining in which data from one table, called the foreign key, is used to look up data in another table.

# F

## flow network

A flow network is a directed graph in which each edge has a capacity and each vertex has a set of incoming and outgoing edges. The sum of the capacity of incoming edges cannot be greater than the sum of the capacity of outgoing edges. The two exceptions to this rule are source and sink vertices. Sources have no inputs but have outputs, whereas sinks have inputs but no outputs.

# G

## gossip protocol

The gossip protocol is a protocol for sharing information between nodes in a cluster. Instead of having every node communicate with every other node, it is more efficient to have nodes share information about themselves as well as other nodes from which it has received updates.

### graph traversal

Graph traversal is the process of visiting all vertices in a graph in a particular way. The purpose of this is usually to either set or read some property value in a graph.

# H

### hash function

A hash function is an algorithm that maps from an input, for example, a string of characters, to an output string. The size of the input can vary, but the size of the output is always the same.

### hinted handoff

The hinted handoff is a protocol designed to preserve update information if a server is down. If a write operation is directed to a node that is unavailable, the operation can be redirected to another node, such as another replica node or a node designated to receive write operations when the target node is down.

The node receiving the redirected write message creates a data structure to store information about the write operation and where it should ultimately be sent. The hinted handoff periodically checks the status of the target server.

### horizontal partitioning or sharding

Horizontal partitioning is the process of dividing a database by documents in a document database or by rows in a relational database.

# I

### intersection of graphs
The intersection of a graph is the set of vertices and edges that are common to both graphs.

### isomorphism
Two graphs are considered isomorphic if for each vertex in the first graph, there is a corresponding vertex in the other graph. In addition, for each edge between a pair of vertices in the first graph, there is a corresponding edge between the corresponding vertices of the other graph.

# K

### key
In key-value databases, a key is a reference to a value. In relational databases, a key is also a way to reference a row in a table. Primary keys refer to the way of uniquely identifying a row. Foreign keys refer to keys stored in one table that are used to reference rows in other tables.

### keyspace
A keyspace is the top-level data structure in a column family database. It is top level in the sense that all other data structures you would create as a database designer are contained within a keyspace. A keyspace is analogous to a schema in a relational database.

# L

### loop
A loop is an edge that connects a vertex to itself.

# M

## multigraph
A multigraph is a graph with multiple edges between vertices.

# N

## namespace
A namespace is a list of key-value pairs without duplicates for holding key-value pairs. A namespace could be an entire key-value database. The essential characteristic of a namespace is it is a collection of key-value pairs that has no duplicate keys. It is permissible to have duplicate values in a namespace.

# O

## order of a graph
The order of a graph is the number of vertices in the graph.

# P

## partition
A partition is a logical subset of a database. Partitions are usually used to store a set of data based on some attribute of the data.

## partitioning
With respect to distributed databases, partitioning refers to splitting documents, tables, or graphs and distributing them to different servers.

With respect to the CAP theorem, partitioning refers to losing a network connection in a way that leaves parts of the network unreachable from some other parts.

**path**

A path through a graph is a set of vertices along with the edges between those vertices. The vertices in a graph are all different from each other. If edges are directed, the path is a directed path. If the graph is undirected, the paths in it are undirected paths.

**polymorphic schema**

A polymorphic schema is a database that allows for documents of different types and forms to exist in the same collection. This term is usually used with reference to document databases.

# Q

**query processor**

The query processor takes as input queries and data about the documents, columns, or graphs in a database and produces a sequence of operations that retrieve the selected data. Key-value databases do not need query processors; they function by looking up values by keys.

# R

**replication**

Replication is the process of saving multiple copies of data in your cluster. This provides for high availability of distributed databases.

**ring**

A ring is a logical structure for organizing partitions. A ring is a circular pattern in which each server or instance of key-value database software running on a server is linked to two adjacent servers or instances. Each server or instance is responsible for managing a range of data based on a partition key.

**row key**

A row key uniquely identifies a row in a column family. It serves some of the same purposes as a primary key in a relational database.

# S

**schemaless**

Document databases do not require data modelers to formally specify the structure of documents. A formal structure specification is known as a schema. Relational databases do require schemas.

**sharding or horizontal partitioning**

Horizontal partitioning is the process of dividing a database by documents in a document database or by rows in a relational database.

**size of a graph**

The size of a graph is the number of edges in a graph.

# U

**undirected graph**

An undirected graph is one in which the edges do not indicate a direction (such as from-to) between two vertices.

**union of graphs**

The union of graphs is the combined set of vertices and edges in a graph.

# V

**value**

In key-value databases, a value is an object, typically a set of bytes, that has been associated with a key. Values can be integers, floating-point numbers, strings of characters, binary large objects (BLOBs), semistructured constructs such as JSON objects, images, audio, and just about any other data type you can represent as a series of bytes.

### vertex

A vertex represents an entity marked with a unique identifier—analogous to a row key in a column family database or a primary key in a relational database. It should be noted that the term *node* is an acceptable replacement for *vertex*. However, this book only uses the latter to avoid confusion with the use of node to describe a service running in a cluster.

### vertical partitioning

Vertical partitioning is a technique for improving database performance by storing columns of a relational table in separate, multiple partitions. This is especially helpful when only a subset of columns is read from a row of data and the columns are read from many rows.

# W

### weighted graph

A weighted graph is a graph in which each edge has a number assigned to it. The number can reflect a cost, a capacity, or some other measure of an edge. This is commonly used in optimization problems, such as finding the shortest path between vertices.

# Index

key-value databases, 103

naming conventions, 145

partitioning, 129, 150-151

rows, 309-310, 337-338

shard, 229

TTL, 163-164

values

*locating, 105-110*

*searching, 160-161*

keyspaces, 287, 309

## L

languages

Cypher, 408-415

query (SQL), 24

*DDL, 24-25*

*DML, 25-26*

standard query, 161-162

latency, reducing, 152-155

laws of thermodynamics, 299-300

layers, abstraction, 120

least recently used. *See* LRU

LevelDB library, 140, 479

levels, consistency, 321-322

licenses, cost of, 31

limitations

of arrays, 84

of flat file data management
systems, 9-11

of hierarchical data management
systems, 14

of key-value databases, 159-162

of network data management
systems, 17

of relational databases, 27-29

of values, 112-113

LinkedIn, 370. *See also* social media

linking records, 15

links. *See* edges

list-based partitioning, 231

lists, 122, 266

locating values, 105-110

location of data, 282-283

locations, modeling, 365

logs, commit, 317-318

loops, 384

for, 253

while, 148

LRU (least recently used), 94

Lucene, 162

## M

machine learning, searching
patterns, 353

magnetic tape, 7. *See also* storage

maintenance

availability of data, 44-48

consistency of data, 42-48

management

applications, 26-27

databases

*design, 4-5*

document databases in
collections, 188-198

*early systems, 6, 17-18*

*e-commerce applications, 5-6*

*flat file systems, 7-11*

*hierarchical data model systems,
12-14*

*network data management
systems, 14-17*

distributed databases, 41

*availability, 44-48*